AFGHANISTAN

WHAT EVERYONE NEEDS TO KNOW®

AFGHANISTAN

WHAT EVERYONE NEEDS TO KNOW®

BARNETT R. RUBIN

OXFORD
UNIVERSITY PRESS

OXFORD
UNIVERSITY PRESS

Oxford University Press is a department of the University of Oxford. It furthers the University's objective of excellence in research, scholarship, and education by publishing worldwide. Oxford is a registered trademark of Oxford University Press in the UK and certain other countries.

"What Everyone Needs to Know" is a registered trademark of Oxford University Press.

Published in the United States of America by Oxford University Press 198 Madison Avenue, New York, NY 10016, United States of America.

© Oxford University Press 2020

Library of Congress Cataloging-in-Publication Data
Names: Rubin, Barnett R., author.
Title: Afghanistan : what everyone needs to know / Barnett R. Rubin.
Description: New York, NY : Oxford University Press, [2020] |
Series: What everyone needs to know |
Includes bibliographical references and index.
Identifiers: LCCN 2019037423 (print) | LCCN 2019037424 (ebook) |
ISBN 9780190496630 (hardback) | ISBN 9780190496647 (paperback) |
ISBN 9780190496654 (updf) | ISBN 9780190496661 (epub)
Subjects: LCSH: Afghanistan—History—20th century. |
Afghanistan—History—2001– | Afghanistan—Politics and government—
20th century. | Afghanistan—Politics and government—21st century.
Classification: LCC DS371.4 .R825 2020 (print) |
LCC DS371.4 (ebook) | DDC 958.104—dc23
LC record available at https://lccn.loc.gov/2019037423
LC ebook record available at https://lccn.loc.gov/2019037424

CONTENTS

vi Contents

7 Reconstruction and Development   **175**
Principal author, Nematullah Bizhan

8 Narcotics and Counter-Narcotics   **204**
Principal author, David Mansfield

9 More War, Insurgency, and Counterinsurgency 230

Principal author, Antonio Giustozzi

10 Peace or More War? 256

ACKNOWLEDGMENTS

Since this book draws in one way or another on everything I have done relating to Afghanistan since 1983, I find myself somewhat at a loss as to how to acknowledge the assistance and support I have received. I will economize by first referring readers to the acknowledgments of all my previous works on the subject. Everyone thanked there deserves to be recalled here as well, most of all my beloved life partner, Susan Blum.

The first person to thank specifically for this book is David McBride, my editor at Oxford University Press. David McBride first approached me in 2009 about contributing the Afghanistan entry in the "What Everyone Needs to Know" series. I negotiated a contract for two books, the one he actually wanted to publish, plus a collection of previously published articles, reports, and book chapters.

At that time, however, I was about to enter the State Department, which informed me that publishing a book called *Afghanistan: What Everyone Needs to Know* was incompatible with my official duties. With some difficulty I persuaded the department that no one could reasonably object to a book collecting works I had published before entering government service. With somewhat less difficulty I persuaded McBride to proceed with the second book in the absence of the first, and *Afghanistan from the Cold War through the War on Terror* came out in 2013.

In October 2013, I resigned from the State Department and
finally set about writing this book. In an attempt to impose the
burden on others, I asked McBride to interview me using the
questions I had drafted for the book outline and have these
interviews transcribed as a first draft. He generously agreed.

Over the intervening years, as I intermittently chipped
away at the manuscript, I benefitted from the generous support of the Carnegie Corporation of New York, for track two
U.S.-China dialogues on Afghanistan, and as always, the government of Norway, for other regional work on Afghanistan
and general support. At Carnegie the goodwill of its president, Vartan Gregorian, sustained me, as did the partnership
of Stephen del Rosso. In Norway our partners included Per
Albert Ilsaas, Kåre Aas, Lisa Golden, Tøre Hattrem, Kai Eide,
and Geir Pedersen.

The Center on International Cooperation of New York
University continued to provide me with the support and
freedom I needed, under the leadership of directors Bruce
Jones and Sarah Cliffe. I benefitted from the multidimen-
sional support provided by Said Sabir Ibrahimi and his predecessors, Thomas Zimmermann, Parnian Nazary, and Tom
Gregg. Ibrahimi scanned this entire text. Gregg's leadership
had enabled our program to flourish even during my extended
absences on duty for the State Department. It was an unex-
pected gift that as I was finishing this book, Rina Amiri, with
whom I had worked for both Lakhdar Brahimi and the late
Richard Holbrooke, came to CIC as a resident fellow to offer
her insights.

As I have mentioned Brahimi and Holbrooke, let me express my gratitude for the opportunities those two men gave
me to participate in the efforts in the United Nations and US
government, which I had hoped would help bring an end to
the armed conflict in Afghanistan. While there is no way that
I can adequately thank the multitudes in Afghanistan who

have helped me learn whatever I have managed to share here, I would like to offer them my regret for the shortcomings of those efforts, as well as my hopes that others will succeed where we did not, perhaps with the aid and encouragement of whatever lessons I have managed to share in this book.

ABBREVIATIONS

AACA	Afghan Assistance Coordination Authority
AED	United Arab Emirates dirham (currency of the UAE)
ANDS	Afghanistan National Development Strategy
ANDSF	Afghanistan National Defense and Security Forces
ANPDF	Afghanistan National Peace and Development Framework
APTTA	Afghanistan-Pakistan Transit Trade Agreement (2010)
ARTF	Afghanistan Reconstruction Trust Fund
ATTA	Afghan Transit Trade Agreement (1965)
BRI	Belt and Road Initiative
CJTF	Criminal Justice Task Force
CLJ	Constitutional Loya Jirga
CNGT	(Office of) Counter-Narcotics and Global Threats
CNJC	Counter Narcotics Justice Center
CNPA	Counter Narcotics Police Agency
COIN	Counterinsurgency
CPEC	China-Pakistan Economic Corridor
CRC	Constitutional Review Commission
DDR	Disarmament, Demobilization, and Reintegration

DEA	Drug Enforcement Administration
DFID	Department for International Development
ECC	Electoral Complaints Commission
ELJ	Emergency Loya Jirga
FAST	Foreign-Deployed Advisory and Support Teams
FATA	Federally Administrated Tribal Areas
GCC	Gulf Cooperation Council
GLOCs	Ground Lines of Communication
HPC	Afghan High Peace Council
I-ANDS	Interim Afghanistan National Development Strategy
ICRC	International Committee of the Red Cross
IEC	Independent Election Commission
IMF	International Monetary Fund
INL	International Narcotics and Law Enforcement Affairs, State Department Bureau
IRGC	Islamic Revolutionary Guard Corps (Iran)
IS	Islamic State
ISA	Islamic State of Afghanistan
ISAF	International Security Assistance Force (was MNF)
ISI	Inter-Services Intelligence Directorate (Pakistan)
ISKP	Islamic State-Khorasan Province
MCN	Ministry of Counter Narcotics
MNF	Multinational Force, later called the International Security Assistance Force (ISAF)
MoU	Memorandum of Understanding
NDS	National Directorate of Security (Afghanistan)
NGOs	Nnongovernmental organizations
NIFA	National Islamic Front (Mahaz) for the Freedom (Azadi) of Afghanistan
NPPs	National Priority Programs
NSA	National Security Agency
NSC	National Security Council
NSS	National Security Strategy
NUG	National Unity Government / NUG agreement

NWFP	North-West Frontier Province (Pakistan; now called Khyber-Pakhtunkhwa, or KP)
OBL	Osama bin Laden
OEF	Operation Enduring Freedom
PPP	Pakistan People's Party
PRSP	Poverty Reduction Strategy Paper
PRT	Provincial Reconstruction Team
QCG	Quadrilateral Coordination Group
RC-E	Regional Command-East
RC-N	Regional Command-North
RC-S	Regional Command-South
RC-W	Regional Command-West
SCN	Supervisory Council of the North
SERC	Special Electoral Reform Commission
SIGAR	Special Inspector-General for Afghan Reconstruction
SNTV	Single Non-Transferable Vote
SRAP	Special Representative for Afghanistan and Pakistan
SRAR	Special Representative for Afghan Reconciliation
SSR	Security Sector Reform
TAPI	Turkmenistan-Afghanistan-Pakistan-India Pipeline
TTP	Tehrik-i Taliban-i Pakistan (Taliban Movement of Pakistan)
UAE	United Arab Emirates
UF	United Front for the Salvation of Afghanistan
UNAMA	UN Assistance Mission in Afghanistan
UNDOC	United Nations Office on Drugs and Crime
UNHCR	UN High Commissioner for Refugees
UNICEF	United Nations Children Fund
UNOCHA	UN Office of Coordination of Humanitarian Affairs

USAID	United States Agency for International Development
USFOR-A	United States Forces Afghanistan
USG	United States government

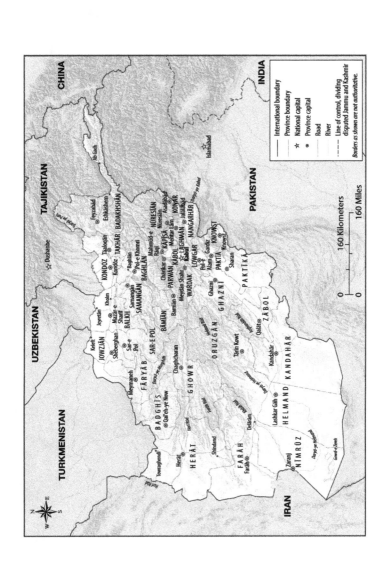

CHINA

TAJIKISTAN

TURKMENISTAN

UZBEKISTAN

IRAN

PAKISTAN

INDIA

N
W   E
S

☆ Dushanbe

Âb Gach

Feyzâbâd

Eshkâshem

Townaghondi

Herât

HERÂT

Shindand

FARÂH

Farâh ⊙

Zaranj ⊙

NIMROZ

Towraghondî

Qal'eh-ye Now

BADGHIS

Maymaneh ⊙

FÂRYÂB

Kelêft

JOWZJÂN

Sheberghan ⊙

Sar-e
Pol ⊙

SAR-E-POL

Chaghcharân ⊙

GHOWR

BÂMIÂN

Bâmiân ⊙

Meydân Shahr ⊙

WARDAK

ORUZGÂN

Tarin Kowt ⊙

HELMAND

Lashkar Gâh ⊙

Delârâm

KANDAHÂR

Kandahâr ⊙

ZÂBOL

Qalât ⊙

GHAZNÎ

Ghazni ⊙

Mazâr-e
Sharîf ⊙

Khôm

Aybak ⊙

SAMANGÂN

Samangân

BALKH

Qondûz

KONDOZ

Tâloqân ⊙

TAKHÂR

Pol-e Khomrî ⊙

Baghlân

BAGHLÂN

Chârikâr ⊙

PARWÂN

Mahmûd-e
Râqî

KÂBOL

Kâbol ☆

LOWGAR

Pol-e
Âlam ⊙

PAKTIÂ

Gardêz ⊙

Sharan ⊙

PAKTÎKÂ

Khowst ⊙

KHOWST

BADAKHSHÂN

NÛRESTÂN

Nûrestân

KÂPÎSÂ

LAGHMÂN

Mehtar Lâm ⊙

KONAR

Asadâbâd ⊙

NANGARHÂR

Jalâlâbâd ⊙

Islâmâbâd ☆

0   160 Kilometers

0   160 Miles

International boundary
Province boundary
☆ National capital
⊙ Province capital
Road
River
Line of control, dividing
disputed Jammu and Kashmir

Borders as shown are not authoritative.

1

AFGHANISTAN SEEN BY OTHERS

Through much of the twentieth century Afghanistan seemed to be a distant concern in the United States. "Afghanistanism" used to be journalistic shorthand for stories about distant places, which editors dismissed as irrelevant. Afghanistan's territory does include some remote, barely accessible regions, but it also includes ancient metropolises such as Balkh, Herat, Kabul, and Kandahar; through much of history these places were centers of civilization, not peripheries, crossroads for commerce and the spread of ideas, including religions and artistic styles. Afghanistan's period of isolation was not an inevitable consequence of its location; it was the result of the policies of the British and Russian colonial empires.

In the late nineteenth and twentieth centuries, those empires agreed to make Afghanistan a buffer state separating their two empires. The only foreign representative would be a Muslim representative of British India, which controlled Afghanistan's foreign affairs. That colonial intrusion into Afghanistan generated imperial studies of Afghanistan by British and Russian officers and scholars, who learned much from the indigenous scholars, while adapting that knowledge to the requirements of colonial conquest and rule. The present work likewise emerged from my personal engagement as a scholar, a citizen, and at times as an official of both the United Nations and the United States, a close observer and a participant in the struggles of the last four decades. I have tried to be fair, and readers will judge differently to what extent I have succeeded, but I cannot claim to be objective. My own actions are among the subjects of this book.

This engagement provided me with a privileged place, in every sense of the word, from which to observe the thorough breakdown of Afghanistan's isolation. The country is now the opposite of a buffer state. Instead of preventing conflict by separating empires or states, it has become an arena where others act out proxy conflicts. The Soviet invasion of December 1979 turned the country into the hottest conflict of a supposedly Cold War. The Afghan state collapsed in the 1990s as a result of that proxy war and the breakup of the USSR, which had been funding the state. The country then became the arena of conflict among regional powers—Pakistan versus Iran, Russia, and India—but also a zone of competition over pipeline routes among the United States, Saudi Arabia, and Iran.

After September 11, 2001, Afghanistan became the first battleground of the so-called War on Terror. The collapse of the state and Afghanistan's falling out of the "international community" enabled al-Qaeda's Saudi leader Osama bin Laden to direct the September 11 attack against the United States. Every one of the world's great (and not so great) powers has competed under the umbrella of the subsequent US-led military and intelligence response, some trying to support it, some trying to undermine it, and some just putting in an appearance. The North Atlantic Treaty Organization, which includes North America and Western and Central Europe, sent tens of thousands of soldiers there for more than ten years. The tensions between Russia and NATO played themselves out over the Hindu Kush. With the destruction of much of the agricultural economy and continual insecurity, Afghanistan became the world's leading producer of opium and its derivatives, linking the country to the global market for narcotics and providing cash incomes that armed groups could tax.

Therefore, after 9/11, which was directed by a Saudi (Osama bin Laden), planned by a Pakistani Kuwaiti (Khalid Shaikh Muhammad), and carried out by fifteen Saudis along with some citizens of the United Arab Emirates, Egypt, and Lebanon, there was a broad international consensus to intervene in Afghanistan, destroy al-Qaeda, remove the Taliban (Persian and Pashto plural of "student" in Arabic) authorities who had hosted it, and establish an internationally approved government there.

Do the United States or other countries have an obligation to help Afghanistan?

No one knows how many people died in the fight: first, against the Soviet Union, in the civil war that followed, the expansion of and resistance to the Taliban, and the war since 2001. The estimates for the anti-Soviet war alone start at one million and rise from there. Millions became refugees and millions more were internally displaced. Afghans sacrificed their livelihoods, their education, and their health. They often feel that the world, the West specifically and the US even more so, owes them a debt for these sacrifices. A young Afghan I met in Kunduz in January 1996 was disappointed at how little help Afghanistan was getting after all its sacrifices. Perhaps I should have just offered my sympathies, but instead I warned him that arguments about moral obligation would not get him anywhere in international politics, not only because people might not be convinced, but because leaders respond to the demands of their own interests and those of their state and people, rather than to moral obligations formulated for them by others. The young man in question, Amrullah Saleh, later became Afghanistan's intelligence chief.

The gap between obligation and action was greatest in the years right after the Soviet withdrawal when the international community effectively abandoned Afghanistan. The country and its people received no aid other than a modest amount of humanitarian assistance, and there was no effort to make peace. Now the US and its international partners have tried to do all of those things, albeit ineffectively, and are giving some priorities over the others. They have incurred obligations to Afghans who have worked with them, whose expectations they raised, and who might now be in danger. The US government and international organizations, however, have inevitably acted in their own interests and have often proven wasteful and ineffective in providing such assistance, which means that the debt will most likely remain unpaid.

How does the situation in Afghanistan affect its neighbors?

In a 1907 agreement, Britain and Russia demarcated Afghanistan's current borders to isolate that country from those two empires and also insulate those empires from each other. At the intersection of four regions, Afghanistan borders on South Asia (Pakistan, including areas of pre-1947 Kashmir claimed by India); Central Asia (Turkmenistan, Uzbekistan, and Tajikistan); the Middle East or Persian Gulf (Iran); and East Asia (China). The border with China, only 57 miles (92 km) long, is at the eastern edge of a narrow corridor of land, the Wakhan Corridor, ceded to Afghanistan to separate Russian territory, now Tajikistan, from British Indian territory, now the Pakistan-administered territory of Gilgit-Baltistan. With the independence and partition of British India and the breakup of the Russian Empire's successor, the USSR, Afghanistan now has six immediate neighbors, with borders as short as the one with China and as long as the one with Pakistan (1510 mi/2430 km). Afghanistan claims not to recognize that boundary, which is based on the 1893 Durand Line drawn between British India and the realm of Abdul Rahman Khan, the Afghan Amir. Pakistan claims that Afghanistan has officially recognized the border in practice but will not admit it for domestic political reasons. This dispute—including the dispute over whether a dispute exists—has made it difficult for the two countries to even discuss how to manage the border.

All of these borders separate ethnically similar populations on both sides, but cross-border relations among Pashtuns on both sides of the Afghan/Pakistan line are especially close. Pakistani Pashtuns sometimes call themselves Afghans, since the word denotes ethnicity as well as citizenship. Pashtuns in Pakistan feel they have a stake in Afghanistan, which some regard as theirs, as many of them also dispute the legitimacy of colonial agreements that separated those territories from the realm of the Afghan Amir.

During the war against the Soviet intervention in Afghanistan in the 1980s, about three million Afghans fled to Pakistan and about two million Afghans escaped to Iran. The process works the other way as well. In 2015, when the Pakistan military staged an offensive into the tribal areas in search of the Tehrik-i Taliban-i Pakistan (TTP, Taliban Movement of Pakistan) and other terrorist groups, tens of thousands of Pakistani Pashtuns fled into Afghanistan. When the Afghan president Ashraf Ghani welcomed the Pakistani refugees, the former president Hamid Karzai protested that they were "fellow Afghans." In the 1990s, after the collapse of the Soviet Union, the civil war in Tajikistan drove tens of thousands of refugees into the Tajik and Uzbek areas of Northern Afghanistan. They have mostly returned, but millions of Afghans remain in Iran and Pakistan, and tens of thousands of Pakistani Pashtuns remain in Eastern Afghanistan. Afghans in Pakistan inhabit not only the border areas but also the port city of Karachi, Pakistan's economic capital. The large Afghan presence in both Karachi and Dubai means that even if Afghanistan is a landlocked state, Afghans are far from being a landlocked people. Their economic, religious, and political networks extend into South Asia and the Persian Gulf countries.

Afghanistan's territory is landlocked. The lack of direct access to either the high seas or international air space makes a landlocked country uniquely dependent on—and vulnerable to—its neighbors. Landlocked countries have slower economic growth rates and lower rates of all indicators of economic and social development than other states. To connect to the international market, or to receive foreign aid or military and security assistance, Afghanistan depends on the cooperation of neighbors for land transit to markets or seaports and access to international airspace.

Before 1947, Afghanistan's foreign trade depended on links to Delhi and the seaport of Karachi, respectively about 1300 km (780 miles) and 1500 km (900 miles) from Kabul. After 1947 the closure of the Pakistan-India border left the country largely dependent on access to Karachi. Thanks to American and allied efforts to build airfields and storage facilities, Afghanistan today exports fruits, like pomegranates, to the Persian Gulf by air, but to fly from Afghanistan, to, for example, the United Arab Emirates, an airplane must cross the airspace of Pakistan, Iran, or both. Nonetheless, as described in chapter 10, the government of President Ghani has done much to diversify the country's foreign trade to lessen dependence on Pakistan. Afghanistan's Central Asian neighbors are also landlocked, and Uzbekistan is double landlocked—a landlocked country bordered only by other landlocked countries. Northward access to the international market or state system requires the cooperation of Russia or China as well. So, while all of the neighboring countries have potential economic leverage over Afghanistan, diversifying trade infrastructure and agreements increases Afghanistan's room to maneuver.

Throughout history, economic activities within this territory have included agriculture, pastoralism, and trade. Trade has fluctuated with the world economy and security. Before 1978 Afghanistan had a predominantly agricultural/pastoral economy (50 percent of GDP) and rural population (80 percent of population). About half of the agricultural production went for subsistence of the cultivators' families. Water was the scarcest input for agriculture. Because of scarcity of water, there was about twice as much arable land in Afghanistan as cultivated land, and today there are frequent droughts that seem to be increasing and becoming more severe with climate change. Afghanistan's economy is no longer primarily agricultural and pastoral, and the agricultural sector is dominated by a single internationally marketed cash crop: opium poppy. Wars, drug trade, foreign aid, and remittances from abroad have funded rapid urbanization and the growth of services.

Flows of water also shape Afghanistan's relations with its neighbors. The snowmelt of the Hindu Kush feeds several rivers whose basins extend into neighboring countries. The Kabul River is one of the five tributaries of the Indus, Pakistan's main water source, and the Helmand River supplies water to the Iranian province of Sistan-Baluchistan. The Kunduz River is a tributary of the Panj-Amu Darya, which defines Afghanistan's borders with Tajikistan, Uzbekistan, and part of the border with Turkmenistan. Use of the water of these rivers requires cooperation, but it has also been a source of conflict.

Afghanistan has often had disputes over water with Pakistan and Iran, as the rivers it shares with those two downstream countries are used for irrigation and power generation on both sides of the border. Use of the water of the Amu Darya is regulated by a 1949 agreement with the Soviet Union, which entitles Afghanistan to a higher share of the water than it is now using. Afghanistan has never used its share of the river water because it lacks the necessary irrigation infrastructure. In the ensuing years, the Amu Darya's flow has been reduced dramatically by extensive irrigation for cotton in Uzbekistan and Tajikistan, leading to the desiccation of the Aral Sea shared by Uzbekistan and Kazakhstan.

All of this is the reason that my boss at the UN, Lakhdar Brahimi, used to say, "Afghanistan cannot be peaceful if its neighbors do not want it to be peaceful."

Is Afghanistan the "graveyard of empires"?

The idea that Afghanistan is an eternally unconquerable nation that will defeat all who enter it and is destined for war and instability seems to be of relatively recent origin. At a meeting at the Wilson Center in Washington, DC, on April 6, 2016, an Afghan American from the Muhammadzai royal clan claimed that Afghanistan had defeated Alexander the Great, Genghis Khan, the British Empire, and the Soviet Union. Those opposed to military intervention in Afghanistan often cite the phrase "graveyard of empires," which also became the title of several books and articles.

Opponents of military intervention in Afghanistan may well be right, but not because Afghanistan has always been the "graveyard of empires." As the anthropologist Thomas Barfield put it, "Until 1840 Afghanistan was better known as a 'highway of conquest' rather than the 'graveyard of empires.' For 2,500 years it was always part of somebody's empire, beginning with the Persian Empire in the fifth century B.C."[1] The cities and regions of Kabul, Balkh, Kandahar, and Herat repeatedly came under the rule of empires and sometimes were themselves the seat of empires. Balkh, known to the Greeks as Bactria, was an important center of Zoroastrianism and Buddhism when Alexander the Great looted its great temple and married Roxana, daughter of the slain king. Kandahar is a derivative of the word "Alexandria," which was founded by Alexander the Great in 329 BCE. Hellenistic rule lasted two centuries, during which sculptors developed the Greco-Buddhist style of Gandhara, named after a kingdom, centered on the city of Peshawar.

Herat, along with Samarkand, was the seat of Persian culture during the Timurid Empire. The first Mughal emperor, Babur, a native of the Ferghana Valley in today's Uzbekistan, conquered Kabul and made it the first seat of the Mughal

---

1. Thomas Barfield, *Afghanistan: A Cultural and Political History.*

Empire. Those with even a glancing acquaintance of Kabul will know of Babur's garden, where he and several of his descendants were buried. Babur's grandson, the Mughal emperor Akbar, founded Jalalabad, which bears his name—his personal name was Jalaluddin, and the name of the city means "built by Jalal."

The Afghan Durrani Empire, a precursor of today's Afghan state, established its center in Kandahar in 1747 and moved to Kabul in 1775. The first Anglo-Afghan War (1839–42) is best known for the massacre of the British contingent as it retreated through the snows toward Jalalabad in the winter of 1841–42, one of the origins of the graveyard of empires trope. It is largely forgotten that the British then fought their way back to Kabul, leveled the bazaar, freed British prisoners, and evacuated Afghanistan on their own terms. In the second Anglo-Afghan War (1878–80), the Afghan Army inflicted a major defeat on the British in the battle of Maiwand in Kandahar province. It was at this battle that the apocryphal Pashtun maiden Malalai threw off her veil and, before being fatally wounded by a British bullet, recited in a famous patriotic couplet: "If you do not fall as a martyr at Maiwand, by God, someone must be saving you for a life of shame!" In *A Study in Scarlet*, Sherlock Holmes deduces that Dr. Watson was wounded in that battle. Despite the heroic memories of Afghan resistance, however, the British achieved their objectives in the war. They imposed the 1879 treaty of Gandamak on Amir Yaqub Khan, taking control of Afghanistan's foreign relations and taking the eastern provinces of Afghanistan into British India, with a buffer zone for the "frontier tribes." Sir Mortimer Durand delineated that boundary under an 1893 agreement with Amir Abdul Rahman Khan. In 1919, after winning a brief skirmish at the Durand Line, Amir Amanullah Khan won the country's full independence, but at the price of accepting the colonial, imposed border in the 1921 Treaty of Rawalpindi.

The Afghan mujahidin did not force the Soviet Union out of Afghanistan as the Afghans under Wazir Akbar Khan forced out the British in 1841. They did, however, inflict severe enough damage that when the reformist Mikhail Gorbachev came to power in 1985, he decided it was more important to improve relations with the West than try to succeed in Afghanistan. The Afghans alone did not inflict that blow on the Soviet Union—unlike any previous war, their resistance received support from major powers, and the strength of that resistance reflected the changing balance of forces in the Cold War. Today the US is again testing the limits of intervention in Afghanistan.

If the "graveyard of empires" trope does not fit the history of all the territory of today's Afghanistan, it is less inaccurate with respect to the mountainous area along today's Afghanistan/Pakistan border, and especially the tribal territories of Pakistan, an area that has always been difficult to conquer or to rule. Before the word "Afghanistan" came to designate a political unit in the nineteenth century, it referred to this area, inhabited by "Afghans" (Pashtuns). In that Afghanistan, people lived in remote valleys, where many tribes depended on nomadism. Such areas were difficult and costly to control and yielded little revenue or commercial advantage. Under the British Empire, the frontier tribes living in the eastern part of this region had a special status. British Indian law did not apply there, nor did Pakistani law from 1947 until the abolition of the Federally Administered Tribal Areas (FATA) in 2018. The population answered to the state through tribal leaders. The British and their Pakistani successors treated those areas like a moat against invaders from the north or west, rather than a part of the state they governed. Changing technologies of transportation and communication, however, have made it much more feasible to communicate with and travel into those areas, and today its inhabitants are demanding full rights as citizens of the states in which they live.

It is also true that the territory of today's Afghanistan, with its sparse population, shortage of water, lack of navigable rivers, and low agricultural productivity, has been difficult not only to conquer but also to rule in its entirety. Those empires that conquered parts of today's Afghanistan essentially held onto the cities and towns and the roads connecting them. The rest of the territory and its population were left largely untouched, as long as they did not interfere with trade or the business of the state.

The main challenge facing today's Afghanistan is not that the martial spirit of its warlike tribal people makes Afghanistan unconquerable or ungovernable, but that the country does not produce enough to cover the costs of governing it. The only way that it ever could produce enough would be to connect to the international markets, which would, in turn, require good relations with its neighbors.

Does Afghanistan threaten the world, or vice versa?

Instability alone does not necessarily give rise to global terrorism. The Democratic Republic of Congo has been unstable and has posed many problems to its neighbors, who also destabilized Congo in order to cope with their own problems, but it never became a source of global threats. Afghanistan was structured by the British to be dependent, and the erosion and collapse of the Anglo-Russian agreement on how to manage that dependence culminated in the war that began in 1978 and continues in 2019. Once the balance of the late colonial period and the early Cold War broke down, the USSR moved in to subsidize the state, generating a global and regional reaction that undermined the state. When the USSR collapsed, and the state lost the subsidy that enabled it to pay for security forces, the Afghan state, too, collapsed. Pakistan briefly consolidated weak control through the Taliban, but al-Qaeda's attack brought the country under US hegemony, which gradually generated a reaction not only from Islamist groups but from the regional powers whose interests the US threatened.

There are many possible scenarios for instability, but only one for stability. Stability requires at least that no regional or global power with the capacity to destabilize Afghanistan sees the political and military order in Afghanistan as a threat. That requires difficult international coordination among states with histories of suspicion and mistrust, as well as a compact among the peoples of Afghanistan itself.

2

THE LAND AND THE PEOPLE

How do people in Afghanistan identify themselves?

To understand a society, it is important to understand the identities of its people; it is equally important to remember that there is no direct causality from identity to belief or action in politics, culture, economics, or anything else. People may have multiple identities, which they deploy in different situations. Identities change. Above all, people have the capacity to reflect on their identities, to accept, reject, or modify them, or even create new ones.

Most Afghans rank "Muslim" as their most important identity.[1] Since the first Afghan empire in the eighteenth century, the predominant and official religion has been Sunni Islam of the Hanafi sect. A minority, mainly Hazara, follow the Twelver Imami Shi'a (they follow twelve imams as successors to Muhammad) like the predominant Shi'a in Iran, Iraq, and Lebanon. Another Twelver Imami Shi'a community is the Qizilbash, descended from units of Turkmen troops recruited

---

1. There are some non-Muslims in Afghanistan, and there used to be more of them. There are Hindus and Sikhs who were trading with the Indian subcontinent before 1947. There was also a small Jewish population in Kabul, Herat, and a few other places. The first constitution of Afghanistan in 1923 said that Afghanistan's official religion was Islam, but that the rights of "Jews and Hindus" would be protected.

in the eighteenth century. "Qizilbash," meaning "red head" in Turkish, refers to the red hats that the guard units wore. There is also a small but influential community of Ismaili Shi'as, many of whom are followers of the Agha Khan, whose investments employ many of them in the hospitality and telecommunications industries.

Islamic belief and practice have been changing rapidly in the past few decades. Under the monarchy, which ruled until 1973, two main Sufi (spiritual) sects played leading roles. Sufis received royal patronage—the Qadiri sect led by the Gailani family and the Naqshbandi sect, led in Afghanistan by the Mojaddedi family. Many eastern Pashtun tribes followed the Gailanis, while the Mojaddedis maintained a network of madrasas (Islamic educational institutions) around the country. Sebghatullah Mojaddedi and Sayyid Ahmad Gailani led the main two "nationalist-moderate" parties of the anti-Soviet mujahidin. Nearly all senior members of the Mojaddedi family, however, were massacred by the communist regime of Nur Muhammad Taraki in February 1979. These Sufi networks have entered politics, but the Sufi practices of both worshiping at shrines where spiritual leaders are buried and of mystical devotion have declined among some sectors of the population in favor of various forms of puritanical militancy.

Since the partition of India, the Deobandi school of Islamic thought and practice has grown, especially in rural Pashtun areas. Named after the town of Deoband in northern India, the Deobandi school was founded in the nineteenth century as a revivalist alternative to Islamic modernism as a way of challenging colonialism. It taught strict adherence to the main works of the Hanafi school but also supported Sufism. When the Deobandis of Pakistan were cut off from the main body of the sect in 1947, they expanded madrasas in Karachi, the Northwest Frontier Province and FATA (now Khyber Pakhtunkhwa) and Balochistan. Religious students (taliban) flocked from Afghanistan to the madrasas in Pakistan, where many paid no tuition and received full room and board.

During the Soviet-Afghan war, Saudi and Kuwaiti aid workers and mujahidin influenced them in the direction of Salafi Islam, which rejects Sufism and worship at shrines. Deobandi madrasas that taught a militant puritanical version of the sect's doctrines, which were often the only educational institutions open to Afghan refugee boys in Pakistan, became incubators of the Taliban.

The mob murder of Farkhunda in March 2015 illustrates some of the tensions in contemporary Afghan Islam. A young woman with an Islamic education, Farkhunda charged that a so-called mullah making and selling amulets at one of Kabul's main shrines was corrupt. These amulets contain inscriptions that supposedly counter the evil eye or bring good luck. Farkhunda's education led her to oppose such superstitions and gave her the courage to speak out as a woman for a purer form of Islam. The mullah charged that she had burned pages of a Quran, which turned out to be false, but a mob of men beat her to death and burned her body. Her case drew attention to violence against women, but it also illustrates the tensions between traditional practices and demand for modernizing orthodoxy among educated youth, including women.

The current constitution of Afghanistan states that the religion of the state is "the sacred religion of Islam," whereas previous constitutions said that the religion of the state is Islam according to Hanafi rites. The current constitution also recognizes Shi'a jurisprudence for personal law among Shi'a.

So far, Afghanistan has escaped the large-scale sectarian conflict and terrorism that has grown in parts of the Arab world, though the rise of the Taliban and especially the Islamic State has stoked sectarian fears.

What are the main ethnic groups in Afghanistan?

Originally, the word "Afghan" referred to Pashtuns, and sometimes it still does. Variants of the term are found in texts dating to the Sassanians in the third century BCE. Both ancient

Sanskrit sources and the Greek historian Herodotus refer to "Pakhtans" or "Paktiai" living in what is now the Afghanistan-Pakistan border area. Pashtun-led governments introduced a new meaning of the word, a citizen of a state called Afghanistan. Since 1923, all constitutions of Afghanistan have stated that a citizen of Afghanistan is Afghan, regardless of ethnicity, but some non-Pashtuns contest the term.

The Afghan constitution of 2004 recognizes fourteen ethnic groups, but only four are large enough to participate as such in the national political arena: Pashtuns, Tajiks, Hazaras, and Uzbeks.[2] Pashtuns have historically been organized tribally, though not all Pashtuns live in tribes. Some of those tribes established and lent their ethnonym to the Afghan state. Some Pashtuns consider Afghanistan as their state, representing their identity, even if they are citizens of Pakistan or another state.

Though no group totally conforms to any model of social organization, Pashtuns have largely been organized in patrilineal tribes. Their Pashto language is an eastern Iranian language like Kurdish or the Shughnani language spoken in the Pamir Mountains of Northeast Afghanistan and Eastern Tajikistan. They have settled in a belt of land from Peshawar up to Kabul and south of Kabul to Balochistan and as far west as Herat. Their nomadic movements enabled them also to become long-distance traders, who settled in India as far as Calcutta. The Afghan monarchy settled many among non-Pashtuns in the north and west, especially along the borders, to guarantee the security of the state in those areas. Like all ethnic groups, many have migrated to cities in Afghanistan, Pakistan, Iran, and the Persian Gulf.

---

2. Article 4 of the constitution states, "The nation of Afghanistan shall be comprised of Pashtun, Tajik, Hazara, Uzbek, Turkman, Baluch, Pachaie, Nuristani, Aymaq, Arab, Qirghiz, Qizilbash, Gujur, Brahwui and other tribes. The word Afghan shall apply to every citizen of Afghanistan."

The largest other group is Tajiks. The origin of the word "Tajik" is unclear. Mountstuart Elphinstone, the first British envoy to what he called the "Kingdom of Caubul and its Dependencies," wrote in 1826, "The name of Taujik is very loosely used," meaning it could have different meanings in different contexts. In contemporary Afghan terminology, a Tajik is a Sunni Persian speaker, which includes people from mountainous areas like Panjshir and Badakhshan and also people from big cities like Herat, Kabul, and Mazar-i Sharif. There are many rural Tajiks engaged in agriculture and related activities, but most of the urban population of Afghanistan is Persian speaking. The second generation of Pashtuns or Uzbeks who move to the city usually adopt the Persian language. Families of mixed origin who assimilate to urban life, adopt Dari (the Afghan form of Persian) as their mother tongue, and lose affiliation with their original group sometimes assimilate to Tajik identity.

Uzbek is an identity redefined in the Soviet Union in the 1920s and '30s. Previously the term designated a tribe speaking a Turkic language in Central Asia, but Stalin consolidated many Turki-speaking groups into a single nationality called Uzbeks, and the term migrated to Afghanistan as well. Their language, which used to be called Turki, or Chaghatay, is now called Uzbeki. In north Afghanistan, contiguous to Uzbekistan and Turkmenistan, there are also a smaller number of Turkmen. Uzbeks and Turkmen in Afghanistan each share their spoken language with co-ethnics to the north, but their written languages are different. The Turkmen and Uzbeks in Uzbekistan and Turkmenistan, who underwent Russification while they were part of the Soviet Union, came to write their languages in Cyrillic script and have switched to Latin script since independence, following the example of Turkey.

Before the urbanization of Afghanistan, Hazaras lived in the central highlands area, which was therefore known as Hazarajat. "Hazara" means "one thousand" in Persian and was at one time a designation for a military unit. There is a tradition that the Hazaras are descended from part of the armies of Genghis Khan, though it is not substantiated by concrete evidence. Many have Central Asian or East Asian facial features. They are almost all Imami Shi'a.

The Hazaras were not ruled from Kabul or by Pashtuns until the late nineteenth century. The Afghan ruler, Amir Abdul Rahman Khan, who was recognized and funded by the British to take control of the territory, conquered their area. Many were massacred, raped, and enslaved, acts supposedly justified by the belief of some Sunnis that Shi'a are not Muslims. Even after the abolition of slavery by the 1923 constitution, Shi'a were not equal subjects. They performed the most menial tasks in Afghanistan's cities.

Their situation has changed in the past decades. When millions of Afghans became refugees, a disproportionate number of Hazaras went to Iran, where they have cultural and religious affinities. In Iran, while they suffered various kinds of discrimination, refugees from Afghanistan had access to better education than in Pakistan. When those refugees began to return to Afghanistan after 2001, educated Hazaras moved into influential positions, not only in the state but in the private sector such as media and telecommunications.

Another important group are the Sayyids (Sadat). They are not an ethnic group—Sayyids are associated with but not members of every ethnic group in Afghanistan. Sayyids are a status group supposedly descended from the family of Ali, the son–in–law of prophet Muhammad. They have played important roles in religion and the bureaucracy and are gaining increased group consciousness.

Is Afghanistan a tribal society?

The tribe is important to some parts of Afghan society and the basis, at least symbolically, of some state institutions. The claim that Afghanistan is "tribal" is a political claim that emphasizes the importance of ethnicity and kinship to national identity. Afghanistan is sparsely populated, with weak state institutions, including institutions of justice. The population includes nomads, people who have no fixed address, who move with their animals from place to place in search of pasture and markets. Farmers bring the water to their land through irrigation; nomads bring their animals to the water through migration. Since nomads have no fixed addresses, they are difficult for a state bureaucracy to govern. Instead of location, kinship becomes an organizing principle among nomads and other groups in weak states.

In Afghanistan and in much of the world, kinship follows strict patrilineage and patriarchy. Family identity is transmitted only through the father. This differs from the bilinear kinship predominant in Europe and the US, although even that form has patrilineal elements. Children in the West have traditionally taken the father's surname, and a wife took her husband's surname, but this is far from universal today. For most purposes, however, the maternal and paternal families have the same status. Tracing lines of descent including both male and female ancestors in a bilinear kinship system becomes virtually impossible within a few generations, as there can be two, four, eight, sixteen, thirty-two, and so on ancestors per generation.

In patrilineal systems, however, identity is inherited only through the father's side, and a genealogy may extend back dozens of generations. These genealogies, whether true or fictitious, constitute the foundation of tribal identity and of relations among tribes and subtribes. As the ancient Israelites had a patrilineal tribal society, this is the same kinship system found in the Hebrew Bible. In such a society, marriage brings the wife into her husband's patrilineal family. The marriage may cement an alliance between the families, tribes, or clans of the bride and groom, but it is clear who belongs to which group. This kind of identity has been reinforced by the structures of property and production, which include land and animals owned and managed by kinship groups. The kinship unit mobilizes labor and distributes the fruits of production.

Families, clans, or tribes have also exercised policing and military activities. Tribes may have oral codes of customary justice and dispute resolution, the best known of which is Pashtunwali, the oral code of customary law among some Pashtuns. Given the pervasive importance of kinship, it has become an idiom for talking about and forming relationships. Kinship does not just define relationships; relationships that originally have nothing to do with kinship may be expressed or strengthened through this system. For instance, in the 1980s Afghanistan was ruled by the People's Democratic Party of Afghanistan (PDPA), a communist party founded in the 1960s. Members of the politburo of the PDPA arranged marriages among their sons and daughters to strengthen the party. A communist party is not a tribe, but tribal norms of behavior strengthened it. Ahmad Zia Massoud, the brother of the United Front (Northern Alliance) military leader, Ahmad Shah Massoud, married one of the daughters of Burhanuddin Rabbani, the political leader of the Northern Alliance, reinforcing and sustaining factional and familial ties. There are many such examples.

A state may try to weaken tribalism, but it can also use it to control the population. Each citizen of a bureaucratic state has an individual identity: a certificate giving date and place of birth, as well as surname and personal name(s); a social security or identity card number; an address; a place of employment; a taxpayer identification number; and, ultimately, a death certificate. The government governs the citizens using this information.

This system is expensive. In Afghanistan and other weak states, the state may instead rely on kinship or residence-based collectivities to provide information and exercise authority, however imperfectly, on the state's behalf. As part of the September 2014 National Unity Government agreement between President Ashraf Ghani and Dr. Abdullah Abdullah, the government promised to issue electronic identity cards (e-Tazkira) to all citizens. Such a database would serve many purposes, including the creation of a permanent electoral register, a major step toward reducing electoral fraud.

One of the obstacles to fair elections in Afghanistan is that the state has very little information about the population. There has never been a complete census, and many people do not have identity cards or addresses. The government has distributed identity cards, tazkiras, for decades but until recently has never tried to distribute them to everyone. People who interacted regularly with the state, like government employees or students at the university, would have the tazkiras, but most of the population did not.

One of my colleagues, an Afghan of Shi'a Sayyid origin, in his early thirties, brought copies of his brother's and his father's tazkiras to me, so that I could see how they differed. In his grandfather's time very few people had tazkiras. His grandfather was the malik, or khan, head of the village, as the tax collector: alaqadar. When the king, Zahir Shah, would visit the village, he would have lunch with his grandfather, and then the king and his grandfather would discuss whatever needed to be discussed. They would make an agreement, on taxes, conscription, or any other matter. The king would leave, and it was then his grandfather's responsibility to deliver the results. The king and his government had no idea who lived in the village; that was his grandfather's responsibility. The state governed through the tribal or clan relationship between the khan and the village. Tribalism does not just structure the state; the state also structures tribalism.

Like all identities, the salience of tribal identity varies with context. Tribal identity is important for a nomad. If the son of a nomad gets a university education, moves to a city, and gets a job in the government, the function of tribal affiliation changes. Getting a job may require asking for patronage from someone from your tribe in the right position. Fellow tribesmen will come by asking for money, jobs for their family members, or some other favor. But there are also competing forms of authority and identity: rank in the bureaucracy, wealth, and political connections. For the past few decades, for instance, control of armed men has become important.

In areas of the country that have been under more stable government control, tribal identities are weaker but can rebound when the state collapses. The monarchy recognized and strengthened some Pashtun tribal identities and weakened others. Tajiks, Uzbeks, and Hazaras have kinship-based collective identities, but their clans are not structured to exercise authority and do not have their own codes of justice, as some Pashtun tribes do.

What is the economy of Afghanistan?

For much of history the territory of today's Afghanistan has been a crossroads, a role the Afghan government hopes to revive. Before the fifteenth and sixteenth centuries and technological developments that made possible long-distance, or "blue-water," navigation, much of the world's trade was transported overland, sometimes over extreme distances. Archaeologists have found items made of lapis lazuli, a blue precious stone found only in Badakhshan, in Northeastern Afghanistan, in tombs from the Old Kingdom of Egypt (third millennium BCE). Four or five thousand years ago, traders took the lapis, probably over the mountains to the River Indus, then by raft to the coast, and then by shore-hugging boats to the shores of the Red Sea.

Because of its position at the intersection of major civilizations, a number of trade routes met and crossed in Afghanistan. The long-distance land-based trade routes between China and the Mediterranean came to be known collectively as the Silk Route or Silk Road, after China's export of that luxury commodity, which was so sought after in Europe and the Middle East.

Those ancient trade routes lost their importance as European countries mastered blue-water navigation, which was much more economical than long-distance overland trade by pack animal. And so the Mughal, Safavid, and Ottoman Empires collapsed in the seventeenth century in part when their trading revenues declined because of the competition from European sea trade. Afghanistan, then, went from being a crossroads to being isolated.

In today's Afghanistan the biggest industry is war. The withdrawal of most of the foreign troops by the end of 2014 meant a loss to the economy of about three hundred thousand jobs, but the continued funding of the Afghan National Defense and Security Forces (ANDSF), not only for salaries but also for construction, food, uniforms, fuel, and telecommunications, assured a continued flow of foreign cash. There may be no reliable sources on how much of the security assistance actually enters the Afghan economy rather than being recycled into the donor's economy.

The second-largest industry is narcotics production and trafficking of opium and its derivatives, marijuana, and hashish. Anecdotal evidence suggests that some Afghans have started labs for manufacture of barbiturates and alkaloids as well. There are only general estimates of the size of some parts of the illegal drug economy, which is not included in national income estimates.

Data collected in the 1970s, the last time the country was at peace, showed that the population of Afghanistan was about 80 percent rural, and that about 50 percent of the GDP came from agriculture, mainly subsistence cultivation of wheat and rice. Afghanistan was also an important exporter of fresh and dried fruits to the surrounding countries; for instance, Afghan melons and other fruits were highly prized in Delhi. By the 1970s Afghanistan had become the world's third-largest producer of raisins, after the US and Greece. It also had exports based on animal husbandry, in particular, karakul lamb from Northern Afghanistan produced by Turkmen who had fled the

Soviet Union. Traders then were able to take the karakul to be sold in European markets.

In the 1930s, the king adopted a proposal from Abdul Majid Zabuli, a visionary trader who provided the capital needed to found a development bank, the Afghan National Bank (Bank-i Milli) in 1931. At that time the government, working closely with Zabuli, used investments by Bank-i Milli to develop the country, largely by investing in cotton cultivation, processing, and marketing, especially in Kunduz and Helmand provinces. The government drained swampland along the Kunduz River, diverting the water into irrigation canals, and then settled Pashtuns from the south and east, which changed the ethnic composition of the area. At the same time, the Soviet regime under Stalin was turning contiguous areas of Central Asia into a cotton bowl.

Afghanistan never became a major cotton exporter, but it had gained importance in the market before the Soviet intervention. The country had no industrial production except for a few government factories like a textile mill in Kapisa province. In the 1970s the Soviets developed natural gas wells in Jawzjan in Northern Afghanistan. It was piped directly to Uzbekistan, which was then in the Soviet Union.

The Roman philosopher Cicero, ca. 63 BCE, had called money "the sinews of war." When war started, money inundated Afghanistan, from the Soviet Union, the United States, Saudi Arabia, and eventually NATO, the World Bank, and virtually every state and development institution—not to mention from drug traffickers and other kingpins of the illicit economy. Before the war, subsistence farmers grew food to eat, rather than to market, which required relatively little money. When young men abandoned agriculture for warfare, they also abandoned a largely subsistence economy for a monetized one: armed groups must buy supplies, including food, which becomes scarcer and more expensive. The money that finances the war also finances food imports. In addition, the people who remain on the land can no longer live off the subsistence economy, because everything is too expensive. They need cash incomes as well, and the way they get cash incomes is by producing opium poppy or migrating to cities where foreigners spend money, or to labor markets in Iran, the Persian Gulf, Pakistan, Europe, the US, or Australia so that they can send money home in what are called "remittances."

As an isolated buffer state, Afghanistan never experienced direct rule by a European colonial power. No foreign companies turned forest or farmland into commercial plantations for cultivation of a single crop, like rubber in Liberia, tea in Sri Lanka, indigo in parts of northern India, or minerals in parts of Africa. The first experience Afghanistan had in mass production of raw materials for the international market was the drug economy.

Millions of Afghans also became refugees. Even before the war, in 1973, the hike in oil prices had expanded the demand for migrant labor in the Persian Gulf. Remittances started to become an important part of Afghanistan's economy. After the war started, remittances from the millions of Afghans living in the neighboring countries became much more important. War, the drug trade, and remittances are the three current mainstays of the Afghan economy.

While before the war 80 percent of the population of Afghanistan lived in rural areas, that country soon became one of the fastest-urbanizing societies in Asia. That is one of the reasons for massive exodus of migrants and asylum seekers from Afghanistan after 2014, which is quite different from the predominantly rural refugees escaping bombing or fighting in the 1980s. The migrants of post-2014 were mostly urban, educated youth, who had either lost their jobs or could see no prospect of getting a job, because of the withdrawal of the international community from Afghanistan.

The current government has considered how Afghanistan can develop a productive economy to become more self-sufficient. Initially Afghanistan would charge fees for the transit of oil, natural gas, and electricity through its territory.

Two projects have kicked off that effort. One is CASA-1000 (Central Asia South Asia 1,000 Megawatts), financed by the Asian Development Bank, which brings electricity produced by hydropower in Kyrgyzstan and Tajikistan across Northern Afghanistan and into Pakistan. The second connectivity project is the TAPI (Turkmenistan, Afghanistan, Pakistan, India) gas pipeline. A consortium is supposed to build pipelines from Turkmenistan gas fields, south through Afghanistan, into Pakistan, and then to India for natural gas and eventually oil. Pakistan is badly in need of natural gas to overcome large gaps in the power supply, but the major source of demand in the region is in India. TAPI is supposedly going to earn Afghanistan about $300 million a year.

Soviet geological surveys and the 2014 United States Geological Survey indicate that Afghanistan has mineral and hydrocarbon resources that might be worth approximately $1 trillion on the international market, but at the moment there is no way to bring these resources to market. China has been the largest prospective investor in Afghanistan and has signed a contract for what would have been the largest copper mine in the world, in Logar province, south of Kabul, but work has stopped because of security problems, the fall in commodity prices after the 2008 financial crisis, and the discovery of a massive archaeological site at the mine's location (Mes Aynak or "little copper well," which includes the remains of a 2,000-year-old Buddhist city).

Is Afghanistan a traditional society living in some past century?

This trope is based on a fallacy of what modernity is and also about what tradition is. Afghans are living fully in modern society, but it is not the idealized modern society of the Western imagination. Afghanistan's economy and social relations have been revolutionized and transformed by their contact with war and the international economy. Previous social relations, beliefs, and values have not disappeared, any more than they have in the West. One of the reasons that some, especially young people, adopt new and even foreign ideologies is the new situations that they are facing, to which their previous values and institutions do not seem adapted. What some see as traditions in Afghanistan are often ideological reactions against these rapid changes brought about by war.

One of the reasons people think that Afghanistan is a traditional society is that some Afghans tell them it is. Here's an example: I was at a meeting in Washington in late 2008 with two US military officers, who had been working in provincial reconstruction teams (PRTs, see chapter 6). These officers gave a presentation called "Traditional Afghan Society" as it might have been described in an Afghan textbook of the 1960s or '70s: Afghans live in tribes, the king is at the top, kinship is the most important relationship, Afghans are moderate apolitical Muslims. The US would succeed, these officers argued, to the extent that it respected those traditions, and that would have led politically to bringing back Zahir Shah as the king in 2001 or 2002. Some Afghans wanted that, but others, including the armed groups that the US relied on to overthrow the Taliban, opposed it. Traditionalism is a political position, not an empirical description of a society.

3

STATE AND POLITICS

What is the origin of Afghanistan?

The place name "Afghanistan" occurs in the tenth-century Persian geography *Hudud al-'Alam* (Frontiers of the world), referring to the region that we would now call the Afghanistan-Pakistan border area. Much of today's Afghanistan, including Kabul, Balkh, and Herat, belonged to what was then the Eastern Persian region of Khurasan, along with Nishapur and Mashhad in today's Iranian province of Khorasan, and Samarkand and Bukhara in today's Uzbekistan. Afghanistan, in its current form, was constructed through the interaction of the British in India, the Russians in Central Asia, and Afghan clans and rulers in the late nineteenth century. The first official use of "Afghanistan" to refer to a state rather than a region seems to have been in the 1879 Treaty of Gandamak between the British government and "Yakub Khan, Amir of Afghanistan and its dependencies." Even that phrase still refers to a region, as it distinguishes "Afghanistan" from other territories ruled by the Amir.

How to recount the history of this state is a political issue: nationalist historiography recounts the history of Pashtun-led empires and states starting in the early to mid-eighteenth century as part of a continuous national history going back to ancient "Ariana." Other versions focus on the history of Khurasan.

The former account identifies the state with Pashtun rule and the latter with its largely Persian-speaking culture, which was adopted by Turkic, Mongol, and Pashtun rulers. For most of history, empires based in neighboring regions ruled all or parts of the territory of today's Afghanistan. Rulers originating or based in Afghanistan sometimes conquered parts of India or Iran. As noted in chapter 1, the common stereotype of Afghanistan as the "graveyard of empires" would have come as a surprise to the Mauryas, Guptas, Macedonians, Sassanids, Kushans, Abbasids, Ghaznavids, Mongols, Timurids, Mughals, Safavids, and Shaybani Uzbeks, among others, all of whom ruled parts of this territory and contributed to its cultural heritage.

Afghanistan began to assume its present form, though not under that name, in the early eighteenth century, when leaders from Kandahari tribes established empires. Mirwais Hotaki, from the Hotak tribe of the Ghilzai confederation ("ulus"), overthrew Safavid rule in Kandahar in 1721. He occupied and looted the Persian capital of Isfahan. That short-lived empire was soon absorbed into the conquests of the new ruler of Persia, Nadir Khan Afshar, a Turkmen whose cavalry were under the command of a Kandahari from a rival tribe, Ahmad Shah Abdali. When Nadir was assassinated in 1747, Abdali returned to Kandahar. He brought with him tools of Persian and Turkic statecraft, including kingship and the use of tribalism structured by the state as an instrument of rule. A member of the Saddozai clan of the Popalzai tribe of the Abdali confederation, Abdali became the first king (padshah) of the Afghans. Upon receiving the kingship he took the title "Padshah-i Durr-i Durran"—king of the pearl of pearls—and the Abdalis then took "Durrani" as their new name. He appointed khans for the tribes, a Turco-Mongol practice never previously used by Pashtuns and assigned them ranks at the court and in the army. He distributed large tracts of irrigated land to the highest-ranking (Zeerak) Durrani tribes, which included, besides the

Popalzai, the Barakzai (including its Achakzai branch) and the Alokozai.

After Nadir Shah's conquest and looting of Delhi in 1739 and then his own assassination in 1747, the empires based in Isfahan and Delhi were badly weakened. Ahmad Shah Durrani took advantage of the situation to found his own empire. Ahmad Shah ruled from Kandahar, as did his son. In 1775 his grandson, Timur Shah, moved the capital to Kabul in an effort to gain greater independence from the Kandahari tribes. Having its capital in Kabul became one of the characteristics of the Afghan state. The Taliban's Islamic Emirate hearkened back to an earlier period; although it kept the ministers and government in Kabul, the supreme religious leader, the amir, remained in Kandahar.

The Durrani Empire grew in a temporary power vacuum at the intersection of three major civilizational areas, the Persian, Turkish, and Indian, also known as Iran, Turan, and Hindustan. In the succeeding centuries, empires from Europe, Britain, and Russia warred over control of territory and populations, notably in the First (1838–42) and Second (1878–80) Anglo-Afghan Wars. The British finally settled on creating a state called Afghanistan, shorn of the Durrani Empire's eastern territories. Russia and Britain agreed on spheres of influence and control in the 1907 Anglo-Russian Convention on Persia, Afghanistan, and Tibet.

During most of the nineteenth century, two conflicts shaped Afghanistan's political development: the rivalry for power among different tribes and clans of the Durrani Pashtuns, and the rivalry between the British and Russian Empires as they approached Afghanistan from opposing directions.

After the Second Anglo-Afghan War, the British, the Russians, and the Muhammadzai clan of the Barakzai tribe of the Durranis reached an agreement on how to resolve both of those questions. The answer was, first of all, that the British would support the rule of Amir Abdul Rahman Khan. He would become an absolute monarch, and the kingship would be passed down only through his lineage. Second, Afghanistan would exercise internal autonomy while the British controlled its foreign relations.

In the past, the Afghan Empire or kingdom had been a tribal monarchy where the king was first among equals in his clan. On the death of a ruler, multiple leaders would stake claim to the throne. Once ensconced in Kabul, that ruler would appoint his cousins, nephews, uncles, and other patrilineal and affinal relatives as governors and other officials. These officials could develop territorial bases of power from which to challenge the ruler or compete for the succession.

Amir Abdul Rahman Khan, however, using money from the British, settled the Muhammadzai elders in Kabul and made them "sharik-al-dawlat," or partners of the state. Rather than appointing them as governors and tax farmers who could challenge the ruler, he educated and paid them to serve in the administration. He built up a large army, with a subsidy from the British, which enabled him to control the territory. The aid from the British did not elicit a hostile response from the Russians, because Britain and Russia had reached an agreement, codified in the Anglo-Russian entente of 1907, which regularized the border regions of the British and Russian Empires. Under the terms of that agreement, Afghanistan would become a part of the British zone of influence, but it would not come under direct British control, and there would be no British troops there.

That entente incorporated or confirmed two bilateral agreements concluded by Amirs Yaqub Khan and Abdul Rahman Khan with British India, the 1879 Treaty of Gandamak and the Durand Agreement of 1893. Under the former treaty, Kabul relinquished to British India much of the territory east of Kabul that it had ruled previously. Amir Yaqub Khan agreed to have no relations with foreign states without the concurrence of the British government, ceding control of the country's external relations. The British government promised that "its Agents shall never in any way interfere with the internal administration of His Highness's dominions." Afghanistan never came under the direct rule of a European colonial power, but it lost its international sovereignty.

The Durand Agreement formalized the "Durand Line," the boundary across which the amir of Afghanistan and the British agreed not to exercise interference. It bears the name of Sir Mortimer Durand, the British official who demarcated the line together with the amir's representatives. Since the partition and independence of India and Pakistan in 1947, Kabul has claimed that it does not recognize that line as the legitimate international boundary with Pakistan.

What political developments shaped the Afghan government since the country took on its present form?

Amir Abdul Rahman Khan changed the government of Afghanistan from a tribal monarchy with a military-feudal administration to a dynastic absolute monarchy presiding over a centralized administration. He also tried to centralize the judiciary and ulama (Muslim scholars of religion and law), though with less success. He built Afghanistan's first internal intelligence agency, the Na'ib Kotwal, which developed a network of informers throughout the country's elites.

Abdul Rahman repressed more than forty revolts, four of which he characterized as civil wars. He imposed the death penalty frequently. He incorporated new regions, tribes, and ethnic groups into the country by marrying the daughters of their leaders himself or to members of his family. He brought to his court the sons and daughters of leaders whom he subdued, creating a nationwide political elite cemented by kinship with the royal family.

He made the Muhammadzais into his partners in the state, not by delegating rulership to their leaders but by offering them high positions within the state that he controlled. He showed particular harshness to the Hazaras when he conquered them, declaring them to be non-Muslims. Thousands were massacred or enslaved. When he conquered Nuristan, however, once the formerly pagan population accepted Islam, he was lenient and incorporated chosen Nuristani leaders into the elite.

All of this state violence succeeded in "stabilizing" the country. The rate of (private) murder declined. The amir died in his bed in 1901, leaving his uncontested throne to his son Habibullah.

Amir Habibullah inherited a realm that was largely subdued, and he did not need to use the violence his father had. He continued the policy of integrating elites into the state through intermarriage—he had more than one hundred wives and concubines. World War I, the Russian Revolution, and the growing movement for Indian independence, however, shook up the environment.

Habibullah established the first modern schools in Afghanistan, for boys only, and introduced other reforms. A group of intellectuals formed a constitutionalist movement, such as existed at that time in Iran and the Ottoman Empire as well. The most prominent of these scholars was Mahmud Tarzi. Tarzi came from a Muhammadzai family that had lived for many years in Damascus, then part of the Ottoman Empire. Historians generally credit Tarzi with introducing modern political thought to Afghanistan, especially through his newspaper, *Siraj al-Akhbar* (literally the Sun of the News, but perhaps better translated as the *Sun Newspaper*). Tarzi's daughter, Soraya, married Amanullah Khan, who appointed his father-in-law as foreign minister and tried to implement some of his ideas.

During World War I, despite overtures by a German mission to Kabul seeking to enlist the Afghans, along with their ally the Ottoman Empire, against their common enemies, Britain and Russia, Habibullah remained neutral, which may have been why he was assassinated in his tent while hunting near Jalalabad in February 1919. The assassin or his motives have never been conclusively identified, but the most likely suspect is the conservative Islamic faction centered on Habibullah's eldest son, Nasrullah Khan. Nasrullah lost the struggle to succeed his father to his younger brother Amanullah.

After World War I, when Britain was relatively weakened, the young new king of Afghanistan, Amanullah Khan, launched a brief war in 1919 for Afghanistan's independence, known as the Third Anglo-Afghan War. Under the subsequent Treaty of Rawalpindi, Afghanistan regained its independence, including full control of its foreign affairs in return for recognizing colonial boundaries.

Amanullah enacted the country's first constitution. He proclaimed independent Afghanistan's arrival on the world stage by traveling to Europe, including Turkey, with his wife, Suraya. Previously, his father and grandfather, Amir Abdul Rahman Khan and Amir Habibullah Khan, had traveled only to British India. In Istanbul, if you walk down Meclis-i Mebusan Caddesi along the Bosporus north of the Golden Horn, you will see photographs of Kemal Ataturk on the wall in front of his old residence, including one with Amanullah Khan and Queen Soraya.

Amanullah Khan came to Turkey looking for ideas on how to transform Afghanistan into a modern country along the lines of what Ataturk was doing in Turkey. Without the British subsidy, however, Amanullah could not build a strong army, even as his reforms placed more stress on his relations with conservative elites. He was overthrown in 1928 after a Loya Jirga (grand assembly) rejected his proposed reforms.

Lacking foreign aid, Amanullah had discontinued subsidies to the Muhammadzai elders and imposed new taxes on both agriculture and cross-border trade. Uprisings started among both Tajiks north of Kabul (cultivators) and Pashtuns to the south and east engaged in cross-border trade. The first to arrive in Kabul were Tajiks led by Habibullah Kalakani, from the village of Kalakan in the Shamali (northern) plain north of Kabul. Kalakani took the title Amir Habibullah, Khadim-i Din-i Rasul Allah, servant of the religion of God's prophet, while his enemies mocked him as *bacha-i saqaw*, son of a water carrier.

It did not take long for a faction of the Muhammadzais to oust him with British support. General Muhammad Nadir Khan had resigned from his position as army chief of staff in 1925 over a dispute with Amanullah over the reorganization of the officer corps. He left as the ambassador to Paris but soon resigned that post and waited in the southern French town of Montpelier. Nadir Khan came from a different Muhammadzai lineage than Abdul Rahman Khan, a clan known as the "Musahiban" or the Peshawar Sardars, as they had been governors of Peshawar before the treaty of Gandamak separated it from Afghanistan.

In 1928 he and his four brothers established a base of operations in Waziristan. The tribal lashkars (militias) they assembled included an Ahmadzai force commanded by Abdul Ghani Khan, the grandfather of the current president of Afghanistan, Ashraf Ghani.

On October 13, 1929, Nadir Khan's army captured and looted Kabul, where they proclaimed him king: Nadir Shah. On November 1, 1929, the new authorities hanged Amir Habibullah II (*bacha-i saqaw*) and moved north. In Shamali and Panjshir they carried out harsh reprisals on the communities that had supported the Tajik ruler.

Nadir Shah established a new dynasty, in which he and his brothers and sons constituted the royal family. Even though he enacted a constitution in 1932, Nadir ruled by force. A student assassinated him during an awards ceremony on November 9, 1933. The student's family had served the family of Ghulam Nabi Charkhi, a powerful Khan from Wardak and former ambassador to Moscow, whom Nadir Shah had beaten to death on that very spot a year earlier. Nadir viewed the Charkhi family as Soviet agents and supporters of Amanullah Khan. Charkhi's nephew Zaid Siddig, now an American citizen, lived in the 1920s and '30s first in Berlin, where his father was ambassador, and then in Moscow, where his uncle gave refuge to the family after Amanullah's overthrow. Siddig describes himself as the only person whose life was saved by both Hitler and Stalin.

The surviving brothers of Nadir Shah named his nineteen-year-old son, Zahir, as king. Zahir reigned in name only as his uncles ruled the country in his name. The dynasty managed to unify the country by force, rebuild the army, establish Kabul University, found the development bank, Bank-i Milli, and introduce cotton cultivation on newly drained former swamplands in Kunduz.

The uncles were in power when India was partitioned into India and Pakistan in 1947. British India was composed of a hodgepodge of directly and indirectly administered territories. Nearly all the indirectly ruled territories were princely states ruled by a maharaja or its equivalent. In those cases the ruler had to choose which state to join. The Pashtun tribal areas, under a different form of indirect rule, were offered a referendum on whether they would join India or Pakistan. Afghanistan, however, claimed that with the demise of British India, the lands ceded by Yaqub Khan should revert to Afghanistan or exercise the right of self-determination in a plebiscite in which independence would also be an option. These claims and the disputes around them became known as the "Pashtunistan" question, after which a central square in Kabul is named.

The most prominent proponent of Pashtunistan in the royal family was Daud Khan, who was first the defense minister and then the interior minister during partition and its aftermath. Daud was the son of Nadir's elder brother, Muhammad Aziz Khan, who was assassinated in 1933 while he was ambassador to Germany. Daud had been raised by his uncle Hashim Khan, the main power in the family after Nadir's assassination.

In 1953 the uncles named Daud as prime minister. Afghans generally consider Daud Khan as the most effective ruler from that dynasty, first as prime minister (1953–63) and then as president of the Republic (1973–78).

During his decade as prime minister, Daud laid the foundations of modern Afghanistan. Taking advantage of Cold War competition to attract aid (he was once quoted as saying, "I feel the happiest when I can light my American cigarettes with Soviet matches"), he expanded the road network, extended schooling to every province, advocated an easing of restrictions on women by, for instance, appearing on National Day with his unveiled wife beside him, expanded the still small investments in industries, and built a new Afghan National Army with aid from the Soviet Union.

A few years after the independence and partition of India, Prime Minister Daud Khan asked the US to develop the Afghan military. But that military would have been deployed mainly against the US's "most allied ally," Pakistan. Pakistan too was looking for funding to build an army, which it wanted to balance India. From the beginning, Pakistan's elites had offered the country to the US as an anticommunist ally in the hope of building a strong enough military to confront India. Pakistan joined both the Baghdad Pact (later CENTO, the Central Treaty Organization, after Iraq withdrew) and SEATO (the Southeast Asia Treaty Organization).

Given the infrastructure and geography, however, all US aid (military and civilian) to landlocked Afghanistan would have had to transit Pakistan, which opposed strengthening the military of a neighbor with irredentist claims on its territory. The US refused. Daud Khan turned to the Soviet Union. The choice of an "atheist" regime as a security partner was controversial enough that Daud summoned a Loya Jirga to approve it. Thus the issue of the Durand Line led to the choice to train the Afghan officer corps in and supply the military with hardware from the Soviet Union, choices that put Pakistan and Afghanistan on opposite sides first of the Cold War, and then of a hot war.

In 1963, as Pakistan-Afghanistan tensions over Pashtunistan mounted (Daud had been arming tribal militias in FATA, the Federally Administered Tribal Areas), Pakistan closed the

Afghan border, setting off an economic crisis in Afghanistan, and the Soviet Union became for the first time Afghanistan's primary trading partner. The crisis was resolved only by Daud's resignation in March 1963.

Zahir Shah had been king for thirty years, but he had never actually ruled. His uncles Hashem Khan and Mahmud Khan, who had run the government from 1933 to 1953, had died, in 1953 and 1959 respectively, and the remaining brother, Sardar Abdul Wali Khan, was in poor health. The latter's son, Lieutenant-General Sardar Abdul Wali Khan, became the main power behind Zahir Shah.

The forty-nine-year-old king differed from every other member of the family: he was uncomfortable exerting power except in the service of his own pleasure and had had little military background—a brief spell in infantry school and a tour as deputy minister of defense. He had spent a substantial portion of his life in France with his uncles and father during their exile in the 1920s. He also studied at French universities for several years while he was king in the 1930s; he seems to have absorbed some liberal ideas, as he immediately set out to create a constitutional monarchy. Because of these efforts, some call the ten years of his direct rule Afghanistan's "Decade of Democracy."

A Loya Jirga that engaged in actual debate approved on October 1, 1964 a constitution drafted by a French legal expert.

The so-called constitutional monarchy never became a functioning democracy, however. The constitution gave the king enough power to prevent parliament from doing anything he opposed, including the right to dismiss the prime minister and call new elections. Zahir Shah did not have to look far to find an excuse, as the political parties that might have enabled the parliament to function were illegal. As a result, the country had three elections and four governments within the span of nine years.

Perhaps the most important political development of the time was the emergence of movements, some of which dominate

Afghan politics to this day. These included ethno-nationalists, leftists, and Islamists. While parties were illegal, Zahir Shah relaxed the harsh repression of Daud's rule so that these movements could hold meetings, publish newspapers, start to organize themselves, choose leaders, demonstrate, and fight with one another without the certainty of swift imprisonment (and torture).

All of these activities directly concerned only a tiny fraction of the country's population, but they had wider ramifications. The expansion of Kabul University (including the Shari'a faculty, the military academy, the Polytechnic, and other institutions of advanced education and training), and the growth of the government bureaucracy and the military all meant that a generation of newly educated rural youth was coming to Kabul, where they were exposed to the new currents. On school vacations they carried these ideas and ideals home, where they would be tested in the coming decades.

Women continued to make small advances. The veil and burqa became rarer in Kabul, though not as rare as the selective culling of miniskirt photographs from the period might suggest. More important, for the first time significant numbers of Afghan girls attended school, including Kabul University, which was coeducational. A few elite women publicly participated in government and politics.

In July 1973, while Zahir Shah was luxuriating in an Italian spa, Daud Khan toppled the hapless government with a military coup without firing a shot. Only one soldier lost his life when his tank fell into the Kabul River.

In one sense, the coup signaled continuity: one member of the royal clan toppled his cousin and took over, as had happened before in the history of Afghanistan. This time, however, the institutional and social basis of the change reflected the changes in Afghan society. For the first time, an aspiring ruler mobilized not tribal and ethnic coalitions from outside Kabul but professional officers of the national army, including Soviet-trained members of the People's Democratic Party of

Afghanistan (PDPA), the closest thing Afghanistan had to a Communist Party. Despite the appearance of dynastic continuity, Daud's coup marked the entry onto the political scene of the newly educated class that came to dominate the leftist, nationalist, and Islamist movements.

During the short five years of his Republic (July 1973–April 1978) President Daud Khan tried to establish the elements of a developmental one-party state. He seized the opportunity afforded by the weakening of Pakistan after the secession of East Pakistan as Bangladesh, and the rise of Persian Gulf oil states after the 1973 embargo and subsequent oil price rise. Daud rejected efforts by the Soviet leader Leonid Brezhnev to shape his government in a pro-Soviet direction. Instead he removed most members of the PDPA. Daud repressed the Islamic movement, forcing several of its leaders into exile in Pakistan. He again raised the Pashtunistan issue.

In 1975 Pakistan premier Zulfikar Ali Bhutto responded by instigating an uprising by Afghan Islamists, notably Gulbuddin Hikmatyar and Ahmad Shah Massoud. Hikmatyar failed, but Massoud set off the two-day "Panjshir Valley Incident" before retreating back to Pakistan. Daud then started negotiations with Bhutto and the Shah of Iran over a package of issues, including the Afghanistan-Pakistan border issue, the Soviet-Afghan-supported uprising in Balochistan, and a potential east-west transportation corridor from Iran to Pakistan through Afghanistan, all of which accorded with the strategic interests of the US.

Knowing that the abolition of the monarchy had left no mechanism of succession to Daud Khan, making an eventual power struggle inevitable, the USSR had reunited the wings of the factionalized PDPA in 1977.

Daud and his cabinet were planning another crackdown on the party in April 1978, when the assassination of a party leader led PDPA army officers to launch another coup, killing Daud and his family and starting a far-reaching purge of the ruling elites. This coup became known as the "Sawr Revolution," after the zodiacal month of Sawr (Taurus) in which it occurred. Members of the newly educated class both launched the coup and seized power for themselves through the mechanism of the PDPA. Daud's plans to free Afghanistan from dependence on the Soviet Union ended, and the region slipped toward war.

How has the Afghan state paid for itself?

For several centuries, states limited to the territory of today's Afghanistan have rarely been able to sustain themselves without revenues originating outside those borders. Going back to the medieval period, Afghan rulers sought to increase their power far less by encouraging commerce and agriculture within their territories than by raiding or conquering territories in India (including today's Pakistan), Iran, or Central Asia. Some dynasties, like the Ghorids or the Ghaznavids, maintained capitals in both Afghanistan and India. The short-lived conquests of Mirwais Hotaki and the longer-lived Durrani Empire followed this pattern. The expansion of the British Empire in India and the establishment of Russian influence in both Central Asia and Iran gradually limited these possibilities.

When the British tried to occupy Afghanistan during the first Anglo-Afghan War (1839–42), they suffered from the same problem. When a fiscal crisis in London forced Delhi to reduce its payments to Kabul, the British resident eliminated the subsidies he had been paying the eastern tribes, which cut down the entire British-Indian contingent during its forced retreat from Kabul in the winter of 1841–42. After the Second Anglo-Afghan War, having forced Amir Yaqub Khan to cede his eastern territories to British India in the 1879 Treaty of Gandamak, the British signed a treaty guaranteeing a subsidy in cash and arms to Yaqub's successor, Amir Abdul Rahman Khan. That subsidy enabled the "Iron Amir" to consolidate his rule and assure India of a secure northwest frontier. Since that time, all Afghan states have required foreign subsidies. The loss of subsidies led to the collapse of Amanullah Khan in 1928 and that of President Najibullah in 1992.

The Afghan state had some domestic revenue as well. Amir Abul Rahman Khan used his army to enforce collection of taxes on agriculture. When his grandson Amanullah Khan tried to do likewise, as well as to impose customs duties on cross-border trade with India, he was quickly overthrown. The dynasty that succeeded him, Nadir Shah and his brothers, followed by his son Zahir Shah and nephew Daud Khan, accepted that they would not be able to levy direct taxes on agriculture or pastoralism. Instead, using the capital raised by the Bank-i Milli, they invested in commercial agriculture (cotton) and husbandry products (karakul lamb) that brought in easily taxable export revenues.

In the 1960s and 1970s the main domestic revenues of the Afghan state were customs duties and licensing of certain sales, like tobacco. In the late 1960s, income from the export of natural gas to the Soviet Union was added. Soviet engineers extracted the gas from fields in Jawzjan, Northern Afghanistan, from where it was piped directly to Uzbekistan. Foreign aid from both the US and USSR and their allies paid for nearly all of the development budget. The USSR trained and financed the army.

In the late 1960s expenditures on the Vietnam War led the US to reduce its foreign aid, which hit the education sector particularly hard, reinforcing a rise in student radicalization. The combined effects of those cuts and a 1973 drought that caused an estimated 20,000 deaths mostly in the Central Highlands populated by Hazaras prepared the way for Daud Khan's coup d'état against his cousin, Zahir Shah. Daud Khan abolished the monarchy and declared Afghanistan a republic. Less than five years later, Soviet-trained army officers killed Daud and his family in the "Sawr Revolution."

Has the Afghan state been centralized or decentralized?

This is a confusing issue for many in Afghanistan, especially those who have arrived and worked there since 2001, after decades of war that weakened the state and led to the rise of competing power centers. Those working in Kabul note that the institutions of the central government have great difficulty governing the provinces and districts, while those working on the periphery observe that the central government often appears as a powerless, alien entity. They understandably conclude that the Afghan state is decentralized. In practice, this led some of the internationals in Afghanistan to advocate working with local power holders in order to get things done and evade the dysfunctional central state.

The paradox of the Afghan state, however, is that it is both centralized and weak. The extreme centralization—virtually every decision or expenditure has to be referred back to Kabul—is a manifestation of its weakness. It does not have the resources to maintain a presence in all districts and villages. It has carried out a narrow range of functions: security, justice, and very few public services. Especially when the state is weakened, as it has been by the past decades of war, local communities and power holders step in to fill the gaps. The emergence of powers outside the state when the latter is weak, however, does not constitute decentralization of the state.

Amir Abdul Rahman Khan used the subsidy he received from the British government to make Afghanistan into a centralized unitary state at the end of the nineteenth century. He monopolized revenue collection, appointments to official office, and the use of armed force, all of which had previously been shared between the monarch and other members of his clan. The Afghan state still has the same unitary, centralized structure, regardless of what power centers exist outside the state. The president makes all appointments, either directly or through ministers, throughout the country.

The constitution provides for elected provincial and district councils, even though only provincial elections have been held. Those councils, however, have only advisory functions. They have no budget and cannot levy taxes. In principle there is a single unitary system of law for the whole country, although that unitary legal system coexists with many forms of customary law in a complex system of legal pluralism.

Afghan rulers established this centralized structure to assure control of the territory and population in alliance with imperial powers, even though it is not at all adapted to the governance of and provision of services to a diverse and widely distributed population. That structure was meant to assure surveillance and the capacity for coercion throughout the land to prevent enemies from entering the territory or revolts from gaining a foothold. It met the needs of the British and successive international hegemons, as it enabled them to pursue their security interests through relations with a single center and deprived rivals of opportunities for subversion of subnational units.

To provide services more effectively, the state would need to introduce some measures of devolution or decentralization of power to provide some accountability to local populations to whom it is providing security, education, healthcare, and other services. As local administrations become more autonomous, however, they are also more easily subject to capture by independent power holders, at times in league with foreign states.

Historically, what was the relationship of Islam to state power, governance, and politics?

Ruling and governing were always carried out by secular elites, but the legitimacy of the ruler depended on his personal piety and enforcement of Islamic law. Once having come to power by force, rulers would seek legitimacy by establishing Sharia courts, building mosques, supporting madrasas, and patronizing spiritual (Sufi) leaders.

In the nineteenth century, the Muhammadzai rulers who succeeded the Saddozai kings of the Durrani Empire added waging (defensive) jihad (struggle) to the duties of the ruler. In 1836, Amir Dost Mohammad Khan was fighting against the Punjab-based Sikh Empire of Maharaja Ranjit Singh, who had captured Peshawar, the winter capital of the Durranis. The British East India Company based in Calcutta had not yet expanded its territory northwest of Delhi. When Dost Muhammad retook Peshawar from the Sikhs, he changed his title from king (padishah) to Amir ul-Muminin, commander of the faithful, denoting his role as a leader of jihad in the defense of Muslim territory. To confirm his Islamic role, he donned the "Cloak of the Prophet," a garment said to have been worn by the Prophet Muhammad. Ahmad Shah Durrani had brought the cloak from Bukhara to Kandahar, where he built the Shrine of the Cloak (*Kherqa Sharif*) to house it in the center of the city.

The Muhammadzai rulers who followed Dost Muhammad Khan continued to use the title of amir, which resonated through the two Anglo-Afghan wars. Amir Abdul Rahman Khan, who settled the conflict with the British at the end of the Second Anglo-Afghan War, depicted himself as a leader of jihad who maintained the independence of Afghanistan against foreign powers. He established Sharia courts throughout the country and tried to regulate them by issuing written handbooks on how they should operate. This was the subject of an early scholarly article by the Afghan president Ashraf Ghani. Such handbooks were intended to reduce the autonomy of the ulama and incorporate the judiciary into the power of the state.

The amir tried to gain control over the mullahs (Islamic preachers) who had enhanced their power during the anti-British resistance, just as they did later through the anti-Soviet resistance. Abdul Rahman Khan, in his autobiography, many times mentions the troubles caused by ignorant mullahs who would declare jihad on their own. He tried to enforce the jurisprudence of the Hanafi school, according to which only a legitimate Muslim ruler could declare jihad.

In 1928, mullahs and Islamic scholars did declare jihad against Abdul Rahman Khan's grandson, Amanullah Khan, and overthrew him. Then there was a short interim of rule by the Tajik Amir Habibullah Kalakani. The next dynasty, the Musahiban, used a softer approach to co-opt the ulama. Since they were concerned about the ulama being trained abroad under foreign influence, they established a faculty of Sharia at Kabul University twinned with Al-Azhar in Egypt. At that time, Al-Azhar was known as the home of Islamic modernists like Sheikh Muhammad Abduh from the late nineteenth century, which the monarchy hoped to instill in the Afghan ulama. Instead, however, returning students from Egypt introduced the ideology of the Muslim Brotherhood.

During the 1980s jihad, there was a struggle among tribal leaders—leaders with secular educations, ulama with a state and university education, and mullahs with a private madrasa education—for different kinds of Islamic leadership. The Taliban represented the Deobandi mullahs with the private madrasa education in Afghanistan and Pakistan, who had been systematically marginalized for more than a century but who made a comeback as the war marginalized other elites. For the first time, the ulama did not just establish Sharia courts; these ulama took power and ordered everything to be done according to their understanding of the law, "Sharia."

Why was Afghanistan stable and peaceful for so long?

Afghanistan was stable from the 1930s through most of the 1970s because there was an international consensus to support the Afghan government more or less as the British and Russians had agreed earlier in the century. During these decades Britain and then the United States had de facto agreements with the Soviet Union over noninterference in Afghanistan. From 1929 the same dynastic family, the Musahiban, ruled. The government belonged to this one family, which placed limits on what was at stake in politics. Not every political movement or prominent man aspired to rule the country, and the government had adequate resources from its international supporters to quell any movement that strayed beyond those lines. Much of the economy consisted of subsistence agriculture and pastoralism; urbanization and political mobilization accelerated only very gradually, and with international aid the government had developed a fairly strong army. The country was just as diverse and religious as it is now but perhaps more tribal.

The obstacles to stability today are, first of all, that so many international actors have developed interests in the outcome in Afghanistan, and second, that virtually all groups in the country have been armed to fight over the ownership of the state, which is no longer the property of any particular group. Internationally, every country's most preferred option for Afghanistan is a stable Afghanistan ruled by its friends. Every country's worst option is a stable Afghanistan ruled by its enemies. In the absence of coordination to produce a better outcome, they ultimately settle on their second choice: an unstable Afghanistan where friends and enemies keep each other at bay.

Afghanistan's poverty is also important but not because the people are poor and therefore extremist. Multiple studies have shown that extremist ideologies are less likely to gain a following among the poor than among the educated. But because Afghanistan's economy is poor as a whole, it cannot finance the institutions of governance or meet people's demands. As a result of nearly four decades of war, people have become somewhat urbanized, whether in cities or in refugee settlements; they have traveled and seen more developed countries. Even Pakistan is more developed than Afghanistan. The demand for education and healthcare has skyrocketed, and the government lacks the resources to meet those needs. The demand for political representation and participation has also grown, along with the demand for education. There are many reasons that Afghanistan is likely to be unstable, but the main cause is not the diversity of its population. When the country is unstable for other reasons, the diversity provides a means to organize politically, but it does not cause the instability.

4

COMMUNIST COUP, ISLAMIC RESISTANCE

How did the war start?

Since 2001, the war in Afghanistan has entered a new phase, but it began on April 27, 1978, when military officers belonging to the PDPA overthrew President Daud and established the Democratic Republic of Afghanistan (DRA). This event marked a double turning point. First, the PDPA leaders who took control of the government were Ghilzai Pashtuns: except for the brief reign of Habibullah II, for the first time since 1842, the ruler was not a Muhammadzai, and for the first time since 1747 the ruler was not a Durrani. What's more, the ruling group was not any tribe, clan, or family: it was an organization: the PDPA. Second, the PDPA came to power through use of force by military officers, men recruited to state service from the school system Daud had expanded in the 1950s, not through a tribal revolt. The coup opened the door to power for the new elite, factions of which would fight for power in the coming decades in a contest without rules.

The PDPA remained divided into the Khalq and Parcham factions. The Khalq faction included mainly Ghilzai and other Pashtuns from rural areas of Eastern Afghanistan, many of whom had been trained for the officer corps in Kabul military schools and then in the USSR. Pashto was the common language among Khalqis. Parcham recruited primarily among those native to Kabul. Many were of Pashtun or ethnically mixed backgrounds, but Dari was their common language, as it is for most of Afghanistan's educated urban population. Except for those with military training, most leaders of both factions attended Kabul University or other Kabul-based institutions of higher education, which incubated radical movements during the 1960s.

In keeping with the mores of the urban elite, Parcham had a few female activists, including Dr. Anahita Ratebzad, a politburo member. One of only four women elected to parliament in 1965, Ratebzad founded the Democratic Organization of Afghan Women, Afghanistan's first women's organization.

The officers who led the April 27, 1978, coup installed the leaders of the Khalq faction, Nur Muhammad Taraki and Hafizullah Amin, as prime minister and foreign minister, respectively. The Parcham leader, Babrak Karmal, was named deputy prime minister. The Soviet Union, which did not seem to know about the coup in advance, sent advisors. To the Soviets' dismay, the PDPA split again within two months. The Khalqis took full control, exiling the top Parchami leaders as ambassadors and arresting others. Within Khalq, Amin consolidated power at the expense of the ineffectual Taraki.

Parcham advocated a gradual approach to social change derived from the Soviet doctrine of "National Democracy," but Khalq under Amin tried to impose a revolution from above. The first step was to expel, detain, torture, or kill members of social or political groups that might threaten PDPA rule. The Khalqis deprived the royal family of citizenship and expelled its members from the country. Successive waves of arrests and executions targeted officials of Daud's cabinet and the governments of New Democracy, army officers, Maoists, Islamists, Islamic leaders, academics, students, ethnic politicians, and notables of any tribe, ethnic group, or region that showed signs of resistance.

The repression supposedly supported the implementation of reform decrees with progressive goals: canceling rural debts and interest payments, distributing land to the landless, granting equal rights to women, enrolling the unschooled, including women, in literacy classes, and limiting bride price. Neither the Afghan state nor the PDPA, however, had the capacity to plan or implement such reforms, nor did the PDPA have a presence on the ground to explain and mobilize support for them. Instead, it sent armed detachments to rural areas, detaining and executing landowners, mullahs, and others it identified as enemies. Whatever message of reform the Khalqis may have intended to impart, the message received was that they meant to impose a bloody monopoly of power. Sima Samar, the founder of Afghanistan's post-2001 Afghan Independent Human Rights Commission, summed up that era: "Any Khalqi could kill anybody."[1]

During its twenty months in power, the Khalqi regime killed at least twelve thousand prisoners in Kabul, principally in the prison of Pul-i Charkhi, according to a list of names made public after the Soviet intervention. The French scholar Olivier Roy estimated that in addition to the more than twelve thousand killed in Kabul, as many as fifty thousand may have been executed in the rural areas.[2] Many disappeared during that time, and ongoing construction projects still unearth mass graves.

In February 1979, Maoists, demanding the release from prison of their leader, kidnapped US ambassador Adolph Dubs, who was killed in a botched rescue attempt by Soviet commandos. Western assistance and presence nearly ended; Soviet aid and advisors filled the gap. Afghanistan, which had managed to balance aid from both the US and the USSR, now found itself unilaterally dependent on the Eastern Bloc.

1. Sima Samar, personal interview, United Nations High Commission on Human Rights, July 26, 2004, Geneva.
2. Olivier Roy, *Islam and Resistance in Afghanistan* (Cambridge: Cambridge University Press, 1990).

The government built an intelligence agency that recruited among loyalists to detain, torture, and interrogate suspected opponents but which functioned mainly in Kabul and a few cities. The spread of revolt in the countryside forced the government to call in the army, a conscript force. Ordered to fight their own people, soldiers began to desert. The revolt crossed a red line in March 1979, when the garrison in Herat mutinied under the leadership of captains Ismail Khan and Allauddin Khan. (In 2001 Ismail Khan returned from exile in Iran to lead the forces that took Herat from the Taliban and later served as governor and minister of water, energy, and power. Allauddin Khan was assassinated in 1995, probably by the Taliban.) The entire city fell out of government control, and fighters killed technical advisors from Eastern Bloc countries. Retaking the city required armored columns backed by intensive bombing, killing an estimated twenty thousand people. Taraki panicked and asked Soviet premier Alexei Kosygin to send troops, but Kosygin demurred.

The Soviet leaders attributed the growing resistance to Amin's extremism, which they believed the US would exploit to recover in Afghanistan what it had lost in the February 1979 Islamic revolution in Iran. At a "Tricontinental" (Asia, Africa, and Latin America) summit in Havana in September 1979, the Soviet leader Leonid Brezhnev and Taraki discussed replacing Amin. Amin, who got wind of the plot, ordered Taraki suffocated with a pillow and assumed full control.

The Soviet Union was led by men in their sixties and seventies, whose formative experience was the Great Patriotic War (World War II). They were deeply sensitive to any hints of external threats and committed to securing Soviet borders. For three decades they had built a buffer of client states around Soviet borders in Europe. These paradigms led Soviet leaders to believe that, especially after its loss in Iran, the US would try to destabilize Afghanistan and arm its proxies to infiltrate the Soviet Union itself. For them, Afghanistan in 1979 was no different from Czechoslovakia in 1968, Hungary in 1956, or Poland in 1945. Afghanistan, however, was a nonaligned country that the US and the West never recognized as being within the Soviet sphere of influence. Against the advice of Soviet experts on Afghanistan, the Politburo decided to send troops to remove Amin, forcibly reunite the PDPA, and subordinate Khalq to the Parcham leader Babrak Karmal, who would implement more "moderate" policies. Karmal had been exiled as ambassador to Czechoslovakia but was living in Moscow.

On December 27, 1979, Soviet armored columns crossed the Friendship Bridge over the Amu Darya from Termez, Uzbekistan, to the Afghan port at Hairatan, in Balkh province. They proceeded to the Soviet-built northern section of the ring road at Mazar-i Sharif. Some turned west to Herat and Kandahar, while most of the force went south and east to Kabul and Jalalabad.

In Kabul, Soviet intelligence had arranged to drug Amin's food. Special Forces were standing by to capture the unconscious leader and force him to transfer power to Karmal. Amin, however, had an upset stomach and did not eat. When the Soviet special operations team moved in, a fully awake Amin fought and died resisting capture. Though it could no longer concoct a cover story about a peaceful transfer of power, the USSR nonetheless flew in Babrak Karmal and installed him as president.

Moscow thought that its "limited contingent" of troops would be welcomed as liberators and stay in Afghanistan for only six months. Most Afghans, however, saw the intervention as yet another foreign invasion of Afghan soil, to be repelled like those that had preceded it. Ulama throughout the country and in the growing refugee camps in Pakistan preached that jihad against the foreign invader was obligatory. Soviet troops would eventually build to a total of 120,000 and remain in Afghanistan for more than nine years, until February 15, 1989.

How did the world respond to the invasion?

The Soviet invasion made the growing conflict in Afghanistan into an international issue. The Soviet military had occupied a nonaligned country. It had bases on the borders of Pakistan and Iran, within striking distance of the Persian Gulf. Just as Pakistan's military president, General Zia-ul-Haq, was starting a program of Islamization, Iran was consolidating its revolutionary Islamic regime, and the new wealth of the post-1973 oil boom was transforming the Gulf countries. Records that became available after the dissolution of the Soviet Union show that the invasion was an ill-considered reaction to out-of-control events, not a planned strategic move toward the "warm waters of the Indian Ocean," but that is how the US government and many others saw it at the time.

The USSR found itself as isolated on Afghanistan as the US was on Israel or Cuba. Joined only by East Germany, on January 2, 1980, the USSR vetoed a resolution condemning the invasion that the UN Security Council otherwise supported by a vote of 12 to 2. On January 3, 1980, a special session of the UN General Assembly voted 104 to 18 to "deplore" the Soviet intervention in Afghanistan and demand the "immediate, unconditional and total withdrawal of the foreign troops from Afghanistan." For the first time, the USSR found itself opposed by almost the entire nonaligned movement (Cuba excepted). American diplomats spoke of turning Afghanistan into the Soviet Union's Palestine.

Just four years earlier the US and the USSR, along with thirty-three other countries, had signed the Helsinki Final Act, signaling a period of détente that led to the Strategic Arms Limitation Treaty (SALT) and other agreements between the US and the USSR. But that détente ended on December 27, 1979. In an address to the nation on January 4, the two-month anniversary of the storming of the American Embassy in Iran, President Carter called the Soviet invasion of Afghanistan "an extremely serious threat to peace" and "a callous violation of international law and the United Nations Charter," which "threatens both Iran and Pakistan and is a stepping stone to possible control over much of the world's oil supplies." He announced that he had recalled the US ambassador to Moscow and asked the Senate to defer consideration of SALT II (the second round of Strategic Arms Limitation Talks). Carter also halted the sale to Moscow of high-technology items, curtailed Soviet fishing privileges in US waters, and canceled the delivery of 17 million tons of grain. He later announced that the US would boycott the 1980 Moscow Olympics.

President Carter also promised to "provide military equipment, food, and other assistance to help Pakistan defend its independence and its national security against the seriously increased threat it now faces from the north." He needed cooperation with Pakistan if the US hoped to assist Afghans resisting the Soviet occupation. As discussed in chapter 2, access to landlocked Afghanistan required transit through either the USSR, which had just invaded the country, Iran, which was holding US diplomats hostage, or Pakistan.

In a pattern that would repeat itself over the years, the need to cooperate with Pakistan to provide aid to Afghans overrode US bilateral concerns over Pakistan, in this case its nuclear program, which had started a few years earlier. During the 1971 Indo-Pakistani war that led to the breakup of Pakistan, the US sent a carrier battle group into the Bay of Bengal as a warning to India. The USSR sent a nuclear-armed submarine to deter US action in support of Pakistan. Indira Gandhi, India's prime minister, saw how nuclear weapons provided strategic autonomy and ordered an acceleration of its nuclear program. In May 1974, India detonated a "peaceful nuclear explosive" in the Rajasthan desert, less than one hundred miles from the Pakistan border. The Pakistan prime minister, Zulfikar Ali Bhutto, promised that Pakistan would "eat grass, even go hungry" to acquire the bomb.

The US, however, sought to forestall a nuclear arms race in South Asia. In March 1979, after uncovering evidence that

Pakistan was secretly building a uranium enrichment facility, the Carter administration imposed sanctions limiting economic and military aid. Those sanctions had to be lifted before the president could deliver the aid he had promised to Pakistan in response to the Soviet invasion of Afghanistan. Carter asked Congress to waive the sanctions. General Zia rejected Carter's initial offer of $400 million in aid as "peanuts." He demanded more military assistance as well as security guarantees against India. In the final days of his administration, Carter reached agreement with Zia on an $800 million package. Before the Soviet invasion, the US had begun providing "nonlethal" assistance to the Afghan mujahidin, but it now began supplying weapons and other military aid, if in modest amounts.

The Reagan administration transformed the US-Pakistan relationship to a strategic partnership, regardless of Zia's dictatorship, nuclear weapons program, or support for Islamic militancy. Reagan fully adopted the interpretation of the invasion of Afghanistan as a Soviet expansionist move and raised Pakistan's importance in American strategy accordingly. Pakistan, along with Saudi Arabia, became a pillar of US strategy in the Persian Gulf, replacing the role previously played by the Shah's Iran. Washington offered Islamabad a $3.2 billion package of military assistance and escalated the program of arming the Afghan mujahidin started by President Carter.

How did the PDPA-led DRA government change after the Soviet intervention?

The Soviet invaders found a collapsing government and growing, though uncoordinated, resistance. In retrospect, as Russian and other former Soviet experts say today, they should have announced national reconciliation with the mujahidin on day one and used models compatible with Afghan society, but they knew nothing about that and were constrained by Soviet ideology. The Soviet leaders tried to do what they knew how to do: turn Afghanistan into a satellite state.

The Soviet strategy was to build institutions at the center, defend against attacks, and then gradually expand those institutions into the periphery. Enforced social change in the rural areas was no longer on the agenda.

Within the cities secured by the Red Army, the new government, aided by omnipresent Soviet advisors, focused on a few main tasks:

- Maintaining control of the cities by a new intelligence agency modeled on the KGB, named KhAD (Khidamat-i Ittila'at-i Dawlati, or State Information Services). Until 1985, KhAD's director was Dr. Najibullah, a charismatic young Parchami whom the Khalqis had exiled to Bulgaria. He ultimately became president of Afghanistan (1987–92). Faced with mass protest and resistance even in the cities, KhAD carried out mass arrests at night. It tortured prisoners systematically, but unlike its Khalqi predecessor it did so to extract information rather than to punish. The government abolished summary executions, though many were executed after brief trials. Following the Soviet model, KhAD recruited informants in major institutions. Over time KhAD became more professional and reduced the use of torture in favor of more effective techniques of interrogation and data collection. Embedded Soviet advisors supervised KhAD closely.

- Rebuilding the armed forces through forced conscription, training, and new equipment. As long as the Soviet Army was in the country, the DRA made only limited progress against desertion. Young male refugees often cited fear of forced conscription as their reason for fleeing the country. The Soviet Union sold Afghanistan so much military equipment (purchased with soft loans that Russia forgave in 2006) that it became the world's third largest arms importer after Saudi Arabia and Japan.

Officers and technical personnel were trained in the USSR or by Soviet personnel in Afghanistan.

• Orienting the educated stratum of the society to serve the new government. The government purged Kabul University, the incubator of Afghanistan political movements, of instructors suspected of disloyalty. The USSR offered university students and young professionals scholarships in the USSR or elsewhere in the Soviet bloc. The school curriculum was rewritten to reflect the party's ideology, and the government established Soviet-style youth organizations such as the Young Pioneers (Peshahangan). Elementary and secondary teachers came under surveillance: KhAD informers reported on teachers' statements and activities. Starting in 1985, the government sent schoolchildren to the USSR to study. The PDPA and its Soviet patrons may have intended this program to expand education, but many Afghans saw it as kidnapping young children to brainwash them.

To the extent possible, the government expanded these programs to other cities. Much of the rest of the country, however, fell out of its control. The security forces collapsed, and the mujahidin gained strength. With rare exceptions the mujahidin put only the most rudimentary governing structures in place, but they denied access to the government and Soviet troops.

The main goals of Soviet military operations were:

• Securing the areas around Kabul and other major cities, the ring road, and roads leading to the borders and customs posts.

• Raiding villages and areas from which mujahidin attacked roads or Soviet and Afghan forces. These raids included indiscriminate bombing campaigns and "cleansing" operations by ground troops. These raids killed many civilians and led to the emptying of entire villages and districts. The population became refugees.

By 1985 the war had evolved into a costly stalemate: Afghan civilians paid the highest price. According to rough estimates, about three million Afghans fled to Pakistan, and two million fled to or could not return from Iran. These five million refugees amounted to nearly one-third of the estimated population of Afghanistan at the time. Including the internally displaced, about half of all Afghans had to flee their homes. As the outbreak of war had interrupted Afghanistan's first ever attempt at a census in 1979, it was virtually impossible to estimate the death toll, but some put it well over one million.

What was the Afghan resistance and who were the mujahidin?

The first revolt came only days after the coup, when the Nuristanis learned that the PDPA had killed Abdul Qadir Nuristani, the minister of the interior and a member of their community. National political organizations had little or no presence in the countryside, and most of the uprisings started in the traditional way: in response to some action of the regime, an influential mullah or other religious figure would preach a sermon calling for jihad, after which the local men would gather whatever weapons they could seize and then capture local government offices, such as police posts or schools.

Sustaining these revolts required external assistance, which came mostly from Afghan groups established in the neighboring areas of Pakistan. Most of the political leadership was headquartered in Peshawar, capital of Pakistan's North-West Frontier Province (NWFP, now called Khyber-Pakhtunkhwa, or KP).

Islamist groups from Afghanistan had sought refuge from President Daud's repression in Pakistan in the early 1970s and, at Pakistan's instigation, staged an abortive uprising against him in 1975. Pakistan kept the Islamist leaders for another day. The core of the group was the exiled leadership of the Islamist movement from Kabul University, headed by Burhanuddin Rabbani, a Sharia lecturer. The main body of the student movement was Jawanan-i Musulman (Muslim Youth), while Rabbani led faculty and others in the Jamiat-i Islami (Islamic Society). The main military leaders in Pakistan were Gulbuddin Hikmatyar, a Kharoti Pashtun from Kunduz province on the border of Tajikistan and student at the Faculty of Engineering, and Ahmad Shah Massoud of the Polytechnic, a Tajik from the Panjshir Valley. Hikmatyar, who had spent several years in prison for the murder of a Maoist fellow student, broke with Rabbani to found his own organization, the Hizb-i Islami (Islamic Party), leaving Jamiat a predominantly Tajik party. Other leaders in Pakistani exile included Mawlawis Yunus Khalis and Jalaluddin Haqqani, who had graduated from the Haqqaniya madrasa in NWFP, a center of the militant wing of the Deobandi movement. Both were from Eastern Afghanistan: Khalis, a Khugiani from Nangarhar, and Haqqani from the Zadran tribe in Khost.

As long as Zulfikar Ali Bhutto was prime minister, the militants were managed by Interior Minister Nasirullah Babar, a Bhutto intimate, but after General Zia staged a coup against Bhutto's government in July 1977, he placed the Afghan militants under the supervision of the ISI (Inter-Services Intelligence), led by General Akhtar Abdul Rahman.

These Islamist political groups were composed almost entirely of young men born in the countryside and educated in the capital. After the coup, they began to send emissaries with arms to organize revolts in their native rural areas. In some places they reinforced or took control of existing uprisings; elsewhere they led initial uprisings themselves.

In the East and South, uprisings were mainly organized tribally with clerical leadership, and they turned to spiritual leaders for organization and support. The two most important Sufi families established themselves in Peshawar and Islamabad: Sayyid Ahmad Gailani, descended from Abdul Qadir Gailani, the twelfth-century founder of the order named after him, was the *pir* (spiritual leader) of the Qadiriyya order. His father had emigrated from Ottoman Mesopotamia (Iraq) to Afghanistan in 1905 at the invitation of Amir Habibullah, who granted him land in Nangarhar. He called his organization (*tanzim*) the National Islamic Front (Mahaz) for the Freedom (Azadi) of Afghanistan (NIFA). Gailani's daughter, Fatima, became the only woman to represent the Afghan mujahidin publicly and internationally. In 2004 she became the president of the Afghan Red Crescent Society, and later joined the International Federation of Red Cross and Red Crescent Societies (IFRC).

Sebghatullah Mojaddedi's family, almost entirely exterminated by the Khalqis, had led the Naqshbandi order. A senior member of the Mojaddedi family had always been Hazrat-i Shor Bazaar, head of the madrasa in Shor Bazaar of Kabul. This was the country's most influential institution of Islamic learning before the establishment of the sharia faculty of Kabul University. The head of that madrasa traditionally confirmed the Islamic legitimacy of Afghanistan's rulers. Mojaddedi's group, which included the Karzai family, took the name National Islamic Front (Jabha) for the Salvation (Nijat) of Afghanistan. To add to the confusion, Gailani's party was known in English by its acronym "NIFA," while Mojaddedi's went by the Persian/Pashto shorthand "Jabha."

Another source of fighters was the rural private madrasas, mostly Deobandi, whose students, led by their teachers, formed "Taliban" (plural of the Arabic for "student") fronts. Some of them, like Mullah Muhammad Omar, later led the Taliban movement. Mawlawi Muhammad Nabi Muhammadi, head of an important Deobandi madrasa in Logar province, led that organization, the Movement of the Islamic Revolution (Harakat-i Inqilab) of Afghanistan. Harakat-i Inqilab represented rural ulama and the Taliban fronts. When the US decided to provide aid such as healthcare and education through the mujahidin parties, it asked them to manage the programs jointly to reduce administrative costs. These three groups (Gailani, Mojaddedi, Muhammadi) joined together as the "moderate nationalist" organizations, generally called "Ittihad-i Seh," the Union of Three.

Yunus Khalis founded a militant Deobandi breakaway from Hikmatyar's group, which was known as Hizb-i Islami (Khalis). It had both tribal and clerical wings. Its main clerical commander was Jalaluddin Haqqani. Khalis had been the prayer leader and preacher in the mosque of the Arsala clan, the leading family of the Jabbarkhel subtribe of Ahmadzai, which had long been given responsibility for securing the portion of the Peshawar-Kabul road around Jalalabad. Leaders of that clan became important commanders. One member, Abdul Haq, executed by the Taliban in 2001, was active in both Nangarhar and Kabul, where he organized an underground network. Haq's older brother, Haji Abdul Qadir, participated in the Bonn Talks (before walking out in protest at "underrepresentation" of Pashtuns) and served as President Karzai's first vice president until his assassination by unknown assailants in July 2002. Haji Din Muhammad, another brother who then assumed leadership of the family, was appointed governor of Nangarhar and then Kabul province, and then became acting head of the High Peace Council.

Haqqani's son Sirajuddin became deputy leader of the Taliban after the announcement of Mullah Omar's death in July 2015 (Omar is reported to have died in April 2013). When an Afghan government delegation met for discussion with a Taliban delegation in Murree, Pakistan, in July 2015, Din Muhammad headed the government delegation, while Jalaluddin Haqqani's younger brother, Ibrahim, was one of three Taliban delegates.

Finally, Abd al-Rabb al-Rasul Sayyaf, a Saudi-educated lecturer at the Kabul University Sharia Faculty who had adopted Salafi ("Wahhabi") Islam, formed a party mainly sustained by

Saudi contributions, known as Ittihad-i Islami (Islamic Union). Today Sayyaf's "Wahhabi" affiliation has faded, and he is a prominent politician and parliamentarian in Kabul, known for his Islamic denunciations of the Taliban. These four parties— Hizb (Hikmatyar), Hizb (Khalis), Jamiat, and Ittihad— joined together as the "Islamist" parties, known as "Ittihad-i Chahr": the union of four.

These were the seven Sunni organizations officially recognized by Pakistan. Pakistan publicly treated them as the representatives of the Afghan refugees, while the ISI used them as the conduits for providing weapons and other supplies to the mujahidin.

In Hazarajat, hastily formed units commanded by Syed Jaghran, a retired army major, repulsed efforts by Khalqis to enter the area in 1979. The Hazaras established their own administration, initially led by local notables and clergy. They named it Shura-i Ittifaq-i Islami (Islamic Unity Council). Young activists inspired by the Iranian revolution and supported by Tehran eventually managed to displace most of the traditionalists. They extended their influence to the Hazara communities in Kabul and Mazar-i Sharif, but the Shi'a parties gained national prominence mainly after the Soviet withdrawal. Hazarajat saw little warfare, as it included no major city and was far from the ring road. Some mujahidin supply routes from Pakistan to Northern Afghanistan crossed the region, and the local authorities profited by taxing them.

A small but effective group of urban Shi'a, mostly Qizilbash and Sayyid rather than Hazara, established the Islamic Movement (Harakat-i Islami) of Afghanistan, led by Ayatollah Muhammad Asif Muhsini of Kandahar, who before his death in 2019 became a prominent leader in Kabul and chancellor of a university funded by Iran. The Islamic Movement engaged in urban operations led by their commander, Sayyid Husain Anwari, who participated in the Bonn Conference as a member of the United Front delegation and later served briefly as governor of Herat. Anwari disrupted Najibullah's 1987 Loya Jirga by firing a rocket at it.

The traditional Hazara groups had an office in Quetta, Pakistan, which has a large Hazara population consisting mostly of descendants of Hazaras who fled Amir Abdul Rahman Khan's subjugation of Hazarajat in the late nineteenth century. Shi'a mujahidin groups also had some representation in Iran, but during the Soviet occupation of Afghanistan, Iran was preoccupied with defending the nation and the revolution from the war launched by Iraq's Saddam Hussein, who was backed by both the Sunni Arab states and the US. Only after the end of the Iran-Iraq War in August 1988, when Soviet troops were withdrawing, did Iran turn its attention to Afghanistan. With Tehran's help, the Shi'a parties established significant presences in Kabul and Mazar-i Sharif after the Soviet withdrawal, becoming influential political actors. At that time, anticipating negotiations over a new government in Kabul, Tehran sponsored a coalition of eight groups that later merged into Hizb-i Wahdat (the Unity Party). Its first leader, Abdul Ali Mazari, died under disputed circumstances in Taliban custody in July 1995. His successors were Karim Khalili, a Bamyan-based leader who served as vice president under both Hamid Karzai and Ashraf Ghani, and Muhammad Muhaqqiq, a member of parliament and vice presidential candidate with Dr. Abdullah Abdullah. After 2014 Muhaqqiq became deputy to CEO Abdullah.

What is notable is the absence of any organization representing Afghan nationalism. The Pashtun nationalist party Afghan Millat (Afghan Nation) maintained a discreet presence in Peshawar under Gailani's protection. Anwar-ul-Haq Ahady, who married Fatima Gailani, was the party's leader for several years. He and Fatima Gailani participated in the Bonn Talks as members of the Peshawar Group. Ahady, who had worked as a banker and professor of political science in the US, later served as president of the Central Bank, minister of finance, and minister of transportation.

In 1983 a group of Afghan intellectuals and tribal dignitaries in Peshawar tried to convene a Loya Jirga. They wanted Zahir Shah to chair the meeting and lead the national resistance. Pakistan, however, banned overt Afghan nationalist activity, including attempts to convene a Loya Jirga, and refused to issue visas to any members of the former royal family.

Afghan nationalism is inseparable from the narrative of how the British deprived Amir Yaqub Khan of the territories east of the Durand Line, and how Pakistan, an "invented" state, incorporated them into its territories. Especially after losing East Pakistan in 1971, Pakistan was not prepared to allow any movement with irredentist aspirations to operate on its soil. On the contrary, it sought to use the resources it received to help the US counter the Soviet Union and to transform Afghanistan from a nationalist state at odds with Pakistan to an Islamic client state of Pakistan.

The doctrine under which the ISI carried out this strategy was the quest for "strategic depth" for Pakistan against India. Under the doctrine of strategic depth, if India attacked into Punjab and the Pakistan army had to retreat, it could use Afghanistan as a rear base or even transfer some assets there. (The development of nuclear deterrence between India and Pakistan is often said to have made strategic depth irrelevant, but elements of the doctrine persist.) Hence Pakistan wanted to support a strong Islamic resistance movement against the USSR, with the help of the US, Saudi Arabia, and China, led by religious or Islamic leaders and preferably of pan-Islamic tendencies. The more radical such leaders also opposed the royal regime or any role for the former king, and they were not preoccupied with grievances against Pakistan, a brotherly Muslim country.

The Pakistani military under Zia also wanted the Afghan leaders to cooperate with right-wing Pakistani religious parties, notably Jama'at-i Islami, that were supporting Zia's Islamization policies. Jama'at became close to Hikmatyar. So soon after the loss of East Pakistan, the establishment deeply distrusted Pakistan's own Pashtun and Baloch nationalist parties, who in their minds were potential leaders of another Bangladesh. Much of their leadership was in prison or exile, and the ISI made sure that the armed Afghan groups did not cooperate with them.

Viewed from Peshawar, the resistance was a national jihad against foreign occupiers and the illegitimate government they had installed. On the ground, however, it was also an uprising that swept away the state structures built over the past centuries by Durranis, and the re-emergence of the political and military power of groups they had conquered and subordinated. The most obvious case is Hazarajat, which freed itself from rule by Kabul, seasonal incursions by Pashtun nomads, and the burden of debts its inhabitants had incurred to those same nomadic tribes.

Tajiks had long been the junior civilian partners of the ruling Durranis. Tajiks staffed the civilian bureaucracy, while the royal family controlled the military in alliance with other Pashtuns. During the resistance against the Soviet Union, however, Tajiks became some of the most powerful commanders. Unfettered by the tribal rivalry that made Pashtun society so difficult to organize or govern, several Tajiks consolidated control of territory and population in quasi-states, especially after the Soviet withdrawal. These included Ahmad Shah Massoud of the Panjshir Valley, Ismail Khan of Herat, and Atta Muhammad of Balkh. They developed larger and better-trained and -disciplined armed forces than most of the other mujahidin groups. All belonged to Jamiat-i Islami, led by Burhanuddin Rabbani of Badakhshan. Jamiat increasingly became the undeclared party of Afghan Tajiks, some of whom contested the identity of Afghanistan as a Pashtun or Pashtun-ruled country.

How did external support shape the Afghan resistance?

The US and Pakistan organized a joint operation with Saudi Arabia and China to finance and supply the resistance against the Soviet Union. Their embassies, including intelligence agencies, held weekly coordination meetings in Islamabad. China participated through 1989, as long as the Soviet troops remained in Afghanistan. The rest of the support for the mujahidin continued until 1991, when the USSR was dissolved.

The US deposited funds in CIA-controlled accounts in Switzerland, and the Saudis matched them dollar for dollar. Private donors in Saudi Arabia, Kuwait, and elsewhere in the Persian Gulf also contributed through the Saudi Afghanistan support committee headed by Prince (king after January 2015) Salman bin Abdul Aziz, who was governor of Riyadh at that time. The use of these contributions was more flexible than the official contributions. For example, they covered gaps in timing and purpose by paying for most of the transport of weapons into Afghanistan. In his book, *The Bear Trap*, ISI colonel Mohammad Yousuf, who for several years directed the aid to the mujahidin under the supervision of General Akhtar, wrote that "Arab money saved the system."

For the sake of (hardly) plausible deniability, all weapons supplied before 1986 had to be models from the Soviet arsenal, whether Egyptian Kalashnikovs provided by President Anwar Sadat, weapons captured by Israel from Egypt in 1967 or 1973, or later in Lebanon, or Soviet-style weapons manufactured in China. The CIA purchased the weapons and was responsible for transporting them to the port of Karachi. There they were transferred to the ISI's Logistics Cell, which trucked them to Peshawar and Quetta. The ISI controlled the distribution of the weapons among the parties. The largest recipient was Hizb-i Islami Hikmatyar, with the three other Islamist groups next.

Sayyaf had direct funding from Saudi private donors as well. The ISI claimed to make these decisions based on operational effectiveness, but the distribution of weapons constituted the

most important political decision along the entire arms pipeline. The criterion for distributing weapons was supposedly
who "killed the most Russians," in the words of William
Casey, the American director of Central Intelligence. By controlling the flow of intelligence information to the CIA, the ISI
initially managed to get the US to fund its project of installing
an Islamist government in Kabul in the interest of "strategic
depth." The ISI also distributed weekly checks to the leaders of
the Mujahidin groups that they recognized in Peshawar.

The transport of weapons and supplies from Pakistan to
the mujahidin in Afghanistan was left to the private sector.
Funding for the transport came mainly from nongovernmental
Arab donors. The Kuwaiti and Saudi Red Crescent offices in
the tribal territories (FATA) distributed these funds. They provided full funding plus 10 percent for contingencies for the
Islamists and only 10 percent for what they called "nationalist" ("watani") organizations. Islamist parties dominated
Northern Afghanistan partly because only those organizations
could afford the cost of moving supplies over the Hindu Kush.

Pakistan also used the party structures to control the approximately three million refugees. To qualify for assistance
every refugee family had to register with one of the seven recognized organizations. The organizations thus became partners with the Pakistan Refugee Commissioner as well as with
the ISI. Those parties with access to more resources could attract more registrations.

How did Arab mujahidin come to Afghanistan, and why did some of them found al-Qaeda?

Bringing Arab fighters and aid organizations to Afghanistan
and Pakistan was part of the Saudi contribution to the US-
Pakistan-Saudi operation in support of the mujahidin. The
Arab fighters made virtually no military contribution to the
struggle, but they played financial and political roles.

Private contributions from Persian Gulf Arab donors bridged gaps in funding. Arab mujahidin also helped advance the US public diplomatic goal of making Afghanistan into the Soviet Union's Palestine. While it had no direct contact with the Arab mujahidin in Pakistan, the US encouraged their leaders to travel, including to the US, in order to raise funds and preach the obligation of jihad (struggle against the enemies of Islam) against the Soviet Union.

Some volunteers came individually. Saudi travel agents even arranged jihad packages for school vacations. Very quickly, however, the recruitment became organized as a joint effort between Saudi Arabia, then ruled by King Fahd, and the Muslim Brotherhood (a Sunni Islamist organization). An important figure in the movement was Abdul Aziz ibn Baz, Grand Mufti of Saudi Arabia and head of the Islamic World League (Rabita), which promoted and preached Salafi Islam around the globe.

The principal ideologue and theorist of the Arab mujahidin was Shaikh Abdullah Azam, an Islamic scholar born in a village near Jenin, Palestine. He left the West Bank when Israel occupied it in 1967. Like many other 1967 refugees, he moved to Jordan, where he joined a group of Palestinian Fedayeen. After a few years he concluded that the secular orientation of the Palestinian leadership made it impossible to wage jihad. He obtained a teaching position in Jeddah, where Osama bin Laden was one of his students.

When the Soviet Union invaded Afghanistan in December 1979, Azam published a fatwa (a legal opinion by an Islamic religious leader) called "Defense of the Muslim Lands, the First Obligation after Faith," which equated the obligation of jihad in Afghanistan to that in Palestine. Abdul Aziz ibn Baz supported this fatwa. Since it was possible to wage jihad in Afghanistan, he advocated emigrating there for that purpose. He persuaded Osama bin Laden to go there in 1980 and soon followed him. In Peshawar, Pakistan, he established an office, "Maktab al-Khidamat," the services office, which served as an overall recruitment and resource center for the Arab mujahidin. It also coordinated the "ansar," supporters of jihad, which included Islamic organizations providing assistance to the refugees.

Azam created and propagated the concept of "global jihad," unconfined by national boundaries. As indicated by the title of his fatwa ("Defense of the Muslim Lands, the First Obligation after Faith"), he was also part of a current in radical Islamism arguing for the revival of jihad, which the jihadists insisted could be defined only in military terms. Azam's teaching resembled that of Muhammad abd-al-Salam Faraj, leader of the al-Jihad group in Egypt. Faraj had written a pamphlet titled "Jihad: The Forgotten Obligation," which argued that jihad was a personal obligation of all Muslims, ranking higher than the five pillars of Islam. Faraj was executed in April 1982 for organizing the October 1981 assassination of Anwar al-Sadat, the Egyptian president. The surviving leadership of al-Jihad, including Ayman al-Zawahiri, joined Azam in Peshawar.

With the approval of the US and Saudi Arabia, Pakistan encouraged and supported the Arab mujahidin. The US even gave Azam a visa to the United States to raise funds in 1988. He had been an advisor to the founders of Hamas, however, and seems to have preached more about Palestine than Afghanistan. While the Arabs were never integrated formally into the organizational format of the seven parties, they needed to cooperate with one or another of them to train and participate in fighting. Because of his Salafi orientation, Sayyaf was the principal host, but Hikmatyar and Khalis played that role as well. The Arabs had nothing to do with the moderate nationalist parties and had few relations with Jamiat. They seemed to suspect that Persian speakers were Shi'a, even though Abdullah Anas, an Algerian who married Azam's daughter, spent ten years working for Massoud.[3] One of them, Wael al-Julaidan,

---

3. Anas has published a memoir of these events with Tam Hussein, *To the Mountains: My Life in Jihad, from Algeria to Afghanistan* (London: Hurst, 2019).

headed the Saudi Red Crescent office in Chitral, which funded virtually all mujahidin logistics into Northern Afghanistan.

While these Arabs contributed relatively little to the military effort, jihadi Peshawar provided a conducive atmosphere for their political organizing. Azam and the leaders of al-Jihad were free to meet, discuss, publish, and preach openly, possibly the only place in the world they could have done so at the time, except for Sudan. One of the most important issues in these talks was the relationship of jihad against the "far enemy" (the US, Israel) to jihad against the "near enemy" (deviant Islamic rulers and foreign occupiers in Muslim lands). These discussions led to the founding of al-Qaeda in Peshawar in August 1988. Azam is often mentioned as a founding member of al-Qaeda, but in fact he never joined: he disagreed with its focus on the far enemy as opposed to the defense of Muslim lands. Leadership of al-Qaeda fell to his former student, Osama bin Laden, who increasingly came under Zawahiri's influence.

Abdullah and one of his sons were assassinated by what we would now call a roadside IED (improvised explosive device) in Peshawar in November 1989. He had recently returned from a trip to Northern Afghanistan, where he had tried to mediate a bloody dispute between Massoud and some Hikmatyar commanders. With his son-in-law Abdullah Anas, he spent time in Panjshir and came to know Massoud. When he returned to Peshawar, he stated that Massoud was a pious Muslim and a brave mujahid, not a Persian-speaking Shi'a. It is possible that this led to his being assassinated by Hikmatyar, who had killed quite a few people in Peshawar as he prepared to become the Pakistan-backed ruler of Afghanistan. Al-Qaeda, however, is another suspect.

From 1989 to 1992 the Arab mujahidin became more important to the effort. Many of the grassroots mujahidin in Afghanistan stopped fighting when the Soviet Union withdrew its troops since the government was no longer trying to impose "communism" on them. For al-Qaeda and the other global jihadists, though, nothing had changed, and the ISI used them to continue the fight. They played an important role, for instance, in the capture of Khost province by mujahidin in April 1991. Afghans increasingly complained about the Arab mujahidin's treatment of the population, since they considered anyone living peacefully under the rule of the government as an apostate who must be executed. They also alienated Afghans by destroying Sufi shrines and trying to convert them to praying according to Salafi (Hanbali) custom, as if the Afghans were not good Muslims.

Between 1989 and 1992, many, including Osama bin Laden, returned home to Saudi Arabia. Others chose to stay or could not go home without risking arrest or worse. They continued to operate out of camps in Eastern Afghanistan, supporting Hikmatyar, Sayyaf, and Jalaluddin Haqqani. And this is where Osama found them in May 1996, when he returned to Afghanistan from Khartoum.

How did the US and Pakistani strategies change?

Initially the US assumed that once the Soviet Union had occupied a territory, it would never leave. Analysts quoted from the autobiography of Amir Abdul Rahman Khan on the subject:

> The Russian policy of aggression is slow and steady, but firm and unchangeable. . . . Their habit of forward movement resembles the habit of an elephant, who examines a spot thoroughly before he places his foot upon it, and when once he puts his weight there is no going back, and not taking another step in a hurry until he has put his full weight on the first foot, and has smashed everything that lies under it.[4]

4. Amir Abdul Rahman Khan, *Autobiography of Amir Abdul Rahman Khan* (1885).

Amir Abdul Rahman Khan's alleged parting message also circulated: "My last words to you, my son and successor: never trust the Russians."

American support for the mujahidin therefore did not aim to defeat the Soviet troops, overthrow the communist government, or establish a new one. It aimed to deter further Soviet expansionism by imposing a heavy cost on Moscow for its Afghan adventure. The common terms for this strategy were "bleeding the Soviets" or "fighting to the last Afghan." Given this goal, it made sense to arm whatever Afghan group inflicted the maximum pain on the Soviets, rather than to try to help the resistance transform itself into a coherent force, one that could present a political alternative to the Kabul regime and stabilize a future Afghanistan.

General Zia shared the goal of deterring Soviet advances, most obviously into Pakistan, but he faced other dilemmas as well. He did not want millions of Afghan refugees on Pakistan's soil to embrace nationalism and ally with Pakistani Pashtun or Baloch nationalists in demanding self-determination for NWFP, FATA, and Balochistan. Instead, Zia extended his domestic policy of Islamization to Afghanistan, where Pakistan supported only Islamic parties. This policy would, Pakistan hoped, enable Pakistan to direct the ire of Pashtuns away from Islamabad and focus it on Kabul and Moscow. The Islamic parties would also become vehicles of Pakistani influence in Afghanistan and eventually Central Asia.

By 1985, it was evident that while the resistance could continue to fight, the war imposed a great cost on the Afghans and Pakistanis without achieving strategic results on the ground. The regime in Kabul continued to build its institutions with Soviet assistance, and the complete dominance of the airspace by the Afghan government and Soviet aircraft deprived the mujahidin of any chance to consolidate territorial control.

After a contentious debate in Washington, the Reagan administration decided to change its objective from imposing costs on the Soviets to helping the mujahidin win. To do so, the guerrillas needed to break the enemy's control of the air space. After experimenting with a Swiss antiaircraft system in an effort to maintain a cloak of deniability over the operation, the US decided (over strong internal objections) to deliver American-manufactured shoulder-held, battery-operated, laser-guided Stinger antiaircraft missiles to the mujahidin. This was the first time these weapons had been deployed outside of NATO, and many were concerned that delivering them to Afghans would lead to their acquisition by terrorists and enemy regimes such as Iran. The CIA, ISI, and mujahidin successfully tested the Stingers in Paktia province of southeast Afghanistan in September 1986. The delivery of other weapons also accelerated.

Since the supply of Stingers required special security measures and made the US role explicit, Washington insisted on delivering the missiles directly to the commanders who would use them rather than going through the ISI and the seven parties. This was the CIA's first attempt to deal with the mujahidin independently of the ISI.

The divergence of views between the US and Pakistan became clearer after the Soviet withdrawal. Zia and ISI chief General Akhtar had been killed, along with Arnie Raphel, the US ambassador to Pakistan, in a still-unexplained aircraft explosion on August 17, 1988. Zia, before his death, had outlined his plans for a post-Soviet Afghanistan: it would be an Islamic state, perhaps even merging with Pakistan, which would expand into or absorb Soviet Central Asia. The Pakistan Army's main instrument for this goal was Hikmatyar's Hizb-i Islami.

The US, however, which by then had accumulated better information, was developing qualms about some of the groups Pakistan was supporting. Hikmatyar, for instance, was generally held responsible for the multiple assassinations of liberal or nationalist Afghan intellectuals in Pakistan. The most notorious such assassination was that of Syed Bahauddin Majrooh, a noted poet, scholar, and writer who had founded the philosophy faculty of Kabul University. In Peshawar he published the *Afghan Information Center Monthly Newsletter*, an invaluable resource for anyone following the conflict. The newsletter publicized the actions, both civil and military, of commanders on the ground rather than the party leaders in Peshawar. After the Soviet withdrawal, Majrooh conducted an informal survey of elders in refugee camps, which found that the refugees overwhelmingly supported the return of Zahir Shah rather than the leadership of any of the Pakistan-supported Islamic parties. And that is probably the reason he was gunned down in his home on his sixtieth birthday, February 11, 1988.

Majrooh's publication expressed a growing trend of thought among resistance supporters that Afghanistan's future would come from the commanders on the ground, not the Pakistan-recognized leaders in Peshawar. The French scholar Olivier Roy argued for this thesis in his influential book *Islam and Resistance in Afghanistan*. In its first divergence from the Pakistani line on the mujahidin, the US decided in 1989 that American funds would no longer support "extremists," identified as Hikmatyar and Sayyaf. The CIA also began to provide direct support to about ten commanders on the ground, who were called "unilaterals." The CIA tried to conceal these relationships from the ISI.

The US, Pakistan, and even the Soviet leadership believed that Najibullah was likely to fall soon after the end of the Soviet withdrawal on February 15, 1989. Saudi Arabia funded a February 1989 "shura" convened by the seven parties in a Rawalpindi hotel to choose an interim government. The open distribution of Saudi cash during the meeting caused a backlash. This was also the first public gathering where the conflict between Pashtun commanders from the south and Tajik commanders in the north found open expression. The divided shura found a traditional solution of agreeing on a weak leader, and Mojaddedi became the powerless interim president.

After Zia's death, the Pakistan Army preferred a partial restoration of civilian rule, and under US pressure it allowed Pakistan People's Party leader Benazir Bhutto to return from exile. The PPP won control of the parliament, and Bhutto became prime minister. Afghanistan policy, however, was not her priority, and it remained under the control of the ISI, now led by Lieutenant General Hamid Gul. Gul concocted a plan for a coordinated assault on Jalalabad by mujahidin forces, supported by the ISI and the Arab fighters. He promised that the city would fall within days. The mujahidin could then escort the Interim Islamic Government of Afghanistan to Jalalabad, where it could raise its flag on Afghan soil and establish a provisional capital. Gul gained the support of Prime Minister Bhutto and the American ambassador Robert Oakley.

Instead, the battle of Jalalabad turned into the high point of Najibullah's career. He rallied his well-trained and supplied security forces, while the tactical, logistical, and political weaknesses of the mujahidin became evident when confronted with a conventional force. The birth defect of being structured as a fragmented group of insurgent bands made coordination impossible. Commanders on the ground began to seek local truces with the government, as foreseen in Najibullah's policy of national reconciliation. Bhutto sacked Hamid Gul in May 1989, usurping what the army considered to be its sole prerogative and assuring that the Pakistan establishment would remove her from office, as it did through a rigged election in 1990.

Why did Mikhail Gorbachev withdraw Soviet troops from Afghanistan?

The common interpretation in the US is that the Stingers did so much damage that the Soviets were forced to withdraw. The final Politburo decision to withdraw all troops from Afghanistan, however, came in November 1986, only two months after the first test of a Stinger and before it had any effect on the battlefield.

Mikhail Gorbachev changed Soviet policy after he became the leader in 1985. His predecessors seemed prepared to keep doing the same thing indefinitely while hoping for different results. Gorbachev, however, redefined Soviet goals in the world and, therefore, in Afghanistan. Much like Presidents Barack Obama and Donald Trump twenty-four and thirty-two years later, respectively, Gorbachev came into office determined to extricate his country from Afghanistan. His main goal was to engage with the US and Europe to modernize the Soviet economy and society, and that depended on ridding the USSR of the distraction of Afghanistan.

At the 27th Congress of the Communist Party of the Soviet Union, which took place in February 1986, Gorbachev signaled a change in direction when he said, "Counterrevolution and imperialism have turned Afghanistan into a bleeding wound." At first, the Soviet military told Gorbachev they could do the job if they had more troops and the right strategy, as the American generals told President Obama in 2009 and President Trump in 2017. Much as Obama conceded on the surge in 2009, and Trump agreed to the "South Asia Strategy" in 2017, Gorbachev gave the military a year to show what it could do. As a result. the 1986 fighting season was the bloodiest yet.

The change in Soviet policy required changing the Afghan government. In May 1986 Gorbachev replaced Babrak Karmal, who was closely identified with the Soviet intervention and the aftermath, with Dr. Najibullah, who had proven to be an effective leader. In December 1986, Gorbachev summoned Najibullah to Moscow to tell him of the previous month's decision to withdraw its troops. From that time on, Najibullah's tasks were to make the security forces stronger and the government more inclusive. The same month, Najibullah announced a policy of national reconciliation, which offered amnesty and reintegration for mujahidin who stopped fighting, provided for a multiparty system, including participation in the government by non-PDPA figures, and called for formation of local shuras, including former mujahidin. In 1987 Najibullah convened a Loya Jirga that not only adopted a new constitution but changed the name of the state back to the Republic of Afghanistan.

Najibullah could not expand the Afghan Army throughout the country as fast and as effectively enough as would have been required to compensate for the loss of Soviet military power. Instead, he created locally based paramilitary groups, which he paid for by printing money. Militia leaders were sometime paid in unopened "containers" of Afs. 10,000 bills.[5]

These militias were organized like the mujahidin, in the "andiwali" (social network) system. Each armed group consisted of a relatively powerful man commanding followers from his kinship, client, or solidarity group. The largest and best known of these militias was the Jawzjanis, led by Abdul Rashid Dostum, who became Ashraf Ghani's first vice president after the 2014 election. Eager as many of these militias were to fight for money, loot, or revenge, they were never fully under the government's control.

How did the USSR withdraw its troops?

Once the Soviets decided to withdraw, they and their clients in the DRA engaged seriously with negotiations on the conflict organized by Diego Cordovez, the United Nations special envoy. The Soviet leadership tried to keep its decision secret, abetted by those in the US government whose Cold War catechism taught that the Soviets would never withdraw. That way it could demand concessions from the US and Pakistan in return for the withdrawal. Eventually, however, the US realized that Gorbachev would withdraw the troops with or without concessions and therefore hardened its approach.

Under the Geneva Accords of April 14, 1988, the Soviets began withdrawing troops from Afghanistan on May 15, 1988,

5. Afs. = the currency of the Islamic Republic of Afghanistan. One US dollar = about 75 Afs.

and completed the withdrawal on February 15, 1989. The withdrawal was "front-loaded": half of the troops left within the first three months, by July 15, 1988.

Cordovez mediated between the government of Pakistan and the government of Afghanistan, originally the DRA and then the Republic of Afghanistan. He also consulted with the US and the Soviet Union, who controlled the resources used to pursue the conflict. They agreed to act as guarantors.

The accord consisted of four instruments. Two constituted the core: an agreement between Afghanistan and Pakistan on "the Principles of Mutual Relations, in particular on Non-interference and Non-intervention," and an agreement signed by Afghanistan, Pakistan, the USSR, and the US on "the Interrelationships for the settlement of the situation relating to Afghanistan."[6]

While the agreement on noninterference came wrapped in a silk cloth of diplomatic language tied with a bow of euphemism, it had one simple goal, which diplomatic convention dictated could not be made explicit: Pakistan would cease to arm, train, support, and, to use contemporary language, grant a safe haven to the mujahidin groups fighting against the Soviet troops and the government.

Diplomatic convention likewise dictated that the agreement on interrelationships stated that the USSR and DRA had reached a bilateral agreement on a schedule for the complete withdrawal of Soviet troops from Afghanistan. Of course, the main negotiations on this subject took place directly between the US and the USSR.

The most difficult issue was the interrelationship, specifically the timing, of the cutoff of aid to the mujahidin and the Soviet troop withdrawal. The timing of implementation of commitments by the parties to the conflict is always one of

6. AF_880414_AgreementsSettlementoftheSituationRelatingAfghanis tan.pdf.

the toughest issues in peace negotiations. Whoever goes first makes itself vulnerable. That is why there is usually an attempt at implementation by stages and monitoring by third parties. In this case, the text of the accords provided that the agreement on noninterference would go into effect on day one, which was May 15, 1988. Pakistan and the US would have preferred that the mujahidin receive aid until the Soviet troops had withdrawn completely. The priority the Soviets placed on withdrawing their troops in dignity and security made that impossible. They compromised on "front-loading" the withdrawal in a way that would effectively confine the remaining troops to bases from which to prepare the rest of the withdrawal.

The highest levels of the Reagan administration never took these negotiations seriously, since they knew that the Soviets would never withdraw. Therefore the text had gone only to the National Security Council staff for approval. The president never saw it until it was ready for signature, and when he did, he judged it unacceptable. The US and Pakistan would end aid to the mujahidin, while the USSR could continue to aid the Najibullah government. No one had ever mentioned or charged that assistance by the Soviet government to the Afghan government violated any international laws, principles, or norms, and it had never been a subject for negotiation.

Now it was, though. The US administration did not try to renegotiate the text of the accords, to which it had already "agreed." Instead, it launched a direct negotiation with the Soviet Union over the issue of "symmetry." If not explicitly, the UN-convened negotiation process had treated aid to the mujahidin and the Soviet troop presence as the items to be negotiated. The US now changed the terms of the negotiation, telling the Soviets that the obligations of the two superpowers had to be symmetrical with respect to their clients. Now, the US offered two options: *negative symmetry*, in which case both would end aid; or *positive symmetry*, under which both would continue arming their clients. The Soviets were furious but could do nothing, since they were committed to withdrawing their troops for reasons that had nothing to do with the content of the accords. They were not willing to prolong their fight in Afghanistan to seek a better deal from the US. The Soviets refused negative symmetry, knowing how unlikely it was that Najibullah could survive even long enough to agree to leave office without Soviet aid. The US therefore declared that it considered the obligations of the US and the USSR to be symmetrical, meaning that it would continue to aid the mujahidin as long as the Soviets aided Najibullah.

Cordovez knew that the withdrawal of Soviet troops would inevitably lead to changes in the Afghan government, including integrating the mujahidin into a different political order. He was unable to make direct contact with the leaders of the mujahidin, though in 1987 he was thinking of various ways to convene a Loya Jirga, as Zahir Shah had proposed in 1983. Positive and negative symmetry, however, had different implications for a political settlement. A peaceful settlement requires the persistence of the state to maintain security and enforce agreements. But that meant that the "communist regime" would survive, even if in a modified form, and that the Reagan administration could not abide. It continued the policy of supporting a resistance movement to eliminate all Soviet influence rather than to present a political alternative for Afghanistan.

Through more than three years (1989–92) of US-Soviet negotiation over a political transition in Afghanistan, one issue above all blocked agreement: whether Najibullah would stay in power at the start of the transition and leave as its result, or whether his departure was a precondition for starting any transition. Until it was clear that the USSR would not survive, Moscow held to positive symmetry and keeping Najibullah in power at least to start the transition.

Why did Najibullah's government collapse in April 1992?

Without the discipline imposed by the Red Army and the thousands of Soviet advisors it protected, old divisions soon resurfaced in the PDPA. The Khalqis had long resented the imposition of Parchami leadership by the Soviets. The rivalry manifested itself in tensions between parts of the security forces dominated by different factions. In March 1990 these tensions came to a head. In an alliance brokered by the Pakistani ISI, the Khalqi Air Force chief Shahnawaz Tanai attempted a coup against Najibullah in alliance with Hikmatyar. Najibullah crushed the coup with his special "Presidential Guard" and militia forces, but he mistrusted the largely Khalqi officer corps of the army and thus increased his reliance on militias.

In addition to the loss of Soviet military support, for which Najibullah tried to compensate by disbursing newly printed cash to militias, the Afghan state was hit by two other shocks reducing its revenue in a few short years. When the last Soviet troops left Afghanistan in February 1989, they closed and capped the gas wells, and the state abruptly lost that income. Then, in September 1991, a month after the failed anti-Gorbachev coup attempt in Moscow, the US secretary of state James Baker and the Soviet minister of foreign affairs Boris Pankin finally agreed to implement negative symmetry, cutting off aid to both sides of the Afghan conflict: the mujahidin and the Najibullah government.

In January 1992 budgetary pressures forced Najibullah, like the British in 1841, to stop paying subsidies to militias guarding his supply lines, in this case north to the former USSR rather than east to India. Once Najibullah stopped paying them, these militias, led by Dostum, mutinied, allied with co-ethnics in both the army and the mujahidin, and seized control of the customs posts, from which they paid themselves. The collapse of the USSR, combined with the loss of control of the security forces and territory, put so much pressure on Najibullah that he agreed to a UN peace plan, which required him to resign as the first step. When the militias, army, and mujahidin saw that Najibullah was leaving, they turned against him quickly if only out of self-preservation. His government fell soon after in April 1992. The army broke up, the bureaucracy was not paid, and the state collapsed.

5

CIVIL WAR: ISLAMIC STATE TO ISLAMIC EMIRATE

What set off the 1992–96 civil war?

Various actors maneuvered to fill the power vacuum in Kabul left by the Soviet withdrawal. After the failure of the offensive on Jalalabad, the US moved away from the Pakistani position. It cut off aid to Hikmatyar and Sayyaf, whom the US then classified as "extremist," though Saudi aid continued. It started a dialogue with the USSR over a political transition involving "moderate" mujahidin parties. The US and USSR negotiated over the terms of a new, more representative government, to be formed under the aegis of the UN Special Mission to Afghanistan (UNSMA), which had been created to monitor implementation of the Geneva Accords. The two sides agreed in principle that, as part of this solution, they would implement negative symmetry, ending aid to both sides, and that Najibullah would resign. Differences remained over the sequence of these events, in particular over whether Najibullah would leave at the start of the transition or as its result. This foreshadowed the identical disagreement twenty-five years later over the departure of Bashar al-Assad in Syria. The interim government would consist of figures chosen by a representative Afghan gathering, to be held in Europe. Commanders on the ground in Afghanistan, including Ahmad Shah Massoud, signaled openness to such an agreement but wanted to be consulted and were wary of ceding power to unknown Afghan exiles.

The US, UN, and USSR (which no longer existed) could not control the tempo of events. As Najibullah lost the ability to pay his government, the armed forces collapsed and split into factions. That, rather than a mujahidin victory, is the reason his government fell.

After the defeat of the Soviet hardliners, who had attempted a coup against Gorbachev in August 1991, the USSR turned its attention inward, lost interest in Afghanistan, and then dissolved. In September 1991 the US and USSR agreed to implement negative symmetry when US secretary of state James Baker met Soviet foreign minister Boris Pankin in Moscow.[1]

The cutoff of assistance to Najibullah made it increasingly difficult for him to pay the militias that guarded the road to the north that had long been Kabul's supply line. Najibullah tried to appoint a loyal Pashtun general to control the northern militias, but instead they revolted. In January 1992, Abdul Rashid Dostum took control of Mazar-i Sharif. Afghan Tajik generals joined Dostum and contacted Massoud. This group acted in concert with factions of the Watan Party (as the PDPA had been renamed) that resented Najibullah for marginalizing Karmal and the Khalqis on Soviet orders.

The UN envoy, Benon Sevan of Cyprus, worked to implement the plan agreed to by the US and UN. He moved up the date of the Afghan gathering to choose a transitional administration to April, but the collapse of the Soviet Union, which might have been able to assure the stability of the Afghan government until a transition was ready, made it impossible to implement the agreed plan. The Afghan government no longer

---

1. Thomas Friedman, "The Soviet Transition; U.S. and the Soviet to End Arms Sales to Afghanistan Rivals," *New York Times*, September 14, 1991. Accessed November 3, 2016, http://www.nytimes.com/1991/09/14/world/the-soviet-transition-us-and-soviets-to-end-arms-sales-to-afghan-rivals.html?pagewanted=all.

commanded any troops that could enforce an agreement, and neither did the UN, the US, or the disappearing USSR. Massoud moved his forces out of Panjshir to Shamali, the plain north of Kabul. Hikmatyar withdrew from the discussions among the seven parties and prepared to fight for Kabul. The ISI built up Hikmatyar's "Army of Sacrifice" (Lashkar-i Isar), which allied with some of General Shahnawaz Tanai's Khalqi forces, intending to use it to capture Kabul.

The remaining six parties agreed on a plan under which Mojaddedi would be president for two months, after which Rabbani would take over. Rabbani would hold a shura within six months to choose a new government and hold elections. Sevan brought candidates for the internationally sponsored transitional government to Pakistan. With the Soviet Union gone, Sevan insisted that Najibullah start the process by resigning, as the US demanded.

As he had no money, and his troops were abandoning him, Najibullah agreed to step down. He gave a televised speech on March 18 announcing his willingness to resign as part of a settlement. But since no one could guarantee the security of the armed forces, the revolt spread, and the Watan Party removed Najibullah as leader. On April 16, as Najibullah tried to drive to the airport to fly to India, where his family had fled, Dostum and Karmal supporters led by Karmal's brother, Mahmud Baryalai, blocked his escape. He sought refuge in the UN compound, where he stayed until September 1996, when Taliban and Pakistani ISI officers accompanying them pulled him from his sanctuary and killed him.

The Kabul garrison commander, General Nabi Azimi, a Tajik, handed the military over to Massoud, whose forces had entered the city from the north. Massoud, who by then saw the international plan as irrelevant, invited the interim government chosen by the mujahidin leaders in Peshawar (minus Hekmatyar) to Kabul. They entered the city and proclaimed the establishment of the "Islamic State of Afghanistan." With Massoud's forces controlling Kabul, the capital was effectively under Tajik control for the first time since 1929 and only the second time since 1747.

Pakistan no longer trusted the government chosen under its control, since once it entered Kabul it would depend on Massoud for its security. Islamabad threw its resources behind Hikmatyar, whose forces entered Kabul from the south. Massoud and his allies Dostum, Khalili, Sayyaf, and others, formed a Northern Alliance (Ittilaf-i Shamali) with the help of Iran and pushed Hikmatyar's forces out of the city. With Pakistan's support, Hikmatyar launched rocket attacks on Kabul. These continued for years, killing thousands of civilians.

Rabbani never managed to convene the promised shura, let alone hold elections. As he remained in office past the term given to him by the Peshawar Agreement, his already tattered legitimacy frayed even more. The Peshawar Agreement had distributed the ministries and provinces among the parties, which treated them as private fiefdoms rather than as institutions of government. Fighting broke out among the groups that initially joined the Northern Alliance. Over the next few years some defected from Massoud to Hikmatyar, sometimes facilitated by the ISI. In both Kabul and the provinces, factional battles took a heavy toll on the population. The International Committee of the Red Cross (ICRC) estimated that approximately fifty thousand civilians died in the factional fighting in Kabul alone during 1992–96.

The fighting took on an increasingly ethnic character. National security forces that included all groups no longer existed. In their place were patronage-based armed groups that assumed an ethnic character because of their recruitment patterns, even in the absence of ethnic ideology. All politics was military, battles were factional, and factions were ethnic; factional battles created ethnic hatreds. Some Pashtuns resented the takeover of Kabul by Tajik forces, which reminded them of 1929, and some Tajiks and others resented what they saw as Pashtun attempts to reassert ethnic supremacy.

Some areas were contested: Dostum and Ismail Khan skirmished repeatedly on the Faryab-Herat frontier, and Dostum contested Kunduz with both Jamiat and Sayyaf. Tajik, Uzbek, Pashtun, Hazara, and other militias battled each other for control of customs posts, factories, and road junctions in Balkh. Pashtun militias from various tribes fought and plundered in Kandahar. There was very little central revenue collection. Police forces were under factional control. Courts still sat, but no state enforced their verdicts. Since judges were hardly paid, and armed strongmen were the ultimate authorities, the judicial system became deeply corrupt. Armed groups set up checkpoints along the highways, extracting illegal "tolls" and sometimes assaulting and even killing travelers and traders. Memories of that period remain traumatic. In Kabul, for instance, people tell of corpses that danced after being beheaded by rival militias.

The situation differed from place to place and changed over time—Kabul was relatively calm during a period in 1995–96 when Massoud had pushed back many of his rivals, and the Taliban had defeated the rest, including Hikmatyar. Herat was stable and even relatively prosperous under the rule of Ismail Khan.

How did the Afghan-Soviet and civil war transform Afghan society, politics, and international relations?

By 1992 fourteen years of violence had eliminated the elites that had governed Afghanistan. The royal family had been expelled, and virtually every Muhammadzai had emigrated to the West. The various groups among the newly educated had repeatedly jailed and massacred each other. The institutions that had employed them had collapsed, as had the revenues and foreign aid that had paid their salaries. By 1992 only a few of the Islamists, like Massoud and Hikmatyar, retained any organization inside the country. Virtually all of the remaining educated class had emigrated or been killed. The leaders of the ulama and the tribes had been decimated by the Khalqis and marginalized by both the destruction of the rural economy and the rise of externally supported Islamist commanders.

As the rural population fled war and lost its young men—the labor force—to armed groups, villagers flooded the cities in Afghanistan, while an estimated five million fled to refugee settlements and cities in Pakistan and Iran. Approximately half of the population was forcibly displaced, mostly to urban areas. There, people from a formerly closed society were exposed to more modern societies and experienced daily the consequences of international politics and warfare. They soon realized that social advancement and access to livelihoods in their new settings depended on education as it never had before, and that girls and women could be—had to be—part of the family's survival strategy. In the village, women could contribute to the family's livelihood by working in agriculture, pastoralism, and food processing. On the family property or in a village, most people were related one way or another, but in exile they could contribute only if they ventured out among strangers, and could contribute much more if they were educated.

Cash flooded the country. It came in the form of both Afghan currency printed by the Kabul government to pay militias and the billions of dollars sent to support the fighting and logistics of the mujahidin. This expansion of the money supply occurred in tandem with the outflow of labor from agriculture to warfare and the destruction of villages and irrigation systems. The country had far more money but produced less food, with the predictable result of inflation, especially of food prices. Those remaining in the rural areas needed a cash crop to survive, and the only one they could market was opium poppy. With the suppression of poppy cultivation in Turkey, Iran, and Pakistan, traffickers were looking for new sources of supply, and the collapse of the state in Afghanistan created just what they needed: an agricultural area capable of producing opium poppy where it was extremely cheap and safe to operate an illegal business. Originally Afghanistan supplied only the raw opium, and the processing into heroin and morphine took place in the neighboring countries, mostly Pakistan. When the opiate economy started expanding in mujahidin-controlled areas during the 1980s, cultivation was concentrated in the provinces of Badakhshan, where poppy cultivation for medicinal purposes had a long history, Nangarhar, and Helmand.

The war inducted practically the entire population of Afghanistan into national and international politics. BBC surveys found extraordinarily high levels of listenership among refugees and Afghans inside the country; one survey "concluded that . . . 50 percent of Afghans . . . regularly listened to the BBC."[2] The Soviet-supported government had been controlled by the PDPA/Watan Party, which tried to mobilize those living under its rule through student, youth, and women's groups, and other organizations. Party literature, posters, and slogans were ubiquitous. In exile, both resistance movement and refugee settlements were largely controlled by the *jihadi* parties (or organizations: *tanzimat*), based in Pakistan for the Sunnis and Iran for most Shi'as.

Mobilization for war changed the political landscape. Virtually every ethnic and tribal group in the country became armed and organized, enabling them to control their own areas, once they had expelled the government. The royal regime had used the centralized administration and the division of the country into ever-smaller provinces to prevent the emergence of regional and ethnic leaders who might challenge the center. Areas now dominated by Tajiks, Uzbeks, and Hazaras had their own armed forces and local administrations. While the state remained centralized de jure, de facto Afghanistan

2. BBC, Radio Education for Afghan Children, http://www.bbc.co.uk/worldservice/people/highlights/010711_reach.shtml.

was a congeries of multiple power centers. Especially in the Pashtun areas, some of these fragments were quite small, inspiring the title of my book, *The Fragmentation of Afghanistan*.[3]

Paradoxically, the development of regional-ethnic-tribal warlordism and fragmentation seems to have strengthened rather than weakened national identity. Not even a whisper of a separatist movement developed. A stronger national identity did not mean less conflict, however. As a result of both history and the process of mobilization, groups developed different conceptions of how the common land of Afghanistan should be ruled. Haji Abdul Qadir, a leader of a senior tribal family in Jalalabad and then first vice president, explained this reality in a May 2002 interview with me two months before his assassination in Kabul: The Pashtuns, he said, want to control everything; the Tajiks think they should share power fifty-fifty with the Pashtuns; and the Uzbeks and Hazaras think power should be divided equally among the four groups.

How did the Afghan-Soviet War change the relationship of Afghanistan to the international community?

The Afghan-Soviet War was part of a historical process, including decolonization and the partition of India, the end of the Cold War, and the breakup of the Soviet Union. Afghanistan was the last Cold War conflict, the first post–Cold War conflict, and the first battle of the "War on Terror."

The US-Pakistan alliance was also a child of the Cold War. The partition of India left Pakistan weaker than the new India, and the breakup of Pakistan in 1971 weakened it further. Pakistan sought a military alliance with the US and, ultimately, access to nuclear weapons, to balance India's demographic and economic advantages; after 1978, as the

---

3. See Rubin, *The Fragmentation of Afghanistan: State Formation and Collapse in the International System*.

Soviet-built Afghan Army came under pressure, Pakistan also sought hegemony over Afghanistan to gain "strategic depth" against India, while portraying its role to the US as a loyal ally against Soviet expansionism. Once the Cold War was over and the USSR disappeared, Pakistan's interests aligned even less with Washington's. Once the US had no further concern that a Soviet presence in Afghanistan brought Moscow closer to the Persian Gulf and Indian Ocean, it agreed to negative symmetry. Lacking the support of any great power, the Afghan state collapsed. Until 1991, flows of resources to the government and mujahidin, allied with the USSR or the US, shaped the conflict as a bilateral one. In 1992 the conflict almost immediately reconfigured itself around the changed flow of resources. The resources available from trafficking or regional actors were captured and redistributed by multiple ethnicized patronage networks, not the state. The war became an ethno-factional conflict in a collapsed state.

Pakistan's response was colored by its army's fear of a repetition of the Bangladesh scenario, in which, the army thought, India intervened in an ethnic conflict to break up the state in 1971. It imagined that any Indian or other hostile presence in Afghanistan could lead to a similar result, this time in alliance with Pashtun or Baloch nationalists.

The Pakistani state, especially the army, had also become more Islamized under General Zia-ul-Haq. This helped Pakistan deepen its relationships with Saudi Arabia, the United Arab Emirates, and other Arab states.

After the 1979 Islamic Revolution in Iran, the Islamic Republic positioned itself as a rival to Saudi Arabia as leader of the Islamic world. While the Iran-Saudi conflict has been and still is linked to sectarian conflict between Shi'a and Sunni, originally Ayatollah Ruhollah Khomeini and his followers downplayed the Shi'a identity of Iran and its revolution in favor of portraying it as pan-Islamic. Afghanistan was one of the first arenas where this struggle took place. Iran saw the US-Saudi-Pakistani alliance in Afghanistan as an attempt to put an anti-Iranian "Wahhabi" government in power, a main reason that it helped form and then supported the "Northern Alliance."

The independence of the former Soviet Central Asian republics created new opportunities and threats. Pakistani Islamist politicians, including Zia-ul-Haq, could now aspire to use an Islamic Afghanistan as a stepping stone to Central Asia. The independence of Central Asia also had the potential to transform the world's energy markets; it was possible to conceive of exporting oil and natural gas from Central Asia, not through Russia but through pipelines going west, south, or east. Such routes would have the advantage, as Washington saw it, of loosening Russia's hold on Central Asia. The easiest and most economical way to bring those products to the world market might be south through Iran, the only country with coasts on the Persian Gulf, the Indian Ocean, and the Caspian Sea. But sanctions imposed on the Islamic Republic by the United States and others precluded such investment. Afghanistan became a potential pipeline route that would help Central Asia become more independent of Russia without empowering Iran, and that meant there was a new strategic stake.

To complete the picture, with the infusion of oil money after 1973, the Persian Gulf became an important entrepôt, not just a gas station. Dubai, one of the emirates that joined to form the United Arab Emirates in 1971, made up for its relative lack of oil reserves by establishing a free port. Until the mid-1980s, oil exports constituted half of Dubai's GDP, but Dubai did not rely on one single sector and diversified its economy. The city became a hub for transportation and logistics.[4] In the third quarter of 2015 Dubai's non-oil trade reached about 271 billion US dollars. Its top four trading partners were China

4. Richard H. K. Vietor and Nicole Forrest, "Dubai: *Global Economy*," Case 709-043 (Cambridge, MA: Harvard Business School Publishing, February 25, 2009).

(AED 132bn), India (AED 74bn), the US (AED 60bn), and Saudi Arabia (AED 45bn).[5] In 2015, Dubai International Airport welcomed 78 million passengers, adding to a total of 700 million passengers since the inauguration of the airport fifty-five years earlier.[6] Kabul is less than three hours by plane from Dubai. Afghanistan's proximity to one of the world's busiest trading centers created new economic opportunities for Afghan traders and migrant workers. Dubai took its place besides Karachi as one of two main ports through which Afghanistan traded with the world.

What conditions gave rise to the Taliban?

The Taliban, like most Afghan phenomena, had both domestic and international origins. The dispute as to which is more important continues to this day. Some see the Taliban as a tool created by Pakistan, while others see them as an indigenous response to conditions after the collapse of the state.

Domestically, the Taliban began as a local movement in Kandahar. The predecessors of the group we now call the Taliban were part of the anti-Soviet mujahidin. "Taliban" means students in madrasas, and that was one of the sources of recruitment for the mujahidin, in particular for Muhammadi's Harakat-i Inqilab and Hizb-i Islami Khalis, both of which followed the Deobandi sect. Because they were not political Islamists, most of these fighters did not continue their jihad after the withdrawal of the Soviet troops in 1989. They were not concerned about dislodging the Najibullah government from Kabul, as the political orientation of the government in Kabul had little if any effect on Kandahar. The fighters went back to their madrasas and villages.

5. AED = currency of the United Arab Emirates (Arab Emirates dirham).
6. Dubai Chamber, Annual Report 2015, http://www.dubaichamber. com/uploads/annualreports/2015/DC_AR15_English.pdf.

In Kandahar the government, such as it was, was extremely fragmented. Some mujahidin commanders had turned into bandits, robbing people at checkpoints and even committing rape. A group of former madrasa students met to discuss how to rid Afghanistan of warlords and bandits and reestablish order, or as they put it, enforce Sharia. They convinced Mullah Muhammad Omar to be their leader, although he was not part of the founding group. They began collecting weapons, which as former mujahidin they knew how to use. According to the origin story told by the Taliban themselves, their first act was to attack, arrest, and execute a commander who had kidnapped and raped two young women from Herat at a checkpoint on the Herat-Kandahar highway. People joined them as they overran more of the checkpoints where criminal fighters were exacting tolls and raping people.

Their efforts coincided with a change of government in Pakistan, which led to a reorientation of policy and opening of new strategic possibilities. In October 1993 the Pakistan People's Party (PPP) won parliamentary elections, returning Benazir Bhutto to the office of prime minister, from which the army and bureaucracy had ousted her in a rigged election in 1990. Pakistan's two main centrist parties, led by feudal or industrialist families, each had a different Islamist party with which it formed coalitions. The Pakistan Muslim League (Nawaz) tended to enter into coalitions with the Jamaat-i Islami, a party following the current of Islamist ideology developed by Abu'l Ala Mawdudi in India and the Muslim Brotherhood in the Arab world. General Zia was a Jamaat sympathizer; Jamaat's natural ally in Afghanistan was Hikmatyar: the two groups collaborated closely. The PPP, however, formed coalitions with the Jamiat-i Ulama-i Islam led by Mawlawi Fazlur Rahman, a Deobandi cleric closely identified with Pashtun politics. Fazlur Rahman supported the PPP in parliament and was a close acquaintance of Bhutto's minister of the interior, General Nasirullah Babar.

Since the breakup of the USSR, Bhutto's foreign minister, Sardar Asif Ali, had argued that Pakistan should refocus its foreign policy toward opening trade with Central Asia. Since there was no immediate prospect of stabilizing Kabul and the route to Uzbekistan, Babar advocated working with anyone on the ground to open the route to Turkmenistan via Kandahar and Herat. Bhutto's cabinet approved the plan in June 1994. While in Ashqabat for Turkmenistan Independence Day on October 25, Bhutto reached agreement with Dostum and Ismail Khan for transit through the territories they controlled. The missing link was from Spin Boldak to Kandahar and up to Farah, where there was no power holder strong enough to control the route.

To open the route, the Pakistan military's National Logistics Cell, the same unit that had transported weapons to the mujahidin, organized a convoy carrying food, clothes, and medical supplies, which left Quetta on October 29, 1994. The convoy was led by Colonel Imam, the nom de guerre of the ISI officer, Sultan Amir Tarar, who had been in charge of training the mujahidin. Soon after crossing into Afghanistan on November 1, the convoy was stopped by Achakzai tribesmen, members of a former regime militia, which now levied unofficial tolls on road traffic. A group of "Taliban" suddenly appeared to free the convoy. It swept out of the refugee settlements of Balochistan with apparent support from the paramilitary Balochistan Frontier Force and took control of a large cache of weapons formerly belonging to Hizb-i Islami. The convoy proceeded to Ashqabat.

The relationship between the Taliban who freed the Pakistani convoy and those who founded the organization to suppress warlordism is disputed: either they were the same group or they soon joined forces. The Taliban proved they could secure roads for traffic and swept into Kandahar, which they captured with little resistance.

Who were the Taliban and who were their leaders, including Mullah Omar?

The Taliban were former students from madrasas in southern Afghanistan, as well as from Karachi, Peshawar, and the Balochistan province of Pakistan. In the 1980s before there was an organization that became known as the Taliban, the French scholar Olivier Roy categorized the origins of the mujahidin and stated that there were four main networks from which they were recruited: one of them was the taliban, students of madrasas.

The taliban were of humble origin, economically and tribal, since well-off or well-connected families did not usually send their sons to madrasas. There were few people of non-humble origin left in Afghanistan, as revolution and war had decimated the elites. For example, Mullah Omar was a member of the Hotak tribe, the Ghilzai tribe from which Mirwais Hotaki had come, but which the Durranis had subordinated for centuries, as reflected in their lack of land and other assets. Omar was the son of a village mullah. He became a mid-level commander of Muhammadi's Harakat-i Inqilab, lost one of his eyes in battle, and was cared for in the hospital of the International Committee of the Red Cross (ICRC) in Quetta. Before becoming the leader of the Taliban he had otherwise never left Kandahar province. After he became Amir al-Mu'minin he visited Kabul once but did not even stay the night (his trip to the ICRC hospital in Quetta is his only known foreign travel). He was known for his honesty and abnegation before 2001.

Almost none of the Taliban leaders came from the high-ranking (Zeerak) Durrani tribes. Virtually none of them had been educated in government schools, secular or religious, and none had attended Kabul University, where most of the other political elites had originated. They were familiar with Arabic, at least for religious purposes, and many spoke Urdu in order to be understood in Karachi, but the only Taliban who spoke other foreign languages were a handful of young refugees who had learned English in Pakistan. Many if not most had grown up in villages without electricity, paved roads, government schools, health clinics, or police stations. Their humble origins and religious qualifications helped them establish rapport with the rural people of Southern Afghanistan: the Persian-speaking middle class they later confronted in Kabul and other cities hardly existed there.

The Taliban did not represent a totally new phenomenon in Afghanistan. The network of teachers and students from private, rural-based madrasas in Afghanistan and the neighboring Pashtun-populated areas of Pakistan (previously India) have played a part in the history of the country for centuries. During the anti-Soviet jihad, ulama and students from these madrasas constituted one of the sources of recruitment for mujahidin in the tribal areas.

This group had become marginalized as a result of years of state-building by the royal regime, which created a new elite (including Islamic scholars and judicial officials) trained in modern schools and universities. The royal regime, the Communists, and the Islamists recruited primarily from different sectors of this new elite. Internecine battles in which one faction after another of that intelligentsia succeeded to power, each decimating its rivals, eventually led to the eclipse of this modernizing group. At the same time, as millions of Afghans became refugees and the country's educational system collapsed, madrasas provided almost the only education available to a generation of Pashtun boys.

The West did little to provide refugees with any other education, leaving the madrasas supported by Middle Eastern donors with a virtual monopoly. The rise of the Taliban occurred as the first of those students were completing the new religious educational process, just as the Communist coup d'état (and Islamist resistance) occurred about twenty years after the massive expansion of the state educational system. The collapse of the state administration and community leadership in many places also increased the importance of the mosques, and the mullahs and Taliban who staffed them.

The madrasa networks created ties among the potential new elite, while other institutions were being destroyed. But the mullahs lost the ties to the landlord-dominated local economy and society that had circumscribed their power. Both the state and the rural economy that had sustained tribal leaders collapsed. The ulama became more autonomous in exile and in warlord-dominated Afghanistan, and as a result they became more extremist and deracinated. In exile they also became linked to international networks, both political and economic, including Pakistani political parties and intelligence agencies along with the Arab Islamists who aided the jihad.

The Taliban attitude toward the state and reforms are not the continuation of some unchanging "tradition" but the result of their own uprooting and trauma, during much of which period a central state dominated by a foreign ideology destroyed the country in the name of progressive reform. Foreign aid, commercial agriculture (opium), and long-distance contraband provided this newly armed elite with the opportunity to mobilize resources for the direct exercise of power, which had been out of its reach before. The mosque network enabled it to penetrate society as well.

The domination of the country by this previously marginalized group reversed the pattern of social, political, and economic bifurcation developed under the royal regime and intensified under the Communists. Under these regimes, foreign financial and military aid enabled an urbanized elite to insulate itself from the countryside and create a parallel society of at least superficially modernized institutions. Under the Taliban, however, foreign aid empowered a network based in Afghan rural areas and refugee settlements in Pakistan to control the capital city, reversing the reforms of past decades. The annihilation of the state and the development and reformist agenda it had pursued under several governments spelled the end of the halting emancipation of urban women through decrees by modernizing male leaders.

Although the leadership of such a state by ulama was unprecedented, the underlying structure reproduced a historic pattern: the state was dominated by a small solidarity group of Pashtuns, in this case Kandahari mullahs (rather than Muhammadzais), dependent on foreign aid and taxing commercial agriculture, now mostly illegal drugs rather than karakul lamb and cotton, and foreign trade, now mostly smuggling rather than exports of natural gas, for its resources.

The social network of the elite at the core of the coalition consisted of Kandahari mullahs, those who studied in the same set of madrasas in Pakistan and Afghanistan and participated in the jihad. Mullah Omar and all but one member of the Supreme Shura were Kandahari Pashtuns.[7] The Kabul shura was also predominantly Kandahari but included more eastern Pashtuns, a few Persian speakers, and at least one Uzbek. Without a single exception all are Sunni mullahs trained in private madrasas. Hence the movement had a strong ethnic and regional character, without its leaders having any intention to form such a movement, and it therefore attracted support from some who sought a Pashtun ethnic movement capable of ruling Afghanistan.

These core leaders follow the Deobandi movement. The movement, which owes its name to the Indian town where a famous madrasa was established in the nineteenth century, developed from conservative reform movements among Indian Muslims. Deobandis reject all forms of *ijtihad*—the use of reason to create innovations in Sharia in response to new conditions—the revival of which is a key plank in the platform of the Islamic modernists. They oppose all forms of hierarchy within the Muslim community, including tribalism or royalty;

7. "Kandahari" here denotes the broad region with Kandahar at its center, including several provinces in addition to the modern province of Kandahar.

they even strive to exclude Shi'a from participation in the polity and take a very restrictive view of the social role of women. All of these characteristics of the Indian and Pakistani Deobandis were found in exaggerated forms among the Afghan Taliban.[8]

The support they received from Pakistan enabled them to capitalize on these endowments. The Pakistan military trained, or retrained, them in military organization and operations. They also received aid from religious networks in Pakistan. In particular, a Mawlawi from Karachi, Mufti Abdul Rasheed Ludhianvi, author of *Obedience to the Amir*, a manual on how to run a militant organization, helped them devise an organizational model that suppressed tribalism and patronage networks more effectively than any other organization in Afghanistan.[9]

What was the goal of the Taliban?

As founding members of the Taliban describe it, their original motivation for banding together in an armed group was to eliminate the warlords and criminals who were looting Kandahar. Their means to doing so was implementation of Sharia. They had no political doctrine other than the implementation of Sharia law, as they understood it. They spoke of a tradition in Afghanistan that in periods of disorder, the students or Taliban would come out of their madrasas, restore order and Islamic law, help a new ruler come to power to provide justice by enforcing Sharia, and then return to their madrasas. During 1994–95, when they were just getting started, some of the Taliban spoke of bringing back Zahir Shah, who at that time was living in Rome. Mullah Omar was reported to have

---

8. Ahmed Rashid, *Taliban: Militant Islam, Oil, and Fundamentalism in Central Asia* (New Haven: Yale University Press, 2000); Barbara Daly Metcalf, *Islamic Revival in British India: Deoband, 1860–1900* (Princeton: Princeton University Press, 1982).
9. Michael Semple first translated and drew my attention to this work.

said later that they had no intention of ruling; they were going to reestablish law and order, so that someone else could rule, but then found that there was no one else . . . (that part may be a bit disingenuous).

The establishment of security in towns and along the roads was a boon for commerce, which also coincided with the Pakistani foreign policy objective of opening the route from Quetta to Central Asia. As a result the Taliban received contributions from associations of Afghan traders in Peshawar and Quetta. The Taliban's operations significantly lowered the cost of transportation, and the traders were willing to share some of their profits with the Taliban to assure that the roads continued to be open and secure.[10]

Mullah Omar made a public decision to turn the movement into a government in April 1996. He convened an advisory assembly or shura, of about fourteen hundred ulama in Kandahar. According to Sharia, community decisions should be taken by *ahl ul-hal o 'aqd*, literally "those who loosen (release) and bind." The term is ambiguous and can be used to legitimate different forms of government, including electoral democracy, in which *ahl ul-hal o 'aqd* would be the electorate. In Kabul Burhanuddin Rabbani, president of the Islamic State of Afghanistan, also tried to convene a shura of *ahl ul-hal o 'aqd*. In the Taliban's interpretation, *ahl ul-hal o 'aqd* should consist of Islamic scholars.

This assembly bestowed upon Omar the title of Amir al-Mu'minin, which means commander of the faithful. While that title has been used by rulers claiming to be Muhammad's successor (khalifa, or caliph) as ruler of all Muslims, it also denotes any leader of an Islamic community, especially one engaged in jihad, not necessarily the caliph of all Muslims. Unlike the leaders of the so-called Islamic State, Mullah Omar and his

10. Aisha Ahmad, *Jihad & Co.: Black Markets and Islamist Power* (New York: Oxford, 2017).

successors never referred to themselves as caliphs or to the territory they ruled as a caliphate. Mullah Omar also symbolized his religious as well as his national legitimacy by donning the supposed cloak of Prophet Muhammad, which Ahmad Shah Durrani had transferred from Bukhara to Kandahar. Mullah Omar took the cloak out of its silver box in Kandahar's central shrine and held it up with his hands in the sleeves. Once Mullah Omar had taken the title of Amir, the Taliban renamed themselves the Islamic Emirate of Afghanistan. The word "emirate" is not necessarily a radical Islamist term but an Arabic word for a territorial domain of governance. There are emirates not associated with militancy, such as the United Arab Emirates and Brunei. There are no emirates, however, associated with representative forms of government.

To sustain the legitimacy of their claim to be the rulers of Afghanistan, they had to capture the capital, Kabul, and unite the entire country under their rule. Some Afghans perceived the Taliban as restoring centralized Pashtun control of the Afghan state. Some Pashtun nationalists who did not share the Taliban's Islamic agenda welcomed their reestablishment of Pashtun rule, while many Islamist non-Pashtuns saw the effort as a threat to their security and rights. The Taliban, however, did not articulate an ethnic agenda and denied having one.

An undeclared but apparent Taliban goal was providing employment to mullahs, especially recent madrasa graduates. The Taliban leaders appointed mullahs to virtually every job. An Islamic government is not a government where every official is a mullah, but the Taliban leaders were responding to the crisis of employment of madrasa graduates. A generation of rural boys were educated in madrasas in Pakistan during the war, when there was no other kind of education available to them.

Their effort to bring the entire country under their rule introduced ethnic conflict and sectarianism into the Taliban's efforts. Once they seized Kabul they devoted their efforts to conquering those areas of the country under the control of non-Pashtun leaders such as Massoud, Dostum, or Khalili. These efforts included brutal incidents involving massacres of members of other ethnic groups as well as the devastation of the Shamali plain, where the Taliban drove out the mainly Tajik inhabitants and tried to burn or uproot grapevines and fruit trees. In 1998, when the Taliban captured Mazar-i Sharif, they may have killed some two thousand men, predominantly captured Shi'a fighters.[11] In early 2001, three hundred unarmed Hazara and Sayyid men, some of whom worked for humanitarian organizations, were executed by the Taliban in Yakawlang, Bamian province.[12]

How was the Islamic Emirate of Afghanistan structured?

The Taliban had no doctrine about how a state should be structured. The only requirement for legitimacy was enforcement of Sharia. Since there is no agreed codification of Sharia, enforcement of that canonical law in practice meant that the decision-makers must be ulama qualified to apply jurisprudence to cases. Political Islamists, in contrast, have a doctrine of the state in which the amir makes political decisions. Gulbuddin Hekmatyar and Osama bin Laden, for instance, had no qualifications in Islamic learning that would entitle them to make decisions in an Islamic emirate like that of the Taliban.

This meant that the judiciary played an extraordinarily important role for the Taliban, while the executive branch did not change much. Wherever they established their rule, the Taliban established Sharia courts down to the village level. The establishment of these courts enabled them to incorporate the clergy into the state structure as previous Afghan states had not. Especially in the rural areas where most Afghans still lived, people sometimes had easier access to these courts

11. https://www.hrw.org/legacy/reports98/afghan/Afrepor0.htm.
12. https://www.hrw.org/reports/2001/afghanistan/afghan101.htm.

than to the official justice system of previous (or later) regimes. While Sharia is sometimes equated to the harsh punishments of the *hudud* crimes (those deemed most egregious), much of the work of these courts involved property, commercial, and family disputes. The ability of the population to resolve these disputes quickly through a system they understood and considered legitimate was one of the chief sources of whatever legitimacy the Taliban enjoyed.

The executive branch consisted of the existing structure of the Afghan state plus Mullah Omar in Kandahar. The Amir al-mu'minin in Kandahar had to approve key decisions and appointments and set basic policy. Otherwise, the emirate took over the existing administration with only one other change: the establishment of a religious police force to Prevent Vice and Promote Virtue (*Amr bil Maroof wa Nahi anil Munkar*), which shared the name with a similar force in Saudi Arabia. The name came from a verse of the Quran. This department was responsible for the enforcement of decrees regarding moral behavior, including those restricting women's employment and dress, enforcing men's beard length and mosque attendance, regulating activities of UN agencies and nongovernmental organizations, commanding destruction of "graven images," and requiring the labeling of religious minorities.

The council of ministers in Kabul was headed by a chairman, who coordinated the government like a prime minister. The Taliban tried to reinforce the centralized structure of the administration, appointing governors who were not natives of the provinces where they served and changing them frequently. They regarded the de facto decentralization that had emerged from the collapse of the state as an aberration, a manifestation of warlordism, which was responsible for the *fitna* (un-Islamic disorder) into which Afghanistan had fallen.

Most of the post-state military structures in Afghanistan up to that time had been organized around *andiwali*, meaning friendship or social networks, so that the basic military unit consisted of a commander and fighters who had personal links to him, which could be tribal, ethnic, educational (studied at the same madrasa), or marital. The commander, not individual fighters, belonged to a party, and if the commander changed parties, the fighters would go with him. These groups were inherently local and would fight only within their own areas. For some, that could mean a district or province, for others a subregion, but the fighters could not be deployed at will by central leadership. Massoud tried to overcome these limitations but met with only partial success.

The Taliban military could transcend parochial or local loyalties, just as religious solidarity could enable ulama to mobilize people across tribal lines. The Taliban recruited fighters individually and could move them around. They were fighting against the United Front (Northern Alliance), which mostly had locally recruited forces. A force from Panjshir could hardly be sent to fight in Herat and certainly not in Kandahar, whereas the Taliban could move their forces anywhere and did not have a significant problem with factionalism.

They were also able to increase state revenues, because they could suppress predatory factionalism and centralize revenue collection. Previously commanders had set up checkpoints on the roads. Anyone with a gun could force anyone coming down the road to pay, whether they were traders or just wayfarers. As mentioned previously, the Taliban received aid from traders' associations in Peshawar and Quetta, because the suppression of predatory factionalism facilitated business. That is also why Pakistan and, originally, the US, thought that the Taliban might be able to create the conditions for building gas and oil pipelines.

The Taliban received training, technical, and strategic military assistance from the Pakistan military, including a cadre of retired officers on contract embedded within the Taliban's command structure. The Taliban also received training and assistance from al-Qaeda, which provided some of their shock troops. The Taliban did not participate in or support global jihad against the "far enemy."

Why did the Taliban ban girls from school and women from work,
as well as enforce other strict prohibitions and requirements?

When the Taliban took control of Kabul, they enacted a set
of draconian decrees. They imposed strict gender segregation, forbidding women from working in offices or teaching
in schools. They closed nearly all girls' schools and arrested
women who tried to hold underground classes. They prohib-
ited women from consulting male physicians or going out to
receive assistance from international organizations. They required that all women wear *chadari* (a garment that covers
most of the head, including hair) and be fully covered to the
ankles. Men were required to attend mosque five times a day
and were forbidden to trim their beards. The Taliban prohib-
ited all manner of Western dress. The Vice and Virtue police
enforced all of these regulations harshly, beating and arresting
both men and women for violations. The Taliban revived the
hudud punishments of stoning for adultery and amputation for
theft, although they soon discontinued carrying them out.

In the West the Taliban were best known for their repressive policies, especially against women, but they boasted in
particular of their policies to restore security. Taliban officials
told visitors, "You can drive from one end of the country to
the other even at night with a car full of gold, and no one will
disturb you." This expression was hardly a metaphor. Driving
across southern Afghanistan from Kandahar to Farah and back
in June 1998, I saw many trucks doing just that; their cargoes
comprised not gold but consumer goods purchased in Dubai
to be sold in smugglers' markets in Pakistan. In two days'
drive I encountered only three unobtrusive checkpoints. The
greater security provided by the Taliban improved the conditions for the trade in opium, even after the government officially proscribed poppy cultivation in 2000–2001.[13] The Taliban

13. United Nations International Drug Control Program (United Nations
Office of Drugs and Crime, UNODC), Afghanistan partner. Strategic

also vaunted their efforts to collect weapons and combat crime, including rape and murder.

For the Taliban, these efforts at restoring order were of a piece with the decrees on women and religious behavior that seem bizarre and repressive to many others, including Afghans, especially the urban and educated part of the population. These policies were all justified as the enforcement of Sharia. The way that the Taliban interpreted Sharia, however, as well as the violent way they enforced it, betrayed a concern with Pashtun conceptions of honor and control, along with a desire to subordinate and even punish the population of Kabul, seen as the source of Afghanistan's ills.

Increased freedom for women, including voluntary unveiling, secular education, and professional employment, had been urban phenomena dependent on the state. They were decreed by the highest (male) leadership of the state in order to implement a (lightly) imposed vision of modernization. The collapse and loss of legitimacy of the weakly modernizing state also meant the weakening of the institutional support for women's public roles.[14] During the Soviet occupation, the Kabul regime expanded women's roles, as men were largely enrolled in the security organs. In refugee settlements and rural areas of Afghanistan, however, patriarchal strictures on women were retained or reinforced. These restrictions resulted from male reaction to both the insecurities of life in exile and the reforms associated with the disaster that had overtaken the country.[15] The Taliban codified and extended many of these

study 2: *The Dynamics of the Farmgate Opium Trade and the Coping Strategies of Opium Traders*, final report (Islamabad, 1998).

14. Nancy Dupree, "Afghan Women Under the Taliban," in *Fundamentalism Reborn? Afghanistan and the Taliban? Afghanistan and the Taliban*, ed. William Maley (New York: New York University Press, 1998), 145–66.

15. For a literary treatment of this process, see Syed Bahauddin Majrooh, "End of a Sojourn in the Abode of Refugees: *Gul andam* [body like a flower], or the Story of Laughing Lovers," trans.

practices, and as a result women were excluded from public life to an unprecedented degree. They were forbidden from going to school (exceptions were later made for religious education up to the age of nine or training in healthcare), from going out in public without a male guardian, and from employment outside the home (with later exceptions for employment in healthcare).

Although the Taliban justified some of these rules under Islamic strictures on sexual mixing, they also frequently referred to the need for security and the prevention of the rapes that had occurred under warlord rule. These restrictions thus constituted a reassertion of male honor through control over women, just as the Taliban's attempted conquest of the rest of the country constituted an attempt to reassert honor by controlling the homeland. The use of Islamic discourse to legitimate protection of honor (*namus*) through control thus asserted the unity of the values often cited by Pashtuns as motivation for participating in jihad: for Islam, for homeland, and for honor (*da islam da para, da watan da para, da namus da para*).[16] Namus also referred to women—women being considered the honor of men, hence "protection" of women by men is deemed obligatory.

Most of the Taliban were unfamiliar with the city of Kabul. Many of their fighters were from rural backgrounds and were even less educated than the leaders. Many of them were illiterate. Their idea of Islam was strongly colored by Pashtun patriarchal tribal traditions. In addition, they had little money, so, given their priorities, they closed the girls' schools and left open the boys' schools.

Ashraf Ghani, in *Ego-Monster* (Izhda-yi Khudi), bk. 1, vol. 5 (Peshawar: Unpublished, 1984). Translated into French as *Le Rire des Amants* (Paris: Phébus, 1991).

16. This was analyzed years before the Taliban. Hakim Taniwal, "The Impact of Pashtunwali on Afghan Jehad," *Quarterly Journal of Writers Union of Free Afghanistan* 2 (January–March 1987): 1–24.

The Taliban never claimed that Islam required or justified denying education to girls and women, nor did they ever explain how they would produce the female teachers and medical personnel that their strict code of gender segregation required without encouraging girls to continue their education through university. They claimed that they closed girls' schools because of insecurity. In practice, closing girls' schools and curbing women's employment were likely to have been concessions to rural fighters' reactionary views. According to former Taliban leaders, the basic concept that informed their policy was that Afghan society had become totally lax and lawless, as shown by the power of warlords and gunmen. To reestablish order, they thought they needed to be very strict and harsh.

How did the Taliban capture control of different regions of Afghanistan?

After the Taliban captured Kandahar in November 1994,[17] they marched west and captured Helmand, Farah, and Nimroz with little or no resistance. When they tried to advance north on the ring road toward Herat, Ismail Khan's allies in the area stopped their advance. They then focused their efforts on moving northeast, joined by an estimated three thousand madrasa students who crossed the border from Pakistan to support them.

In February 1995, the Taliban routed Hikmatyar's forces in Logar, effectively ending the shelling of Kabul. They pushed into southern Kabul, where they captured the leader of Hizb-i Wahdat, Abdul Ali Mazari. Mazari died in the Taliban's custody under disputed circumstances, which intensified the antagonism between the Taliban and Hazaras.

17. Zachary Laub, Council of Foreign Relations (CFR), "The Taliban in Afghanistan," July 4, 2014. Accessed November 4, 2016. Available at: http://www.cfr.org/afghanistan/taliban-afghanistan/p10551.

The Taliban launched a new assault on Herat in April 1995.[18] Pashtun militias in Shindand defected to them, leaving the city defenseless from the south. Traders financed this offensive, as Ismail Khan, facing big expenses defending Herat on two fronts, had raised taxes. Dostum had also turned against Jamiat and was attacking Herat from the east, in Faryab, diverting Ismail Khan's troops. In September 1995 the Taliban captured Herat. Ismail Khan first fled to Iran and then returned to lead troops in Faryab against Taliban-controlled Herat.

By this time the Taliban had developed bigger ambitions, whether by themselves or under the influence of the ISI. They aimed not just to restore law and order in Afghanistan by implementing Sharia, but to restore the unity of Afghanistan under a single Islamic government. They perceived the control of the central Afghan government by Tajiks and the control of much of the territory of Afghanistan by different warlords, as the division of Afghanistan.

The Taliban made their way up the east of Afghanistan through other Pashtun areas. They gained the allegiance of Jalaluddin Haqqani and his network in early 1995, enabling them to establish their rule in Paktia, Paktika, and Khost. With Haqqani's support, their advance picked up. Hikmatyar, having lost his bases outside Kabul, finally accepted the post of prime minister in the Rabbani government in the spring of 1996 and immediately focused on the country's most important problem: insufficient veiling of women in Kabul.

Over the spring and summer of 1996 the Taliban consolidated their hold over southern Afghanistan, from Herat to Paktia. In September, with the help of the Haqqanis, the ISI, and a new influx of Pakistani madrasa students, they captured Jalalabad, where the Taliban first encountered Osama bin Laden. They then went on to take Kabul. Massoud, who

18. Larry P. Goodson, *Afghanistan's Endless War: State Failure, Regional Politics, and the Rise of the Taliban* (Seattle: University of Washington Press, 2001).

had lost the support of most of his former allies, evacuated his forces to Panjsher rather than try to defend the city. In Panjsher Massoud is reported to have told his men that they deserved to lose Kabul, as they had failed to provide security and governance.

After consolidating their hold on Kabul by imposing their draconian regulations and flooding the city with armed madrasa students from southern Afghanistan and Pakistan, they prepared to move north by taking advantage of the ubiquitous divisions on the other side. At that time Abdul Rashid Dostum, who controlled Mazar-i Sharif and the customs point and bridge to Uzbekistan, was engaged in a dispute with Ghulam Rasul Pahlawan, an Uzbek commander who had sided at various times with both the mujahidin and the government to expand his personal power. Rasul was assassinated in Mazar-i Sharif in May 1997, and his supporters and family held Dostum responsible. The Taliban were approaching from the west (Herat) and south (Kabul), blocking roads and sparking food shortages. Dostum had been unable to pay his troops for months. Rasul's brother, a former PDPA functionary named Abdul Malik Pahlawan, had been in secret contact with the ISI and the Taliban. Malik offered to expel Dostum, capture and hand over Ismail Khan, and allow the Taliban to fly troops into the airport. In May 1997 he delivered all three. Dostum fled Mazar-i Sharif to Uzbekistan and then Turkey. The Taliban transferred Ismail Khan to a prison in Kandahar (he escaped two years later with the help of a guard). Pashtun commanders in the north joined the Taliban, notably giving them control of Kunduz, with its airport and crossroads location. Not only did the Taliban immediately occupy Mazar, but Pakistan moved quickly to ratify the military advance politically, indicating that it had helped plan the events and knew of them in advance. The Pakistani foreign minister Ayub Gohar air-dashed to Mazar to announce that the war was over, and that the Taliban had won. Pakistan formally recognized the Taliban's "Islamic Emirate of Afghanistan."

The Pakistani delegation barely made it back to the airport before an uprising pushed the Taliban out. Whatever promises the ISI and the Taliban had made to Malik, he expected that they would recognize him as the de facto ruler-warlord of the north, replacing Dostum. Instead, they set about extending the writ of the Islamic Emirate. The Taliban went house to house collecting weapons, as they had done elsewhere. Malik had not cleared his deal with Hizb-i Wahdat, the main party of the Hazaras in Mazar, where it was led by Muhammad Muhaqqiq. Rather than surrender their weapons, some Hazaras started an uprising against the Taliban. A disgruntled Malik soon joined them and routed the Taliban. They massacred about fifteen hundred Taliban fighters they had taken prisoner and scattered the bodies in the desert of Dasht-i Laili. The Taliban demanded a UN investigation, but the UN High Commissioner for Human Rights finally did not investigate.

Throughout the following year the Taliban strengthened their position in Herat and moved closer to Mazar. Hizb-i Islami commanders, mostly from the settler communities of Pashtuns in the north, joined up with the Taliban. Dostum had returned to northwest Afghanistan, and his forces were also advancing against Malik. In August 1998, the Taliban swiftly captured not only Mazar but also Bamiyan and the rest of Hazarajat. In Mazar they gave their troops license to take revenge for several days, and the estimates of those murdered, mostly Hazaras, reach into the thousands. Many were killed in Bamiyan as well, where the local Tajiks sided with their fellow Sunnis in the Taliban against the Shi'a Hazaras, who had previously burned their houses in another change of power. As parts of Hazarajat changed hands several times, the Taliban exacted reprisals, including the well-documented torture and massacre in May 2000 in Yakawlang of at least three hundred Hazaras. The Taliban further extended their control by capturing Massoud's headquarters in Taluqan in September 2000, forcing Massoud to retreat to Badakhshan and Tajikistan and isolating Panjshir.

What was the strategy of the Northern Alliance resistance to the Taliban?

In October 1996, less than a month after the fall of Kabul to the Taliban, the groups that had lost Kabul met again in Northern Afghanistan. With the support of Russia and Iran, they formed an alliance called the Supreme Council for the Defense of the Motherland. That entity, however, was almost purely symbolic. The northern areas had four main administrative and political centers: Mazar-i Sharif, which some wanted to make a temporary capital for the government of the ISA, but which instead became a locus for conflict among Dostum's Junbish, Wahdat, and Jamiat, as well as factional warfare within Junbish; Takhar, the headquarters of Massoud's SCN; Shiberghan, Samangan, Dostum's headquarters; and Bamiyan, headquarters of the Hezb-i Wahdat administration of Hazarajat.

In June 1997, a month after the temporary recapture of Mazar from the Taliban, the Supreme Defense Council was reshaped into the National Islamic United Front for the Salvation of Afghanistan (UF). This political grouping, commonly if erroneously known as the Northern Alliance, supported the Islamic State of Afghanistan (ISA), which continued to hold Afghanistan's seat in the UN. The UF included Jamiat, Junbesh, the main faction of Hezb-i Wahdat, the Shi'a Harakat-i Islami, which recruited among Sayyid rather than Hazaras, Sayyaf's Ittihad-i Islami, and the remnants of the ousted Jalalabad shura.

The United Front was intended to act as the political support mechanism for a new government to be based in Mazar-i Sharif, but that attempt suffered a major setback in August 1997, when a plane carrying forty UF leaders, including Abdul Rahim Ghaffurzai, the prime minister–designate, crashed, killing all passengers. Ghaffurzai, a Muhammadzai with extensive foreign affairs experience, would have given this alliance a more national image and a better international presence.

Thereafter the United Front was unable to agree on a prime minister.

Massoud worked both to unify the UF, so it would have something resembling a chain of command, and to mobilize international support, especially through public campaigns against the Taliban. As a result of the latter efforts he was invited to address the European Parliament in Strasbourg in April 2001, soon after the Taliban destroyed the Bamiyan Buddhas. He tried to reach out to Pashtuns, in particular by signaling a new willingness to collaborate with Zahir Shah's plan for a Loya Jirga. He sought to establish a unified military command by reaching agreement with his Iranian and Russian suppliers that future military aid would go entirely through him, as defense minister of the ISA, rather than directly to commanders. Through a series of meetings in Uzbekistan and Iran, he reached agreements with Dostum and Ismail Khan and brought both back to Afghanistan in the spring of 2001. Massoud also met with such key Pashtun former mujahidin leaders as Abdul Haq of Nangarhar and Hamid Karzai of Kandahar. These efforts, which laid the foundation for his posthumous victories after September 11, no doubt intensified the determination of the Taliban to expel him from his last foothold in Afghanistan and of al-Qaeda to eliminate him before Western attention would turn to Afghanistan after September 11, 2001.

What was the relationship of the Taliban to Osama bin Laden and al-Qaeda?

The Taliban became increasingly linked to the transnational fringe of global Islamist politics, including Osama bin Laden (OBL), especially as their isolation from the global mainstream grew. They provided a haven to the Islamic Movement of Uzbekistan, some Chechens and Uighurs, and assorted militants from other countries. Although these links began opportunistically, various forms of structural integration complemented them as they persisted.

The links to Afghanistan and Pakistan of the first bombing of the New York World Trade Center in 1993 drew attention to the activities of the Arab networks based in Afghanistan, but it was not until May 1996, when OBL returned from Sudan to Afghanistan, that the country became the center of his network, known as al-Qaeda.

Bin Laden, one of the first Arabs to join the mujahidin's struggle against the Soviet Union, stayed throughout the war. He helped fund the participation of Arab and other international volunteers. Throughout that time, he worked in collaboration with the Saudi intelligence agency, which worked closely with its Pakistani and US counterparts. OBL turned against his erstwhile sponsors at the time of the first Gulf War, when he opposed the invitation of American troops to Saudi Arabia. He left Saudi Arabia for Sudan in 1991, and Saudi Arabia deprived him of his citizenship in 1994. Under pressure from Egypt, which held al-Qaeda responsible for an assassination attempt on President Mubarak in Addis Ababa, Sudan expelled bin Laden in 1996. In May he returned to Afghanistan, having chartered a plane from Ariana Afghan Airlines, supposedly for a cargo flight from Khartoum to Jalalabad. OBL, together with a group of his followers, lived under the protection of the Jalalabad shura until the Taliban captured the area in September 1996.

Neither the United States nor Pakistan, through whose territory bin Laden's plane flew, seem to have objected to his taking up residence in Afghanistan. Although he had gathered a group of followers from throughout the Arab world in Sudan, and, with the support of Sudanese Islamist leaders, had tried to form a worldwide front of radical Islamists, he was at that time considered a threat mainly within the Middle East. The Taliban promised Riyadh that OBL would not use his refuge to support any acts of violence abroad, but in February 1998 he issued a public fatwa calling for worldwide jihad against "Jews and Crusaders." As a result, Riyadh reduced its aid to the Taliban in summer 1998. After the bombings of the US embassies in Kenya and Tanzania in August 1998, and the subsequent US reprisals, Mullah Omar reneged on what Saudi authorities thought was a commitment to hand over bin Laden, and Saudi Arabia withdrew assistance and froze diplomatic relations. Until then, Saudi Arabia had been one of three countries, along with Pakistan and the United Arab Emirates, that maintained diplomatic relations with the Islamic Emirate of Afghanistan.

The embassy bombings led the Clinton administration to fire cruise missiles at training camps in Eastern Afghanistan and a pharmaceutical factory mistaken for a chemical weapons plant in Sudan. These actions also awakened the Clinton administration to the broader dangers posed by OBL's organization. Together with subsequent intelligence, this prompted a series of escalating sanctions imposed on the Taliban. In 1999 the UN Security Council imposed sanctions against Taliban-controlled Afghanistan. The US also began intelligence cooperation with Massoud against the common foe.

What was the relationship of the Taliban to Pakistan once the Taliban gained power?

The Taliban were effectively a transnational organization, reflecting the multifaceted links between some Afghan Pashtuns and parts of Pakistani society, links that became even denser after 1978. At least until the change in Pakistan's declared policy after September 11, 2001, the Taliban's military structure included Pakistani officers. Their decision-making process included routine consultation with Pakistani Deobandi religious leaders. Their foreign relations depended on access to the outside world through Islamabad and on Pakistani advice and logistical assistance. Their military force recruited fighters from Pakistani madrasas, whose students were estimated to form as much as 20–30 percent of the total. Extremist Pakistani Deobandi organizations (Sipah-i Sahaba, Lashkar-i Jhangvi, Harakat-ul-Mujahidin) had bases in areas under their control.

The Taliban's economic resources derived from networks linked to the Pashtun diaspora in Karachi and Dubai, and to the Pakistani administration in FATA, the Northwest Frontier Province (now Khyber Pakhtunkhwa), and Balochistan. The Pakistani rupee was so widely used as currency in areas under Taliban control that the Pakistan banking authorities launched an investigation of the impact of that practice on their economy. The integration of Pakistani elements into the Taliban at all levels was not simply a result of a policy of the Pakistani government or military. Instead, the Pakistani state used and responded to pressures from these transnational links, which reflected changes in the social and political structures of the region.

How did the Taliban and the United Front fund their institutions and operations?

This war, with its transnational linkages, was supported by the growth of a regional war economy, including smuggling of consumer goods, the drug trade, and the gem trade. These economic activities provided resources for the warring parties and cemented their ties to the social groups that profited from these activities. As elsewhere, the war economy entrenched interests in maintaining the social linkages that supported the conflict.

The security enforced by the Taliban corresponded to an economic need. Before the ascent of the Taliban, predation by commanders imposed heavy costs on commerce, blocked Pakistan's access to Central Asia, and prevented consolidation of Islamic or any other kind of order. Hence, a coalition of Pakistani authorities, Afghan and Pakistani traders, and ultraconservative Afghan and Pakistani religious leaders supported the Taliban. The Taliban's control by 1998 of nearly all the country's roads, cities, airports, and customs posts drastically lowered the cost and risk of transport and consolidated Afghanistan's position at the center of a regional war economy.

The war economy was built on structures that developed during the anti-Soviet war and even before. The infrastructure of support for the resistance had poured cash into several social networks. Before reaching its intended beneficiaries, both military and humanitarian aid passed through many international, Pakistani, and Afghan intermediaries, some of whom skimmed off cash and resold arms and commodities. These resources provided capital to expand smuggling and other businesses. While the Pakistani military delivered arms to mujahidin parties in its own trucks, private teamsters moved the supplies to the border region and into Afghanistan. Many of these trucks were already active in Pakistani-Afghan smuggling that exploited the Afghan Transit Trade Agreement (ATTA). Under this agreement, listed goods could be imported duty-free in sealed containers into Pakistan for onward shipment to landlocked Afghanistan. Many, if not most, of the goods were instead sold in smugglers' markets (*bara* bazaars) in Pakistan. During the war the trucks used in this lucrative trade were also leased for arms transport, the income from which expanded the capital available for investment in smuggling linked to the ATTA, as well as the growing drug trade.

The breakup of the Soviet Union raised the economic stakes in Afghanistan and pitted Iran and Pakistan against each other in competition for access to the oil- and gas-rich Central Asian states. Pakistan saw commercial and political connections to Central Asia via Afghanistan as key to the development of "strategic depth" in its confrontation with India. The US defined an interest in the independence and economic diversification of the Central Asian states, without relaxing sanctions on Iran, which would have provided an economically feasible pipeline route. Pipelines through Afghanistan would reconcile those contradictory goals. Various companies, including the US-based Unocal Corporation in alliance with the Saudi company Delta (whose consortium received American government encouragement) and its Argentine rival Bridas, began negotiations with the Rabbani government and de facto power holders. Traders chafed at the growing insecurity along the major routes crossing the country. The projected oil and gas pipelines were stymied by the continuing war and the Taliban's harboring of OBL. The war economy in Afghanistan consisted of the transit trade, the drug trade, the gem trade, service industries stimulated by the growth of the former three, and the emission of currency. Foreign exchange earned by exports financed Afghanistan's imports of war materiel as well as food and other necessities.[19] The Taliban controlled the transit trade, which seemed to be the largest of these sectors; Massoud and his successors controlled the gem trade. Until 2000 opium production and trade expanded in regions controlled by both sides, but in 1999, areas controlled by the Taliban produced 97 percent of Afghanistan's poppy.[20] During 2000 and 2001, however, with the Taliban's ban on poppy cultivation in effect, the UF-controlled areas appeared to have a higher production. Sales of opium and its derivatives continued, drawing on the stocks of two consecutive bumper crops. Traders sold off these stocks in the aftermath of September 11, causing raw opium prices to fall by about two-thirds.

Control by the Taliban of most of the main road system cleared a corridor for the smuggling of duty-free consumer goods from Dubai to Pakistan. Until a ban on international flights from Taliban territory imposed under UN Security Council sanctions on November 14, 1999, some goods were flown directly to Afghanistan from Dubai. Most goods crossed the Persian Gulf by ship to Iran, where truckers hauled them

19. Z. F. Naqvi, *Afghanistan-Pakistan Trade Relations* (Islamabad: World Bank, 1999).
20. United Nations International Drug Control Programme, *Afghanistan Programme: Annual Opium Poppy Survey 1999* (Islamabad: UNDCP, 1999); United Nations International Drug Control Programme, Strategic study 5: *An Analysis of the Process of Expansion of Opium Poppy to New Districts in Afghanistan*, 2nd report (Islamabad: UNDCP, 1999).

to Afghanistan and then into Pakistan.[21] This trade complemented smuggling into Pakistan under cover of the ATTA. In June 1998 I observed that many of the trucks appeared to be carrying automotive vehicle tires and spare parts rather than the electronic appliances I had heard so much about. I later learned that because automotive parts had recently been eliminated from the list of goods eligible for import under the ATTA, they were being imported by this alternate route.[22]

A World Bank study estimated the value of unofficial re-exports to Pakistan at $2.1 billion in 1997 (out of a total of $2.5 billion in exports), the first year after the Taliban had captured Kabul. The total re-exports amounted to nearly half of Afghanistan's estimated GDP, and those to Pakistan constituted around 12 to 13 percent of Pakistan's total trade.[23] A follow-up study found that unofficial re-exports had decreased to about $1.1 billion by 2000, of which $885 million went to Pakistan, probably due both to a liberalization in Pakistan's trade regulations that reduced the incentive for smuggling and to tighter controls. The earlier World Bank study estimated that the Taliban derived at least $75 million in 1997 from taxing Afghanistan-Pakistan transit trade. The effective tax rates (taking into account the difference between valuations at official and market exchange rates) were less than 10 percent for all commodities in 2000.[24] Although this is a significant income in the context of Afghanistan, it is far less than the amount of

21. In protest against the murder of Iranian diplomats and a journalist by Taliban troops in Mazar-i Sharif, Iran closed the Afghanistan-Pakistan border between August 1998 and November 1999. During that period the goods took a detour via Turkmenistan.
22. Naqvi, *Afghanistan-Pakistan Trade Relations*.
23. Ibid.
24. World Bank, "Trade and Regional Cooperation between Afghanistan and Its Neighbors," February 18, 2004, http://siteresources.worldbank. org/INTSARREGTOPINTECOTRA/1385530-1139318607199 /20810980/TradeAndRegionalCooperation.pdf.

Pakistani duties that would be owed on these goods, so the more indirect contraband route was still profitable.

Before the appearance of the Taliban, Afghanistan was already a major opium producer. About 56 percent of the poppy crop was grown in the areas of Southern Afghanistan that the Taliban captured in the fall of 1994, and 39 percent was grown in Eastern Afghanistan, which the Taliban took two years later. These remained the principal opium-growing areas, though the poppy crop also spread to new regions.[25]

Afghans, including the Taliban, earn relatively little from this crop. Superprofits in the global drug market derive from the risk premium of marketing an illegal commodity in wealthy societies. Producers and marketers of the raw material share in these profits only if they develop vertical integration through to the retail markets, as the Colombian cocaine cartels did in the 1980s.[26] Afghan opium traders, however, generally sell only to the border; a few are involved as far as the Persian Gulf, but not in the lucrative retail markets.[27]

Within Afghanistan, although opium growing and trading involved economic risk, neither the Taliban nor their opponents originally treated these as criminal activities, and there was consequently neither a high-risk premium nor any violent competition for markets. After the ban on opium cultivation, the Taliban continued to permit the opium trade, leading some to speculate that the ban was an attempt to increase profits by raising prices. The opium trade in Afghanistan at that time was, by and large, peaceful and competitive.[28]

It is difficult to estimate how much revenue the Taliban derived from this trade. Growers paid the Islamic tithe (*ushr*) at the farmgate (goods purchased directly from a farm) on opium

25. UNDCP, Strategic study 5: *Opium Poppy*.
26. Manuel Castells, *End of Millennium*, vol. 3 of *The Information Age: Economy, Society, and Culture* (Oxford: Blackwell, 1998), 166@-205.
27. UNDCP, Strategic study 2: *Dynamics of the Farmgate Opium Trade*.
28. Ibid.

and other produce, mostly in kind. Less consistent reports indicate that the Taliban also levied *zakat* of 20 percent on traders in opium and opium derivatives. Some evidence indicates that this *zakat* was collected only in the south, not in the east, where Taliban control was less stable.[29] (For more details, see chapter 8.)

The transit and drug trades were complemented by service industries, such as fuel stations, shops, and tea houses. Much of the fuel was smuggled from Iran, where its subsidized price was approximately nine cents per liter, less than a soft drink. The official budget in Kabul (which did not include military expenses) seems to have been paid for by direct foreign aid from Pakistan (Rs. 500 million, or about $10 million in 1998) and a few tax revenues from Kabul itself. Until the summer of 1998 the Taliban also received direct financial assistance from Saudi Arabia, which provided subsidized fuel as well as cash grants. These were ended in protest over the Taliban's failure to expel or curb Osama bin Laden.

Although the Taliban controlled all major branches of the central bank, Da Afghanistan Bank, they did not print their own money. The Taliban continued to recognize the notes delivered to the Massoud-Rabbani forces, despite their protest against this funding of their enemies and the resulting devaluation of their currency. Taliban banking officials said they recognized the Rabbani currency because they did not wish to undermine national unity by circulating two currencies.[30]

29. Bizhan Torabi, "Entretien avec Mollah Mohammad Omar," *Politique internationale,* 74 (1996–97): 141–42; UNDCP, Strategic study 2: *Dynamics of the Farmgate Opium Trade,* p. 13; Ahmed Rashid, *Taliban.* According to Sharia, *zakat* is a tax on wealth levied at 2.5 percent, or one-fortieth. It is unclear on what legal basis the Taliban imposed this tax at a much higher rate and on a flow of commerce rather than a stock of wealth. It is also unclear whether the *zakat* is assessed on gross income or on profit.
30. Interviews with director of Bank-i Milli Afghanistan, Kandahar, and deputy director of Da Afghanistan Bank, Kabul, June 1998.

In practice, the Taliban would probably have had difficulty obtaining professionally printed notes.[31]

Northeast Afghanistan, controlled by Massoud until his assassination on September 9, 2001, produced only 3 percent of Afghanistan's opium before the Taliban's ban. Commanders levied *ushr* on opium farmers, and at least some local authorities taxed opium traders as well.[32] There were a number of heroin refineries, though authorities destroyed some of them. Besides the aid it received, mainly from Iran, and the continued delivery of new Afghan currency, the United Front's main income (actually SCN's income) came from the gem trade. Massoud taxed trade in lapis lazuli and emeralds, collecting *ushr* from mine owners and *zakat* from traders. In 1997 Massoud established a monopoly in purchase of the gems, and in 1999 he signed an agreement with a Polish firm, Inter Commerce, to market them. His aides estimated that the trade had previously brought in $40 to $60 million per year and that the new joint venture might make as much as $200 million in annual income.[33]

Both of these officials were graduates of Pakistani madrasas, with no economic, commercial, or financial background or experience.

31. The international legal regime for currency printing is complex and decentralized. In controversial cases the few companies that do "security printing" (of currency, passports, and other official documents) look to their host governments (usually their major customers) for guidance. These governments generally use political criteria in giving opinions about such contracts. The major security printers are in the United States, the United Kingdom, Germany, and France, none of which look favorably on the Taliban. I thank R. Scott Horton for clarifying these points for me.

32. Bernard Frahi, Tony Davis, personal communications.

33. Françoise Chipaux, "Des mines d'émeraude pour financer, la résistance du commandant Massoud," *Le Monde*, July 17, 1999.

What relations did the Taliban have with the US and the rest of the international community?

The Taliban knew absolutely nothing about the United States and the rest of the international community. They neither knew about them as they conceive of themselves, nor did they know about them as they were conceived to be by Osama bin Laden. Their experience with the US was that it had supported them in their jihad against the Soviet Union. They wanted to be accepted by the international community, as long as it was on their own principles and terms. They sent a delegation to New York in January 1997 to try to get Afghanistan's UN seat at the General Assembly. The Taliban had banned the planting of opium mainly as an effort to obtain international recognition, but the ban did not extend to trafficking from the large existing stockpiles. The Taliban had identified counter-narcotics as a policy area where they could meet the demands of the international community.

The Taliban's relations with Afghanistan's neighbors other than Pakistan mainly derived from their relationship to foreign Sunni Islamist groups. Iran's policy sought to break out of the isolation imposed by US sanctions. It sought to link up with Central Asia by supporting groups in Western, Central, and Northern Afghanistan against what it saw as attempted encirclement by a US-led grouping including Saudi Arabia and Pakistan. The competition between Pakistan and Iran, which also took on a Sunni-Shi'a sectarian dimension, became a cultural confrontation between an Arab-Pashtun alliance and Persian and Turki speakers. In 1998, eleven Iranian diplomats were killed by Pakistan-based militants as the Taliban captured the city of Mazar i-Sharif. Taliban-Iran relations became strained even further, to the extent that Iran deployed seven thousand troops on the Afghanistan-Iran border preparing for a possible war.[34]

34. Douglas Jelh, "Iran Holds Taliban Responsible for 9 Diplomats' Deaths," *New York Times*, September 11, 1998, http://www.nytimes.com/1998/09/11/world/iran-holds-taliban-responsible-for-9-diplomats-deaths.html.

Afghanistan provided weapons and refuge (facilitated by cross-border links among Tajiks) that helped intensify the 1992–95 war in Tajikistan, set off by the Soviet collapse. The drug trade also penetrated Tajikistan and its neighbors, drawing in the Russian mafia and corrupting the Russian border guards, as well as Central Asian governments. Pakistan and Iran each became home to hundreds of thousands if not millions of opium and heroin addicts, and HIV and AIDS began to spread rapidly in Central Asia, as a result of both intravenous drug use and the related increase in prostitution.

Members of a repressed Islamist group in Uzbekistan's Ferghana Valley fled to Afghanistan and Tajikistan in 1992. Some of the Uzbek fighters, reorganized as the Islamic Movement of Uzbekistan, established bases in opposition-controlled areas of Tajikistan as well as in Afghanistan, where they developed links to al-Qaeda. After the implementation of the 1996 Tajikistan peace accord, members of this group sought to fight their way back to Uzbekistan directly from Tajikistan and across southern Kyrgyzstan, taking hostages and setting off international crises. Some of their fighters established bases in FATA, where they received training in some of the same Pakistani madrasas that gave birth to the Taliban.

Even before September 11, 2001, massive displacements caused by both war and drought had placed all the neighboring countries under pressure once again, but now, unlike in the 1980s, Afghan refugees were not welcome anywhere. Pakistan, Tajikistan, and Iran—all in different ways and for different reasons—rejected them, refusing to register them and/or forcing them to return.

Since the bombings of the US embassies in Africa in August 1998, terrorism dominated the international agenda on Afghanistan. UN Security Council resolutions passed in 1999 and 2000 imposed increasingly stringent sanctions against the Taliban on the grounds that they were harboring Osama bin Laden, al-Qaeda, and other terrorist groups and training centers.[35]

---

35. United Nations Security Council, Resolution 1363 (July 2001); Resolution 1333 (December 2000); Resolution 1267 (October 1999).

Their policies often brought the Taliban into conflict with the international aid community, led by the United Nations. A dialectic of confrontation and concession developed. Especially after the imposition of the first round of UN sanctions against the Taliban at the end of 1999, the core leadership seemed to conclude that it was unlikely to win the acceptance of the international community and drew closer to OBL and his allies. The Taliban considered the July 2000 decree of Mullah Omar banning the cultivation of opium poppy a final test of the goodwill of the international community. The Taliban had identified one demand they could meet without violating their religious principles, but the response seemed to them inadequate. International actors reacted not only to the opium ban but also to new restrictions on aid workers and the continued harboring of terrorists, as well as the Taliban's violations of human rights—not only by the measures limiting women's rights but also by the massacres of Hazaras. The destruction of the Bamiyan Buddhas in March 2001 symbolized the Taliban's new direction: by destroying a key symbol of Afghanistan's pre-Islamic glory, they showed they were not nationalists but pan-Islamists and under "Wahhabi" influence to boot. This decision alienated some within their own ranks and solidified relations between the Arabs and Mullah Omar.[36]

How did the Taliban respond to 9/11, and why did they refuse to hand over the al-Qaeda leaders?

As far as we know, the Taliban had no advance knowledge of the 9/11 attacks. Their first reaction was to condemn the attacks. In October 2001, President George Bush gave the Taliban an ultimatum: "hand over bin Laden or . . . ," while preparing to topple the regime in cooperation with the United

36. Barnett Rubin, *Fragmentation of Afghanistan*, 2nd ed. (New Haven: Yale University Press, 2002).

Front. Mullah Omar delayed, trying to find an Islamic solution; Pakistan's leader General Musharaf sent a delegation to Kandahar. Omar convened a council of ulama to determine what was the right Islamic thing to do with Osama bin Laden. The council of ulama decreed that Afghanistan was not hostile to any country, but if anyone invades the country, then it will wage defensive jihad against them. Some in the Taliban leadership advocated the expulsion of OBL and al-Qaeda, but Mullah Omar ultimately rejected President Bush's ultimatum. He claimed to be willing to hand over bin Laden for trial by an Islamic country, but not to the United States.

On October 7, 2001, US and British forces launched a military offensive against al-Qaeda and the Taliban in Afghanistan.

6

9/11, INTERNATIONAL INTERVENTION, AND THE ISLAMIC REPUBLIC OF AFGHANISTAN

What happened in the run-up to 9/11?

Osama bin Laden and Ayman al-Zawahiri, the leaders of al-Qaeda, returned to Afghanistan from Khartoum, Sudan, in May 1996. There they joined a small but growing group of international radical Islamists belonging to different groups. Uzbeks were the largest foreign group, followed by the Arabs, who were divided into various factions. Of all the factions only al-Qaeda advocated direct attacks on the "far enemy," the United States.[1]

In November 1996, two months after the Taliban captured Jalalabad and came into contact with al-Qaeda for the first time, Mullah Omar sent an armed delegation to bring bin Laden to Kandahar. OBL feared he would be executed, but instead Mullah Omar convened him and other leaders of foreign fighters in an ultimately failed attempt to gain control over them.

Bin Laden began the planning for 9/11 several years before the event. In an effort to keep the plot secret from the Taliban,

---

1. Abdullah Anas and Tam Hussein, *To the Mountains* (London: Hurst, 2019), and Mustafa Hamid and Leah Farrell, *The Arabs at War in Afghanistan* (London: Hurst, 2015).

key meetings were held outside Afghanistan, in Kuala Lumpur and Hamburg. Neither the Taliban nor most of the other Arabs in Afghanistan knew of the plan.

Bin Laden intended to draw the US into war in Afghanistan, trapping it like the Soviet Union. In that case the US would need allies on the ground, which it would find among the Afghans led by Ahmad Shah Massoud. The CIA had restarted intelligence cooperation with Massoud, mainly on al-Qaeda, after the August 1998 bombing of the US embassies in Kenya and Tanzania.

OBL planned to assassinate Massoud before 9/11 both to cripple the US's response and to ingratiate himself with the Taliban, whose reaction to 9/11 he could not anticipate. Working with supporters in Europe, he arranged for two Tunisians masquerading as Belgian journalists of Moroccan origin to interview Massoud in Afghanistan. On September 8, as their secret deadline approached, after waiting for three weeks in the town of Khwaja Bahauddin, on the Afghanistan-Tajikistan border, they threatened to leave if Massoud did not grant them an interview. When he did so the next day, the assassins detonated an explosive device hidden in their camera, killing Massoud and an aide and wounding two others. Both assassins were killed, one by the blast and one by pursuers.

Had the assassination occurred earlier, as planned, the Taliban might have been able to exploit the United Front's leadership vacuum to occupy more territory and undermine its organization. Events moved more quickly, however, awarding Massoud a posthumous victory.

How did the US and other international actors respond to 9/11?

President George W. Bush announced the way the US would respond to the al-Qaeda attacks in a speech to a joint session of the US Congress on September 20, 2001. He identified the attackers as "a collection of loosely affiliated terrorist organizations known as al-Qaeda," which "has great influence in

Afghanistan and supports the Taliban regime." That regime, he said, "is not only repressing its own people, it is threatening people everywhere by sponsoring and sheltering and supplying terrorists."

Bush made no demands of al-Qaeda: the US would destroy it. Of the Taliban, however, he demanded,

> Deliver to United States authorities all of the leaders of al-Qaeda who hide in your land.
>
> Release all foreign nationals, including American citizens you have unjustly imprisoned. Protect foreign journalists, diplomats, and aid workers in your country. Close immediately and permanently every terrorist training camp in Afghanistan. And hand over every terrorist and every person and their support structure to appropriate authorities.
>
> Give the United States full access to terrorist training camps, so we can make sure they are no longer operating.

He concluded by saying that "these demands are not open to negotiation or discussion," and that the Taliban "will hand over the terrorists or they will share in their fate."

The US relied on Pakistan to deliver the message to Mullah Omar, but the first delegation that General Pervez Musharraf sent to Kandahar counseled the Taliban leader that the Americans were bluffing and advised him to resist. When the US learned of this, it forced a reshuffle of personnel at the ISI.

The Taliban leadership was divided. Mullah Omar convened a shura of ulama, which issued a declaration thanking bin Laden for his services to jihad but asking him to leave Afghanistan. OBL first told Mullah Omar he had nothing to do with the attack. Fearing that the Taliban might turn on him, though, he fled Kandahar and holed up in the Tora Bora Mountains south of Jalalabad, where he had helped finance the construction of a base for Jalaluddin Haqqani in the 1980s. The

CIA engaged in secret negotiations with Mullah Obaidullah, the Taliban minister of defense, but even if Mullah Omar had wanted to make a deal (indications are that he did not), he could not have done so with the alacrity necessary to satisfy the outrage of the American public. Military operations began on October 7.

The US benefitted from broad international solidarity and support. For the first time, NATO's Atlantic Council voted to activate Article V, designating the 9/11 events as an attack on a NATO member, which all member states would consider an attack on them. The US secretary of defense Donald Rumsfeld, however, refused the offer of a formal NATO operation, fearing that a NATO-led coalition would hamper a rapid and decisive response.

The administration used diplomacy mainly to obtain logistical access to landlocked Afghanistan for the military. US-Iran relations made the western route impossible despite common interests, but the US started contacts with Russia and Central Asia to the north and Pakistan to the east and south. President Putin intervened with Central Asian leaders to assure that the US would obtain the required transit and basing rights. Acquiring his assistance was relatively easy, as the US had effectively joined Russia and Iran in supporting the United Front.

On Pakistan, which had supported the Taliban, the US had two options: target Pakistan or coerce it into cutting off support for the Taliban. The US gave Pakistan an ultimatum. According to his memoirs, General Musharraf war-gamed resistance but concluded it was futile. He prepared to cooperate while preserving as many of Pakistan's Afghanistan assets as possible.

The US sent CIA teams by helicopter from Tajikistan to contact UF commanders. Iranian intelligence provided logistical assistance in Tajikistan and on the ground in Afghanistan. The first stop was Panjshir, where Massoud's successors, Muhammad Qasim Fahim (military commander), Abdullah (foreign affairs), and Yunus Qanuni (political affairs), agreed to participate in the US-led effort, with Amrullah Saleh acting as interpreter. The US did not, however, support the efforts Massoud had made to centralize command and control over UF forces. Instead the CIA contacted individual commanders to assure that it, rather than the UF leadership, exercised strategic control.

The next step was to fly in small teams of Special Operations Forces to guide operations in the north, particularly by Dostum and Atta. With US air support those commanders captured Mazar-i Sharif on November 10. The next day Taliban fighters began to withdraw from Kabul. Fahim's troops had gathered north of the city as American airstrikes decimated the Taliban defenders. Whether and when Fahim's men should enter the city became a political issue. One of Pakistan's conditions for assisting the US was that the "Northern Alliance" should not be allowed to capture Kabul. Despite calls from some quarters for the US or British special forces to secure the capital rather than letting it fall to the control of one Afghan group, the US and UK were unprepared to do so, and the UF forces under Fahim's command walked into the undefended city on November 12.

The remaining Taliban in the north fled into the city of Kunduz, along with hundreds of foreign fighters and Pakistani military advisors. They came under the command of Mullah Fazl, the northern zone commander, and Nurullah Nuri. The Taliban leaders in Kunduz, seeing that they were surrounded, decided to negotiate terms of surrender with Dostum. To do so they had to disarm foreign fighters despite some resistance. General Musharraf negotiated the air evacuation of the Pakistani officers with the US; Fazl and Nuri surrendered to Dostum in return for a promise of amnesty and safe passage. The other Taliban and foreign fighters were locked in shipping containers and loaded onto trucks to be moved to Dostum's fortress at Qala-yi Jangi, Samangan.

En route some of Dostum's men began firing into the shipping containers in which prisoners were being transported.

Several hundred were killed in Dasht-i Leili. After arriving in Qala-i Jangi, some of the foreign fighters, who had smuggled bombs and other materials, started an uprising in which CIA agent Johnny Michael Spann became the US's first casualty in Afghanistan. Hundreds of the detainees and forty UF military personnel also died.

In the south and east there was no single partner for the US comparable to the United Front. Anxious not to trigger an ethnic conflict, the US prevented General (later Marshal) Fahim from sending his Tajik troops south of Kabul. In the east two groups loosely linked to the UF shared power: The ethnic Pashai militia of Hazrat Ali controlled northern Nangarhar and the military garrison in Jalalabad. The "Eastern Shura" led by the Arsala clan controlled southern Nangarhar in partnership with local tribes. This area included Tora Bora, in Khugiani district, where bin Laden made his last stand in Afghanistan. In Loya (Greater) Paktia (Paktia, Khost, and Paktika provinces) local tribes formed shuras that took on functions of governance.

Loya (Greater) Kandahar (Kandahar, Zabul, Uruzgan, and Helmand) remained in the hands of the Taliban. US Special Forces were active in the area searching for al-Qaeda leaders. The main commander they tried to support was Hamid Karzai, from a prominent Popalzai family.

Who is Hamid Karzai?

Hamid Karzai is a member of Ahmad Shah Durrani's Popalzai tribe. His father, Abdul Ahad Karzai, was a prominent elder of the tribe and deputy speaker of the upper house of parliament in the 1960s. Hamid Karzai describes himself as a "tribal man" from a "parliamentary family." In an interview on March 1, 2014, he told the *Washington Post*, "I am a pacifist, I am a total, absolute pacifist. I don't believe in war, and I don't believe in guns, and I don't believe in politics." He is the only ruler of Afghanistan (and possibly of any other country) to have made such a statement.

During the resistance against the Soviets, Karzai was the spokesman for Mojaddedi. When the mujahidin government came into power, Mojaddedi, who was president for the first six months, appointed Karzai as Afghanistan's permanent representative to the UN in New York.

Back in Kabul in the fall of 1992, Karzai became deputy minister of foreign affairs under President Rabbani. He would sometimes act as Rabbani's English interpreter, because he had attended the University of Simla in India. At one point members of Jamiat became suspicious of him, and he was arrested by the National Directorate of Security (NDS), then headed by Fahim, who later served as Karzai's minister of defense (2001–04). According to the story, during Karzai's interrogation Gulbuddin Hekmatyar fired a rocket at the jail, and he escaped. He rejoined his father in Quetta, where he became active in the Loya Jirga movement and the Rome Group around Zahir Shah.

When the Taliban captured Kandahar in 1994, the Karzai family provided some initial assistance. Karzai has said that of all the groups in Kandahar at that time, the Taliban seemed to be the most honest. The Taliban considered making him their unofficial representative at the UN, but Mullah Omar finally decided not to give such an important job to someone who was not a member of the Taliban movement. Karzai saw signs of the Taliban's increasing radicalism and dependence on Pakistan and Arab jihadists, while the Taliban realized that Karzai would never join the movement.

The Loya Jirga movement became an anti-Taliban movement, although it had started before the Taliban. Karzai supported Zahir Shah and made several trips to Rome. Within the Zahir Shah camp, he was one of those who supported cooperation with the Northern Alliance. The other side, led by Abdul Haq of the Nangarhar Arsala clan, urged Zahir Shah to mobilize fighters himself. Abdul Haq hoped to be the commander of the king's forces. The group to which Karzai belonged argued that if the king had his own army, he would become just another faction, rather than a symbol of national unity.

In 2000 and 2001 Karzai traveled to Dushanbe to meet Massoud. He had been thrust into a leadership position when Taliban gunmen assassinated his father in Quetta in July 1999. He continued his father's work on the Loya Jirga movement, which by then had merged with Zahir Shah's office in Rome. Karzai tried to enlist the US in supporting and unifying the anti-Taliban forces.

Karzai was in Quetta on 9/11, and Pakistan soon revoked his visa. He had no military experience—he had been a political figure during the anti-Soviet jihad and the initial years of the Islamic State of Afghanistan. Nonetheless, he rode back into Afghanistan on a motorcycle. Accompanied by a CIA officer, he gathered a following of armed Popalzais and some others. By late November, he and his men had reached the village of Shah Wali Kot, about fifty miles northeast of Kandahar. Karzai and Mullah Omar held discussions through a mediator. On December 5 the news came that the Bonn conference had chosen him as the leader of Afghanistan's interim administration.

From that point on, his personal story merged with Afghan history.

How was the new government, led by Hamid Karzai, established, and what was the Bonn Agreement?

On November 10, 2001, President Bush told the UN General Assembly, "The United States will work with the UN to support a post-Taliban government that represents all of the Afghan people."

During the 2000 election George Bush had campaigned against American involvement in "nation building." Secretary of State Colin Powell persuaded him that the US had to do something to replace the Taliban regime. Assigning responsibility to the UN checked that box without the US taking responsibility for it.

UN Secretary-General (SG) Kofi Annan recalled Lakhdar Brahimi to resume his service as special representative (SRSG) to oversee this mission. Brahimi's consultations led to the convening of the UN Talks on Afghanistan in Bonn, Germany, from November 29 to December 6, 2001.

From the beginning, the US and the UN had differing objectives. For SG Annan and SRSG Brahimi, the war had started in 1978. When the 1988 Geneva Accords and 1989 Soviet withdrawal failed to end the war, the UN launched new peacemaking efforts. Brahimi had led those efforts from 1997 to 1999, and Annan recalled him to try once again to bring a twenty-three-year-old conflict to an end. Peacemaking and peace building were the principal goals. For the US, though, the war started in 2001. The Bonn Agreement and civilian operations in Afghanistan were part of the war effort against the Taliban and al-Qaeda, not part of a peace effort on behalf of the people of Afghanistan.

Four Afghan delegations participated in the Bonn talks. The most important were the United Front (UF), commonly called the Northern Alliance, and the Rome group. The UF was a coalition of non-Pashtun and Islamist armed groups that had resisted the Taliban in the name of the Islamic State of Afghanistan, the government headed by President Burhanuddin Rabbani, which the Taliban had expelled from Kabul in 1996. By the time the Bonn Conference opened, the Supervisory Council of the North (SCN), the UF's shock troops built by the late Ahmad Shah Massoud, had already reoccupied Kabul. The ethnic composition and geographical origin of those forces resembled those that had overthrown Amanullah Khan and installed Amir Habibullah Kalakani (Bacha-i Saqaw) in 1928.

Habibullah had been routed and hanged by Nadir Khan, father of Zahir Shah, who led the Rome group, which also participated in the Bonn negotiations. Named after the city where the former king had lived since his 1973 ouster, the Rome group included exiled elites from the royal regime. They had gathered around Zahir Shah since 1983, when the former king called for a solution to the Afghan conflict based on the institution of the Loya Jirga.

The other participants were the Peshawar and Cyprus groups, which supposedly safeguarded the interests of Pakistan and Iran, respectively. The Peshawar group, led by the Gailani family, was chosen at a jirga of Pashtun tribal elders convened by the ISI in Peshawar. The Cyprus group's members, of various views and backgrounds, had convened on Cyprus with Iranian support as an alternative to the Rome group. They were led by a son-in-law of Gulbuddin Hikmatyar, who was under house arrest in Tehran.

The UN convened the meeting in Bonn. Other international stakeholders sent representatives who did not participate in the drafting sessions but whom Brahimi and the Afghan participants could consult. The presence of American, Iranian, and Russian representatives enabled the UN to reach back to the Afghan leadership on the ground when necessary.

The conference drafted and approved an agreement on "interim arrangements pending the re-establishing of permanent institutions of government in Afghanistan." The two items on the conference's agenda were:

- Choosing an internationally recognized interim authority to take control of the state after the defeat of the Taliban; and
- Setting out a roadmap for how the interim authority would preside over a political process to broaden its base of support and reestablish a fully legitimate government.

Of the Afghan participants, only the SCN came with a political strategy, and only the Rome group came with a plan for

the transition. Though Yunus Qanuni, head of the UF delegation and one of Massoud's principal aides, did not say so, it
soon became evident that the SCN sought to use negotiations
to form a coalition with the Rome group and sideline Rabbani.
On November 17, 2001, supported and funded by Russia,
Rabbani had entered Kabul, where he proclaimed himself
president. He instructed Qanuni to listen and report back from
Bonn, but not to reach any agreement. Instead, after making a
show of resistance, Qanuni stayed on to negotiate the composition of a new government. (He had little choice, as he and his
delegation had been transported to the meeting on a British
military aircraft, and Secretary Powell instructed his envoy
James Dobbins to assure that they would not leave.)

American diplomats, reinforced by the military on the
ground, pressed Rabbani to transfer power to the new government. After initial hesitation, Russia and Iran joined the US
in supporting a settlement at Bonn, leaving Rabbani with no
choice but to agree.

Tensions over the ethnic balance pervaded the meeting,
though participants rarely spoke of them explicitly. The weakness of non-Taliban Pashtun leadership in most of the country,
plus the occupation of Kabul by Tajiks mainly from Panjshir,
inspired anxiety that Pashtuns would be marginalized. No
one spoke Pashto at the opening session. The leaders of the
UF, Rome group, and Cyprus group spoke in Persian, while
the leader of the Peshawar group spoke in English. Midway
through the talks, Haji Abdul Qadir, from the Arsala clan in
Jalalabad, whose "Eastern Shura" had allied with the UF and
was there as part of their delegation, walked out, claiming
there was insufficient Pashtun representation. He later became
governor of Nangarhar and then vice president, the office he
held when he was assassinated in July 2002.

At the end of the meeting, the Peshawar group's Anwar
ul-Haq Ahady refused to sign the agreement on the grounds
that it was insufficiently representative, which referred to the
underrepresentation of Pashtuns. He was the leader of the

Pashtun Nationalist Afghan Mellat Party. He later became governor of the central bank, commerce minister, and finance minister.

At Bonn, the UN tried to help the Afghans design a process to address the ethnic balance equitably. The same process, starting with the Emergency Loya Jirga, might have been able to bring the Taliban into the new system.

As the UF came to Bonn with no ideas on how to manage a transition other than staying in the positions of power they now occupied, the conference relied on a plan drafted by the Rome group. The plan called for stages of transition legitimated first by an Emergency Loya Jirga (ELJ) and then a Constitutional Loya Jirga (CLJ). Neither of these bodies had clear definitions, but the understanding was that the ELJ delegates would be chosen according to makeshift procedures appropriate for a country emerging from war, while the CLJ would conform as much as possible to previous laws defining the Loya Jirga. The interim government would last for six months, during which it would appoint an Independent Commission for Convening the Emergency Loya Jirga. The ELJ's task would be to choose a "transitional" government. The transitional government, which would be chosen in Afghanistan, would be more representative than the interim authority named at Bonn, since the ELJ would include all those who, in Brahimi's words, "for one reason or another could not participate in Bonn." Brahimi and the UN understood that to include the Taliban, but the US and others did not.

The UF reluctantly accepted the Loya Jirga, because they had no alternative process to propose, but they feared that the elites of the old regime would manipulate it to reestablish the former system. The Rome group had come to Bonn expecting Zahir Shah to preside over the transition. Short of that, they proposed that he chair the ELJ. After strong resistance by the UF, the conference agreed finally that the ELG would "be opened" by Zahir Shah as a symbol of historical continuity.

The role of the king was the subject of other disputes as well. If only because the UF had no alternative proposal, the conference agreed that the legal framework for the new government would be the applicable parts of the 1964 constitution, the last one widely considered legitimate. It was, however, a monarchical constitution, and, together with Zahir Shah's return to play a role in the ELJ, it was hard for Iran to accept. At the insistence of Iranian envoy Javad Zarif, the agreement specified that the constitution of 1964 would be applied except for "those provisions relating to the monarchy, and the executive and legislative bodies." The UF also demanded that the agreement's preamble say that its purpose was to establish a republican form of government. The Rome group, which did not want to rule out the restoration of the monarchy, opposed that language. Brahimi resolved the issue by saying that since there is no king in Afghanistan, language addressing the issue was not necessary.

The transitional government elected at the ELJ would appoint a constitutional commission and convene a CLJ within eighteen months to adopt the constitution. At the insistence of the US and Iran, the agreement required the transitional government to hold "free and fair elections" for a "fully representative government" within two years of the ELJ, namely about six months after the adoption of the constitution. Since the form of government (presidential, parliamentary, or mixed) was yet to be determined, the agreement did not specify what kind of elections.

The parties also disagreed about the transition of armed groups to security forces. The UN had drafted a standard article on the demobilization, disarmament, and reintegration (DDR) of armed groups. The commanders in the UF delegation opposed any mention of disarmament as dishonorable. Instead the agreement provided for these forces to be "reorganized" as required under the "command and control" of the interim authority.

To protect the new government and the political process from pressure by armed groups, Annex I of the agreement called on the UN Security Council to authorize a multinational force to secure Kabul and surrounding areas. The MNF (Multinational Force), later called the International Security Assistance Force (ISAF), was also to train new security forces for the Afghan government. According to the same Annex, all military groups were to withdraw from Kabul and any other area to which the UN-mandated force might be deployed, so that the politically neutral ISAF would be in full control of security. This never happened, and Fahim's troops remained the predominant Afghan armed force in Kabul, together with the police and intelligence apparatus that the SCN also controlled. The Annex also provided for ISAF to expand to other "urban centers and other areas." Secretary Rumsfeld, however, vetoed such expansion, as he did not want another security force in the same battle space as his kinetic counterterrorist forces. He relented in 2003 when the force requirements of the Iraq War made it necessary to supplement US with other NATO troops.

An article drafted by the UN prohibiting the interim authority from giving amnesty for war crimes or crimes against humanity met opposition from the commanders present and, by satellite telephone, those on the ground. UF commanders in the field rebelled against what they were hearing—that the UN would send troops to Afghanistan to disarm them and try them for war crimes. Omitting the article on amnesty and including a clause thanking the "mujahidin" for their sacrifice kept them on board.

The structure and composition of the interim authority was the most contentious issue, as it determined the initial distribution of power. The new government's political legitimacy would depend in part on convincing the non-Taliban majority of Pashtuns that the Taliban's overthrow and the capture of Kabul by a Tajik armed force would serve national, rather than ethnic, goals. Agreement on a Pashtun interim head of state would help avoid the appearance of an ethnic victory.

According to his associates, Massoud had come to the same conclusion before his death. At Bonn, Karzai was the candidate of the UF, UN, and US. He had little support within his own Rome group, however.

In deference to the former king, the Bonn Agreement stated, not entirely accurately, that Zahir Shah had declined the participants' request to lead the government. Zahir Shah agreed to the statement and showed no inclination toward power or politics, despite the ambitions of others in his family. The Rome group claimed that, as they were the representatives of the former king, they had the right to choose the leader. The participants agreed that the Rome group could nominate a leader, who would be approved if no other group objected. The Rome group voted for the chair of its delegation to Bonn, Abdul Sattar Sirat, to become head of the interim authority, which would have contradicted the UN-UF-US strategy of assuring at least symbolic Pashtun leadership. (Sirat, a former chief justice, is variously reported to be Uzbek or Tajik.) When Brahimi asked for the UF's opinion, Qanuni said that he could not object, because Sirat was married to his wife's cousin. It was left to Hamid Gailani, head of the Peshawar group, to veto Sirat. The delegates agreed to the pre-cooked choice of Karzai.

The SCN then proposed that under Karzai as head of state, Qanuni would become prime minister, while other SCN leaders, all natives of the Panjshir Valley, would control all power ministries and agencies including foreign affairs, defense, interior, and intelligence. The final agreement maintained the SCN monopoly on those positions, but it did not include the post of prime minister. Karzai, the interim president, became head of both state and government, with a monopoly over appointments, setting the stage for changes to come.

Combined with the adoption of the 1964 constitution as the legal framework for the government, the establishment of a presidential-like system left Afghanistan's much-weakened centralized structures in place. It is commonly said that the US and UN "imposed" an inappropriately centralized system on Afghanistan. The centralization of the Afghan state's legal framework may be inappropriate, but all the Bonn Agreement did was to leave it in place. How the state actually operated was a different matter and was determined more by the distribution of money and weapons than anything agreed upon at Bonn.

When the agreement that made him president was announced, Karzai was still in Shah Wali Kot. On December 6, the day after the signing of the Bonn Agreement, he and the Taliban leadership in Kandahar agreed to a truce. The Taliban agreed to hand over the four provinces they still controlled to the interim administration. In return, Karzai promised the Taliban an amnesty and that Mullah Muhammad Omar would be able to live in dignity in Kandahar. No documentary evidence of this agreement is known to have survived. This account is based on the testimony of participants.

The limits on Karzai's power became obvious immediately. Secretary Rumsfeld disavowed Karzai's agreement with the Taliban in a press briefing at the Pentagon, where he responded to repeated questioning about Karzai's agreement with the Taliban by saying that there would be "no negotiated solution." The US implemented the policy that "those who harbor terrorists will share in their fate" by detaining all senior Taliban leaders (and some not so senior ones) they could find, even those who surrendered and offered to help find bin Laden. It nullified any promises of amnesty in return for surrender given by Afghan leaders in accord with tradition. Dostum had to turn over Nuri and Fazl, whose release the Taliban demanded in November 2010 at their first post–9/11 direct talks with the US, and who joined the Taliban negotiating team in Doha in 2019.

The US sought a place of detention that would not, in the Bush administration's view, be subject to US domestic or any other legal system. That is how it ended up opening the detention center on Guantanamo Bay Naval Base, where neither US nor Cuban law applied. They sought to exempt the facility from international humanitarian law as well by categorizing the detainees as "illegal combatants." Many Taliban who had initially gone back to their villages fled instead to Pakistan.

What was the political role of the UN in Afghanistan?

The UN played and still plays many roles in Afghanistan. Besides the political role of officials reporting to the UN Secretary-General in fulfillment of the SG's good-offices role, the UN also worked on human rights, with a particular emphasis on women's rights, economic development, coordination of international assistance, elections, legal and judicial reform, DDR of combatants, building and monitoring the police force, cultural and historical preservation, public health, education, census and demography, humanitarian assistance, and more. In its most visible and public role, however, it represented the community of nations in providing good offices to Afghans trying to reestablish government after the virtual collapse of both the state and nonmilitary politics.

The UN was effective in its political role when the senior representatives of the US and UN cooperated. At Bonn, Brahimi worked closely with James Dobbins from the Department of State and Zalmay Khalilzad of the National Security Council (NSC). Khalilzad, an Afghan immigrant to the US, had worked on Afghanistan during the 1980s in the Reagan administration and knew most of the Afghan leaders. He knew Ashraf Ghani, then an advisor to Brahimi, from his adolescence in Kabul, and he knew me, also an advisor of Brahimi's, from the 1970s, when we were both graduate students in the Department of Political Science at the University of Chicago. When Brahimi moved to Kabul as SRSG and head of the UN Assistance Mission in Afghanistan (UNAMA) , he continued to work with Khalilzad, first as presidential special envoy and then, from November 2003, as ambassador to Afghanistan. Ghani and Khalilzad also had long-standing relationships with Hamid Karzai.

The Bonn Agreement charged the SRSG with monitoring and assisting implementation of the agreement. His first task was "establishing a politically neutral environment for the holding of the ELJ in free and fair conditions," an aspiration that could be only approximated after twenty-three years of continual war involving every group of the population and most of the country's neighbors. The UN subsequently supervised and assisted in convening the Emergency and Constitutional Loya Jirgas, and elections of the president (2004, 2009, 2014, and 2019) the parliament (2005, 2010, 2018), and provincial councils (2005, 2009). To carry out this mission, the UN established offices not only in Kabul but also in regional and provincial centers throughout the country.

The principal tool through which any government manages the state is the budget, including both mobilizing resources through taxation, borrowing, and other means, and allocating those resources to various purposes. In a democracy, parliament approves and monitors the budget to assure the proper use of the nation's resources. In Afghanistan and other countries with international operations after protracted conflict, however, much, most, or nearly all public expenditures are financed by international aid from donor countries either directly or indirectly: through UN agencies, development banks, or nongovernmental organizations (NGOs). Aid comes through both civilian and military agencies.

The donors provided only a small portion of the aid directly to the government, which at least initially lacked the capacity to implement major projects. The result was a confusing, uncoordinated bazaar of foreign aid, in which donors chose their own priorities. Such assistance weakened rather than strengthened the state's ability to govern. There was no budget for the entire public sector but only for the relatively small part managed by the government. Revenue did not flow to the state, and expenditure was executed by many different organizations using different accounting schemes, definitions, currencies, and fiscal years, making it virtually impossible to determine who was spending how much on what, rendering governance virtually impossible.

Over opposition from the UN Development Programme (UNDP) and the World Bank, Brahimi insisted that all UN funds and programs in Afghanistan should report to the SRSG. The SRSG could then, in principle, assure that assistance supported the UN's goals. Members of his team advocated that all aid should go through a single UN fund that would channel funds to the government, to the extent possible. The World Bank set up the Afghanistan Reconstruction Trust Fund (ARTF), through which donors could provide funds to support the government budget. The donors could not earmark contributions for any specific purpose, so they funded Afghan government priorities, but the World Bank oversaw the expenditure on the ground. As most aid was provided bilaterally, the ARTF, however, became one of many aid mechanisms, rather than an overall coordinating mechanism.

UNAMA has a mandate from the UN Security Council that is reviewed and renewed each March. As the Afghan government gained competence, its leaders—particularly President Karzai—began to resent what they saw as infringement on their sovereignty by the political UN, especially in the conduct of elections. Their opponents would charge that the government was using sovereignty to shield itself from charges of voter fraud.

What was the International Security Assistance Force and what was its mandate?

ISAF, as it was called, was originally a multinational force, whose mandate the Security Council renewed every six months, to maintain security in Kabul and surrounding areas. In practice that meant Kabul, Bagram Airbase, and the road connecting them. Every six months the command would rotate. The UK founded ISAF, followed by a German-Dutch command and then a Turkish one. Mobilizing volunteers every six months was cumbersome and assured that no institutional learning took place.

As mentioned previously, Rumsfeld had originally opposed bringing NATO in. In 2003, however, faced with a growing insurgency in Iraq, the US reconsidered and proposed that NATO assume the command of ISAF to provide continuity. The structure of Operation Enduring Freedom (OEF) had also changed in ways that made it resemble ISAF more. The commanders in the field had found that kinetic operations to capture or kill suspected terrorists were not sufficient. To win over the population so they would provide intelligence and to marginalize the warlords whose abuse of power was driving people to the Taliban, the US would have to increase its presence and provide assistance. It still did not want to invite ISAF into its battle space, but it wanted to alter the pattern of deployment and the goals and tasks of the military to produce "the ISAF effect without ISAF." This proposal led to the founding of Provincial Reconstruction Teams (PRTs). A PRT consisted of a military force deployed to a provincial capital and tasked with providing a secure environment for "reconstruction" programs financed by the country deploying the forces, in partnership with the governor. After several years, when the framework of state building gained greater ascendance, a joint task force of the US, UN, NATO, and the Afghan government redefined the task of PRTs as extending the reach of the Afghan government to the local level.

At first only the US set up PRTs, solely in provinces on the Pakistan border where the heaviest fighting was taking place. In the summer of 2003, however, Germany took the initiative of setting up a PRT in Kunduz. That fall, NATO's Atlantic Council voted to take command of ISAF, and the UN Security Council approved plans to expand ISAF into all the provinces.

The PRTs became the template for ISAF expansion as a NATO project. Since each troop contributor had different rules of engagement, NATO decided to expand by placing different member states in charge of PRTs, which were organized into four regional commands. The expansion took place in a counterclockwise direction on the map, starting with the Germans in Kunduz (see Figure 6.1) in Regional Command-North (RC-N). Most countries agreed to provide troops only on the assurance that they would *not* have to engage in combat. The more risk averse or weakest were assigned to Regional Command-North (RC-N) or West (RC-W). The US shared Regional Command-South (RC-S) with the British and Canadians and dominated Regional Command-East (RC-E) with a few partners. The expansion of

Regional Command-South:
Kandahar, Kandahar (Canada)
Lashkar-Gah, Helmand (Britain)
Tarin Kowt, Uruzgan (Netherlands)
Qalat, Zabol (Roisman, USA)

Regional Command-North:
Kunduz, Kunduz Province (Germany)
Mazar-e Sharif Balkh (Sweden)
Feyzabad, Badakhshan (Germany)
Pol-e Khomri, Baglan (Hungary)
Meymaneh, Faryab (Norway)

Regional Command-West:
Herat, Herat (Italy)
Farah, Farah (USA)
Qala-e Naw, Badghis (Spain)
Chaghcharan, Gowr (Lithuania)

Regional Command-East:
Bayman, Bayman (New Zealand)
Bagram, Parwan (USA)
Nurestan, Nurestan (USA)
Panjshir, Panjshir (USA)
Gardez, Paktia (USA)
Ghazni, Ghazni, (Poland, USA)
Khowst, Khowst (USA)
Sharan, Paktika (USA)
Jalalabad, Nangarthar (USA)
Asadabad, Kunar (USA)
Mihtarlam, Laghman (USA)
Wardak, Wardak (Turkey)
Logar, Logar (Czech Republic)

Figure 6.1 Provincial Reconstruction Teams, Lead Nations

Source: https://web.archive.org/web/20091109012206/http://www.nato.int/isaf/docu/epub/pdf/isaf_placemat.pdf.

ISAF coincided with the launch of the industrial-strength insurgency in 2006, and many of the contributing nations were caught unprepared.

Who were the "warlords," and how did the US and other actors deal with them?

The state as it operated on the ground differed in many ways from the legal framework established by the Bonn Agreement and the constitution. Many foreigners arriving in Afghanistan for the first time quickly concluded that the government was "traditionally" decentralized and that the current government should be as well. What they observed is that the processes of governance, though not the institutions of government, were not only decentralized but also derived from sources of power outside the state structure. Governance was deinstitutionalized rather than decentralized, as much—if not most—governance took place outside of government institutions.

The men commonly called "warlords" (in Dari, *jangsalaran*) in the years immediately following the Bonn Agreement were leaders who exercised a combination of institutional and extra-institutional power to control territory, population, and economic resources. Most had been commanders in the jihad against the Soviet Union, but Abdul Rashid Dostum is a former militia commander for the government of Najibullah. As the army and administration collapsed, especially after the fall of Najibullah, these men consolidated control over territories, generally inhabited by kindred ethnic or tribal groups.

Removing them from power was the most popular accomplishment of the Taliban. With the support of Russia and Iran, most of them banded together to form the United Islamic Front for the Salvation of Afghanistan, commonly known as the Northern Alliance. The US revived and rearmed them as its major allies in Afghanistan after 9/11. In the predominantly Pashtun south and east, where the population was more segmented, the US relied on local Pashtun commanders, mostly of tribal background. Many of the Pashtun mullah commanders had joined the Taliban.

The warlords had access to a variety of economic resources. In Kabul, control of the state itself was the main resource. Those on the border took control of customs or drugs or other smuggling revenues. They operated independently from state institutions, which, to the extent that they functioned at all, did so under warlord control rather than by authority established through a constitutional process, which did not yet exist.

In the non-Pashtun areas, where there was no tribal system and the social structure was flatter, relatively few warlords consolidated control over larger areas, like Central Asian autocrats. In the Pashtun tribal areas of Afghanistan, the society was fragmented into clans and tribes, each of which had multiple leaders. Few if any leaders could become full-scale warlords by exercising control over a major city and its hinterland. Only the Taliban's harsh measures justified by religion brought some order by imposing a rudimentary system of justice.

By September 11, the Taliban had defeated all but one of these regional power holders. Only Massoud still held territory in Afghanistan, in the northeast, bordering on Tajikistan. He largely operated out of Dushanbe. General Dostum spent time in Uzbekistan, Turkey, and Iran. Ismail Khan had escaped Taliban detention to Iran and had returned to Afghanistan only recently. Several other leaders were in Pakistan.

When the US government decided to overthrow the Taliban regime, it faced, in theory, several alternatives, but only one that it took seriously. There were people with various proposals for trying to organize at the grass roots, like the Loya Jirga movement, but the US was looking for military allies on the ground. Donald Rumsfeld answered accusations that the US had "created" the warlords by saying, "We didn't create them, we just took them where we found them."

Because the US had already established intelligence cooperation with Massoud, who had created the most effective anti-Taliban fighting force, the US approached his successors first.

As the offensive progressed, and the Taliban withdrew from the cities and retreated to either their villages or Pakistan, the military commanders took control of territories that they had ruled before the Taliban. In the absence of a legal framework for the exercise of power, they did so as warlords. They could hardly have done otherwise. During this period, the warlords held a variety of official positions as they were integrated into the new order. Some were military commanders, some were governors, some were both, and some went from one role to the other. At the beginning, Ismail Khan in Herat was both the commander of the Herat garrison and the governor of Herat, while exercising influence throughout the Western Zone. He chose to be governor until being forcibly removed in 2004. Atta Muhammad was the commander of the army's Sixth Corps in Mazar-i Sharif, but he shifted over to being governor of Balkh. Abdul Rashid Dostum was at first commander of the Seventh Corps, but he was then removed and given a purely symbolic position. Gul Agha Sherzai was the governor of Kandahar but also maintained control over the operatifi (ministry of the interior special forces). Part of the struggle over what to do with the warlords was what influence they would have over the appointment of officials. Some of them were removed from governorships and appointed as cabinet ministers, which was a way to contain rather than increase their power.

Such was the fate of Ismail Khan, who became minister of water and power. Some of these warlords were moved to governorships in areas outside of their native areas, where they had to rely more on formal institutions. That was the case of Gul Agha Sherzai, who was moved from Kandahar to Nangarhar.

Over time, the warlords moved away from exercising direct control over territory and armed forces. Instead, they accumulated wealth from the aid, contracts, and payments they received from the United States, control over customs posts, drug trafficking, and other forms of commerce, legal and illegal. They invested in businesses, starting with contracting with the US military and NATO. They probably would be best described now as rich and powerful political figures with various degrees of formal or informal authority over patronage networks including armed men.

How were the Afghan National Security Forces, and the security sector more generally, built?

In April 2002 the UN invited the new government of Afghanistan and the G-7 (US, UK, France, Germany, Italy, Canada, and Japan) to Geneva to plan security sector reform (SSR) in Afghanistan. The participants discussed how to implement the mandate in Annex I of the Bonn Agreement to help "the new Afghan authorities in the establishment and training of new Afghan security and armed forces." The participants defined SSR as consisting of building the army, police, and judiciary; combatting narcotics; and the disarmament, demobilization, and reintegration (DDR) of nonstate militias.

These tasks are interdependent parts of any effort to secure a territory from terrorists and build a political order capable of providing security over the long term. The US-led coalition, including the UF and other militias, had taken tenuous control of the national territory. Maintaining and defending that control in support of a state authority would require a combination of demobilization and transformation of the militias, leading to creation of a professional army. The intelligence organizations of the militias also had to be demobilized or reformed. Within the areas secured by the military, the state would need to introduce policing to patrol and monitor communities.

In Afghanistan's civil law system, investigating violations of the law is the responsibility of the prosecuting magistrate, or saranwal, who can then instruct the police to detain criminal suspects. After further investigation, the saranwal must either release the suspect or hand him over to the judiciary for trial. The judiciary also hears civil disputes. Such disputes risk developing into criminal cases if the judiciary cannot settle them peacefully. For purposes of SSR, strengthening and reforming the saranwali is considered part of judicial reform.

The army, intelligence agencies, police, and judiciary cannot exercise a law-bound monopoly of the use of force unless unofficial militias are dissolved; DDR requires decisions about whether the existing fighters will be reintegrated into the new defense and security forces or into civilian life, which requires guarantees of security and opportunity.

The inclusion of counter-narcotics as a component of SSR was a forerunner of problems that ultimately made this policy into the international operation's most spectacular failure. Treating the narcotics (mainly opiate) industry as a security and law enforcement rather than a development issue made it impossible to succeed. The narcotics industry was generally located in areas outside of government control. A focus on crop eradication in ungoverned areas led to a militarized policy that alienated farmers, who looked to the Taliban for protection. Later changes in policy were unable to reverse the trajectory. (See chapter 8.)

All sectors of SSR are interrelated and need to be coordinated to function properly. Only the US could have coordinated SSR, although the UN could have helped in areas other than the military and intelligence services. The Bush administration, however, opposed involving the US in "nation building." It defined the US mission narrowly as "counterterrorism," capturing or killing suspected terrorists and their facilitators. The US, with help from France and Canada, therefore took responsibility only for restructuring the military forces and intelligence services. It called on others to become "lead nations" for other parts of SSR, effectively putting them in silos, with independent funding and programs.

Germany became the lead nation for police reform, the UK for counternarcotics, Italy for judicial reform, and Japan for DDR. The US pressed to form the police more as a paramilitary force against the insurgency rather than as a law enforcement body. Many of the soldiers who were demobilized out of the Afghan militia forces went into the police, which is one of the factors that accounts for the high level of corruption and predation in that institution. Italy took responsibility for judicial reform out of President Silvio Berlusconi's desire to do a favor for President Bush, much to the surprise of the Italian officials charged with implementing that responsibility.

A judiciary system is essential for the legitimacy of the state, and the ability to provide justice in an accessible and timely way was one of the major factors that strengthened the Taliban. The concept of justice in Afghanistan is largely based on Islam and Islamic law (Sharia). Written legal codes cannot conflict with Sharia, and Islamic jurisprudence is recognized as a source of law where the codes are silent.

Any system of law and law enforcement requires legally trained personnel and a population that understands and believes in the legal system. In Afghanistan, there are virtually no lawyers except in a few major cities. The functioning legal system for most people has been either customary law in their villages, which is a combination of decisions by elders and rulings by clerics, or Sharia courts. Sharia is familiar to everybody in Afghanistan, and there is a mullah in every village. Italy could not address or reform customary or Islamic legal practices.

The British prime minister, Tony Blair, had largely sold the war to his public on the grounds that most of the heroin sold in Britain was refined from opium grown in Afghanistan, so addressing that challenge was essential to maintaining domestic support. Japan supported DDR out of the commitment to peace in its postwar constitution, but that same constitution forbade it to station its military in Afghanistan to help implement the policy. That role was limited to funding a program carried out by the United Nations Development Programme (UNDP) and, later, the US.

How DDR would be related to the formation of the army and police became one of the most contentious issues. The Bonn Agreement urged "the United Nations and the international community, in recognition of the heroic role played by the mujahidin in protecting the independence of Afghanistan and the dignity of its people, to take the necessary measures, in coordination with the Interim Authority, to assist in the reintegration of the mujahidin [United Front fighters] into the new Afghan security and armed forces."[2]

Fahim wanted to make retrained UF forces into the core of the army. A group that came to be known as the "Pashtun technocrats," which eventually gained the support of the US military, advocated demobilizing most of those forces and building a new army. Fahim's eventual successor as the minister of defense, Abdul Rahim Wardak, argued that it was easier to train recruits with no military experience than to retrain guerrillas as disciplined soldiers. Fahim's plan would have institutionalized the military power of his commanders, while the alternative plan also integrated Western- or Soviet-trained officers into the command structure. Demobilized fighters excluded from the army largely joined the police or the private security companies that guarded US bases and other international installations.

After 2005, under the Afghanistan Compact, the successor to the Bonn Agreement agreed to in London in January 2006, the lead nation system was supposed to be transitioned into a more coordinated security-sector building system. The Obama administration put a lot more effort and funding into building the army and the police, because it was necessary under the counterinsurgency doctrine adopted in the last years of the Bush administration. It established a single position in ISAF overseeing SSR.

2. The Bonn Agreement, December 22, 2001, Annex III, #4.

What was the purpose of the Emergency Loya Jirga and what happened there?

According to the Bonn Agreement:

> An Emergency Loya Jirga shall be convened within six months of the establishment of the Interim Authority. The Emergency Loya Jirga will be opened by His Majesty Mohammed Zaher, the former King of Afghanistan. The Emergency Loya Jirga shall decide on a Transitional Authority, including a broad-based transitional administration, to lead Afghanistan until such time as a fully representative government can be elected through free and fair elections.

The ELG would "decide on a Transitional Authority" by electing a head of state and approving proposals for the structure and personnel of the administration (cabinet). The administration was to be "broad-based," as the interim authority was not. The broad-based administration constituted another step in the transition to a "fully representative government." The agreement specified that the ELJ would have mechanisms to represent the "settled and nomadic population," Afghan refugees, civil society, scholars, traders, intellectuals, and a "significant number of women."

The main subject of tension around the "unrepresentative" character of the interim authority was the control of security forces by representatives of SCN from Panjshir. Many understood that the main way the ELJ would make the government broad-based would be by reducing Panjshiri predominance in the security forces.

The return of Zahir Shah from his twenty-nine-year exile in Rome just after Nawruz 1381 in March 2002 set off speculation about restoration of the monarchy and ending the domination of Kabul by northerners, as his father had done in 1929. Zahir Shah's role opening the Loya Jirga raised expectations, especially among Pashtun delegates, that he might play an official role, restoring the old order at least symbolically. Fahim strongly opposed any restoration, and, after talks with Zahir Shah, Khalilzad announced that the former monarch was not interested in an official position but supported Hamid Karzai's candidacy for president.

The ELJ made history as the first representative national gathering in decades, but it fell short of expectations. The presence of ISAF in Kabul made it possible for Afghans to express different views, but not without some risk of intimidation, as happened on the eve of the gathering when Fahim's military and intelligence services took control of the meeting's security from ISAF, in apparent violation of the Bonn Agreement, Annex I.

According to the rules drafted under UN supervision by the Independent Commission for Convening the Emergency Loya Jirga, leaders of armed groups could not participate in the meeting. Nonetheless, major warlords and commanders who had not been elected occupied reserved seats in the front row. They dominated the gathering, pressed through a motion to change the state's name to the Transitional Islamic State of Afghanistan, and demanded official status as "mujahidin." Taliban or those suspected of being Taliban could not participate without risking arrest and detention. Hence the ELJ made only limited progress toward national reconciliation and broadening the government. Contrary to expectations the Emergency Loya Jirga consolidated the position of the warlords and the exclusion of the Taliban. Some have argued that this result contributed to the rise of the Taliban-led insurgency.

The delegates elected Hamid Karzai as chairman (president) without much controversy. After two weeks of secret negotiations, Karzai presented a list of members of the government. Qanuni resigned as interior minister and was replaced by a powerless Pashtun from Wardak. Qanuni became minister of education. Fahim remained in place. Karzai made Ashraf

Ghani, a former senior official of the World Bank, finance minister, which Ghani transformed into a powerful position.

How did Afghanistan adopt a new constitution, and what happened at the Constitutional Loya Jirga?

The Bonn Agreement provided:

> A Constitutional Loya Jirga shall be convened within eighteen months of the establishment of the Transitional Authority, in order to adopt a new constitution for Afghanistan. In order to assist the Constitutional Loya Jirga prepare the proposed Constitution, the Transitional Administration shall, within two months of its commencement and with the assistance of the United Nations, establish a Constitutional Commission.[3]

The CLJ convened on December 13, 2003, and adopted the constitution on January 4, 2004. It deliberated on a text first drafted by a small commission that sat from October 2002 to March 2003. That commission submitted the text to a Constitutional Review Commission (CRC), which examined and revised it from March 2003 to September 2003. In September 2003 the CRC submitted its draft to the National Security Council chaired by President Karzai, which made significant changes before submitting the draft to the CLJ.

At the CLJ, there was a strong feeling that, as one delegate put it, "The Pashtuns are back." What many Pashtuns perceived as disproportionate representation of non-Pashtuns, especially Tajiks, in the previous government was now over. Pashtuns won the major issue by establishing a centralized

3. Bonn Agreement, I:6. https://ihl-databases.icrc.org/ihl-nat/a24d1c f3344e99934125673e00508142/4ef7a08878a00fe5c12571140032e471/ $FILE/BONN%20AGREEMENT.pdf.

government and state headed by a directly elected president. Members of the constitutional commission and delegates to the CLJ from other ethnic groups had proposed various forms of power sharing and decentralization, including a parliamentary system where the head of government (prime minister) would represent a multiethnic coalition in parliament; a mixed system with both a president and prime minister with authorities to check each other's power; the election of local authorities such as governors and district governors; or the nomination of local authorities by elected councils. The draft submitted to the palace by the CRC proposed a mixed system, with both a president and prime minister, but the NSC changed it to a pure presidential system, and that was the draft that went to the CLJ.

While Pashtuns won their favored outcome on the form of government, on explicitly ethnic issues the constitution reached a hard-fought balance, making it in some respects the most inclusive constitution the country has had. Pashto and Dari are given parity as "languages of the state," while speakers of other languages enjoy the right to have educational institutions and media in their mother tongues. The constitution reinstated a requirement that the national anthem should be in Pashto (Rabbani's government had adopted one in Dari), but in return for that the constitution required the anthem to mention all of the fourteen ethnic groups listed as components of the nation in Article 4.

In an attempt to reassert the predominance of the Pashto language, figures close to President Karzai inserted language into the constitution, after it had already been approved, requiring the use of "national nomenclature," which is the use of Pashto terms for certain institutions, like *Stara Mahkama* for Supreme Court, and *pohantun* for university.

The constitution established Islam as the religion of the state, but did not specify, as had previous ones, that official religious rituals be carried out according to the (Sunni) Hanafi rite. While the Hanafi school alone was prescribed as the source of residual jurisprudence where the written law is silent, the constitution recognized Shi'a jurisprudence in family law cases among Shi'a.

Under US pressure the constitution did not use the word "Sharia," but Article 3 used other language to assure that governance accorded with Islamic law. This "repugnancy" clause states that "In Afghanistan, no law can be contrary to the beliefs and provisions of the sacred religion of Islam." This was significantly stronger than the equivalent clause of the 1964 constitution, "There shall be no law repugnant to the basic principles of the sacred religion of Islam and the other values embodied in this Constitution." In the 1964 constitution the king was named the guardian of the "basic principles of the sacred religion of Islam." In the new constitution, however, the Supreme Court had the power of judicial review of laws and executive actions, including review of whether laws complied with Article 3. Islamists had advocated a separate "Constitutional Court," which, they said, would function like the Council of Experts in Iran, but the NSC review eliminated it from the draft. The CLJ inserted an article establishing a Commission for the Implementation of the Constitution, but it had only advisory rather than judicial powers. Established after years of delay, it has turned out to be powerless.

The constitution established a bicameral parliament, as in the constitution of 1964, but left the president with strong powers of legislation by executive decree. Parliament had the power to check the behavior of individual ministers by "interpellating" (questioning) and censuring them, but it did not have the power, as in parliamentary systems, of voting no confidence in the government as a whole. The constitution provided for elected provincial and district councils, which had advisory rather than legislative authority. The government formed provincial councils but has not been able to hold elections at the district level.

The constitution maintained the Afghan tradition of defining a Loya Jirga (LJ) as the ultimate institution of state power. Rather than a tribal gathering, however, the constitution of 2004 followed that of 1964 in defining the Loya Jirga as composed of both houses of parliament, representatives of provincial and district councils, members of the government, and members of various social groups such as women, Islamic scholars, and academics. The LJ has the power to amend the constitution or to enact emergency measures.

Many of these decisions were controversial, and the losers felt that the result was pushed through by President Karzai and his international supporters in the US and UN. As subsequent elections showed, many of the major issues about the structure or legitimacy of the Afghan state have not been resolved.

What is the role of elections?

The constitution provided for direct elections by universal adult suffrage of the president of the republic every five years, of the Wolesi Jirga (lower house of parliament) every five years, of provincial councils every four years, district councils every three years, and municipal councils for terms and at intervals to be determined by law. The country has held presidential elections in 2004, 2009, 2014, and 2019; parliamentary elections in 2005, 2010, and 2018; and provincial council elections in 2005, 2009, and 2014. The lack of constitutionally chosen district councils meant that the upper house of parliament or Senate (Meshrano Jirga) could not be formed in a constitutional manner, nor could the Loya Jirga.

The constitution requires Afghanistan to hold more elections than it actually can. Every election relies on foreign assistance and expertise. Elections are much cheaper in India, where the civil service conducts them, but Afghanistan's lack of a well-functioning local administration in much of the country means that elections require establishing a dedicated nationwide administrative body each time. Supplying polling stations with voting materials initially required logistical help from the international armed forces. The electoral commission established by the constitution cannot call elections freely as required by law: mobilizing sufficient funding, largely from foreign assistance, is necessary first and cannot be assured in accord with the constitutional timetable.

According to the constitution, the president must win a majority of valid votes cast; if no candidate does so, the government must hold a second round of elections between the two front-runners. This system prevents the election of a weak president whom the majority opposes. The majoritarian principle, however, undiluted by any requirements for regional or ethnic representation, virtually guarantees that in any presidential election where the two main vote-getters are Pashtun and Tajik, the main issue is whether Pashtuns are the majority of the population. Disputed presidential elections in 2009 and 2014 boiled down to a contest over how many votes from Pashtun areas should be disqualified as fraudulent. Similar issues arose in determining the results of the 2019 presidential elections, but in a very different form, due to the use of biometric identification of voters linked to ballot papers.

For elections to the lower house of parliament and provincial councils, the electoral law instituted the Single Non-Transferable Vote (SNTV) system. The lack of accurate population data made it impossible to draw single-member districts with equal populations. The alternative was multi-member districts, and all agreed to use the province as the unit. The reason for using SNTV, rather than a system of proportional representation within provinces, was that many Afghans, and President Karzai in particular, are hostile to political parties. The concept of party is associated with an unaccountable armed faction.

Each province received a number of seats in the parliament in proportion to its estimated share of the national population. Candidates can run as individuals or with a party affiliation, but the affiliation is for identification only and does not affect voting, tallying, or the outcome. Each ballot lists all candidates in that province, including both a general list and a separate list of women candidates. Each voter votes for one general candidate and one woman. (For example, if there are N seats, then the N-2 general candidates with the highest number of votes are elected, as are the two women candidates with the most votes.)

President Karzai and other leaders supported SNTV, a system in use in no major country and which produces perverse results because of its focus on individual candidates rather than parties. SNTV provides no incentive for candidates to cooperate with each other. It produces individualistic legislators with no party discipline whom the executive can manipulate relatively easily.

What were the results of the two presidential elections won by President Karzai?

Hamid Karzai won the first presidential election, in September 2004, with 55.4 percent of the votes. The main opposing candidates were warlord/politicians from each of the three main non-Pashtun ethnic groups: Qanuni (Tajik), Dostum (Uzbek), and Muhaqqiq (Hazara). In the run-up to the election, the US ambassador Zalmay Khalilzad led an effort to remove Ismail Khan as governor of Herat, so that the central government could control the voting in that populous province.

After the balloting, the losing candidates challenged the result, and there is no doubt that the tally included many votes cast either tribally or fraudulently, but the dispute did not escalate. Everyone knew that President Karzai would win with the clear backing of the United States.

Once elected, Karzai, with international support, removed Fahim as minister of defense and replaced him with General Abdul Rahim Wardak, a Pashtun professional military officer trained in India and the US under Daoud Khan. He had served as the military commander of Pir Gailani's resistance group. Karzai established an ethnic balance among the leaders of the security forces. The ministers of defense and interior were always one Tajik and one Pashtun, but neither ethnicity always controlled either ministry. Equally important, Karzai did not reappoint Ashraf Ghani as minister of finance or any other government post, naming him as chancellor of Kabul University. Ghani soon resigned and prepared to run for president.

When the time came for the second presidential election, the situation was quite different. The election came soon after the 2009 presidential transition in the US. According to the constitution, elections should have been held thirty to sixty days before Karzai's term ended on May 5. The outgoing Bush administration, however, had decided without much consultation that the elections should take place in the fall, five years after the September 2004 elections. When President Obama took the oath of office on January 21, 2009, he found on his desk awaiting his signature an order to send seventeen thousand additional troops to Afghanistan to secure the fall election. After some agitation by the political opposition claiming that Karzai had no authority to rule after his constitutional term ended, the elections were set for August, just before Ramadan.

The Obama administration came into office determined to refocus on Afghanistan and suspicious of President Karzai. Many Americans who had served in Afghanistan, both military and civilian, had concluded that the corruption and incompetence of the Afghan government had become a major cause of the Taliban-led insurgency. Many blamed Hamid Karzai for accommodating the warlords the US had imposed on him and tolerating the corrupt disbursement of aid money over which he had virtually no control. They had sought the help of President Bush, who held weekly videoconferences with Karzai, but Bush continued to treat Karzai as a friend and avoided difficult issues. The videoconferences, senior officials believed, ended up insulating Karzai from US pressure rather than influencing him.

Obama canceled the weekly videoconferences. He and his team also heard from the British that it would be impossible to improve governance and counter the insurgency as long as

Karzai was in office. A number of senior Afghan officials privately made it known that they would prefer if Karzai withdrew rather than run for another term.

In the ensuing brief but intense debate, Richard H. Holbrooke, appointed by Secretary of State Hillary Clinton to the new position of Special Representative for Afghanistan and Pakistan, emerged as a harsh critic of Karzai. He was known to be the source of highly critical leaks to the press, including one to the *New York Times* that said the new administration would work with Karzai when it could and around him when it had to by engaging with regional leaders, that is, warlords.

Obama decided against such a risky course of action in the first months of his presidency and did not try to dissuade Karzai from running. Inevitably, however, Karzai learned of the effort. The mistrust it generated colored his relationship with the Obama administration over the next eight years. Holbrooke, tasked with defining US policy toward the upcoming election, continued pushing against Karzai. The aim of US policy, he said, was to make the election as competitive as possible to either remove Karzai or pressure him into improving governance. To this end he encouraged the potential opposition candidates Dr. Abdullah Abdullah and Ashraf Ghani, which they misinterpreted as promises of US support. Holbrooke also advocated US intervention to assure a "level playing field" for all candidates. His office instructed Lt. Gen. Karl Eikenberry (Ret.), then the US ambassador, to attend opposition candidate rallies, though without declaring support for any candidate.

This policy was already in place when I joined Holbrooke's team as his senior advisor on April 23, 2009. At the first meeting I attended in the Special Representative for Afghanistan and Pakistan (SRAP) office, on April 24, Holbrooke presented the policy to the team. I commented that the policy was misguided (I may have used the word "crazy"). Electoral or "democratic" institutions had not developed in Afghanistan to the point that one could settle who was in power by arithmetic. Elections, I said, were needed to provide popular affirmation of an elite consensus, and that the role of the US should be to shape and support that elite consensus to mitigate rather than stimulate conflict. Thereafter I stayed away from the electoral effort and focused on laying the groundwork for a political settlement.

Holbrooke coordinated with UN Deputy SRSG Peter Galbraith, a longtime friend of Holbrooke's who had been the Clinton administration ambassador to Croatia during the Dayton Accords in 1995. Holbrooke had assured Galbraith's appointment over other US candidates. Karzai considered them to be a team trying not so secretly to overthrow him.

The election, which took place on August 20, 2009, failed to produce a clear result. The two main candidates were Hamid Karzai and Dr. Abdullah, with principal bases of support, respectively, in predominantly Pashtun and Tajik provinces. Turnout was low overall, but it was particularly low in Pashtun areas that were controlled or contested by the Taliban, who threatened reprisals against voters and polling places. Massive reports of fraud came from everywhere but especially in the Pashtun areas. Abdullah's supporters interpreted the reported fraud as an illegitimate effort to bolster the Pashtun majoritarian claim, regardless of facts. Karzai both denied the magnitude of the fraud but also saw efforts to invalidate his votes as part of the US-led plan to replace him with a more pliable leader.

The practical issue was whether Karzai had won more or less than 50 percent of the valid votes cast, a result dependent on decisions made by the Electoral Complaints Commission (ECC), which included international members whom Karzai regarded as under American influence. As tensions mounted, Richard Holbrooke set off a crisis when he asked Karzai what he would do if the results required a second round. Karzai, who believed (with some evidence) that Holbrooke and Galbraith were hoping and even working for a second round, interpreted the question as pressure to agree to a second round, despite his claim that he had won. After weeks of international pressure and discussions with John Kerry, chairman of the US Senate Foreign Relations Committee, Karzai agreed to a deal that satisfied no one. On October 20, two full months after election day, Karzai accepted decisions by the Electoral Complaints Commission (ECC) that invalidated nearly a quarter of the ballots (1.26 million) and resulted in the certification that he had won 49.67 percent of the vote, with 30.59 percent going to Dr. Abdullah. The runoff was scheduled for November 7, but amid escalating ethnic and political tension and under heavy international pressure Dr. Abdullah withdrew on November 1, saying that the runoff could not be credible.

Who is Ashraf Ghani, and how did he become president?

Ashraf Ghani comes from a distinguished family in Eastern Afghanistan. His grandfather was one of the military commanders who brought down the government of Amir Habibullah II (Bacha-i Saqqaw) in 1929 and helped bring Nadir Khan to power. His family belongs to the Ahmadzai tribe, Ghilzai Pashtuns, from Logar. He graduated from the American University in Beirut and was pursuing his doctorate in anthropology at Columbia University when the Communist coup took place in 1978. After that, he remained in the US and completed his doctorate. He was involved in solidarity efforts with Afghan mujahidin in the 1980s, though he was always critical of the fundamentalist orientation promoted by their supporters. He moved from the Johns Hopkins University, where he was a professor of anthropology, to the World Bank, because he wanted to prepare for the reconstruction of Afghanistan.

Ghani and I had worked closely together in advising UN envoys. Then, in 2001, in early October, UN Secretary-General Kofi Annan redrafted Brahimi as his special representative and put him in charge of what became the Bonn Conference.

Brahimi immediately reached out to Ghani and me as his two principal advisors.

Ghani decided that he would go to Afghanistan, which he did initially as a member of the UN staff. But he soon left the UN and joined the government. With President Karzai's authorization, he set up an aid coordination body, the Afghan Assistance Coordination Authority (AACA), which led to his being appointed minister of finance during the ELJ.

During a period when Ghani was out of government, from 2005 to 2009, he and his long-term associate from the bank, Clare Lockhart, wrote a book called *Fixing Failed States*, a technocratic manual about how to build states. The book argued that proper design of institutions can have autonomous political effects, and that the most important element of designing institutions is to assure the accountability for how funds are spent. As finance minister, Ghani devoted his main efforts to recentralizing control over Afghanistan's finances. He also became quite outspoken about corruption and ran against Karzai for president in 2009, largely on an anticorruption platform. He got 3.5 percent of the vote. He had expected to get much more assistance from the United States than he did. In his view such assistance would have been essential to create a level playing field, so that he would have the same kind of resources that Karzai had as president, complete with helicopters and security. He lost, but Karzai appointed him as the director of the board managing the security transition as NATO forces would withdraw. It gave him the opportunity to travel to every province of the country, and he used it to build a base for himself to run for president again.

The 2014 presidential elections took place at the constitutionally mandated time, on April 5, 2014. Dr. Abdullah, running again with the support of the major Tajik and Hazara power holders (ex-warlords) from the former United Front, won 45 percent of the vote. Ashraf Ghani easily surpassed six other Pashtun candidates, winning 32 percent. He had established his credibility as a serious candidate when he announced in October 2013 that Dostum had agreed to be his running mate. In return, Dostum issued an apology to those harmed in the civil war. Dostum brought with him a vote bank of Uzbeks amounting to about 10 percent of the electorate and a ground game across Northern Afghanistan. Ghani and Dostum were known to detest each other, so by taking on Dostum as an ally Ghani showed willingness to play the dirty game of real politics, convincing many Pashtun power holders in Eastern Afghanistan to back him. Ghani had opted for the Pashtun plus one (Uzbek or Hazara) ethnic formula to cross the 50 percent line. The alternative, a Pashtun-Tajik unity ticket, was impossible, as neither Pashtun nor Tajik political leaders were willing to cede first place to the other. The electoral map reflected the tribal and ethnic composition of the tickets. Abdullah won in the predominantly Tajik and Hazara provinces. Ghani, an Ahmadzai (Ghilzai) Pashtun, swept Eastern Afghanistan and Uzbek areas in the north. In the predominantly Durrani areas he ran behind Karzai's former foreign minister Zalmay Rassoul, a Muhammadzai.

The second round, on June 14, was marked by widespread fraud, disputes over which delayed the announcement of a final outcome until September. Abdullah's supporters produced tapes, allegedly of intercepted telephone calls, in which Karzai loyalists used coded language to discuss ballot box stuffing. The vote count was subject to multiple audits, including those supervised by UNAMA, but the level of fraud and the intensity of political tensions overwhelmed the institutions. Abdullah's backers came to believe that fraud and international pressure would lead to a fraudulent outcome intended to assure Pashtun rule. They mounted demonstrations, which began peacefully. Soon, however, pressure built for a coup to install Abdullah as president, despite Abdullah's personal opposition. Telephone calls from President Obama clarified that the US would not support any government that came to power illegally, and he sent Secretary of State John Kerry to seek a solution.

After weeks of bargaining, Ghani and Abdullah agreed to form a National Unity Government (NUG). Abdullah would recognize Ghani as the legitimate president, even though he and his followers were certain they had won the election. In return, Ghani would appoint Abdullah as chief executive officer (CEO), a post similar to a prime minister except that it depended on executive decree rather than the constitution for its authority, and its incumbent is not accountable to parliament. The two leaders promised to make appointments in a balanced and equitable way between both sides (power sharing), as well as through a "merit-based mechanism." The inherent contradiction of these approaches, as well as the lack of agreed criteria for either "balance" or "merit," plagued the NUG.

In an attempt to end the conflict over the form of the state, both parties agreed that within two years from the signing of the agreement (by September 2016) the government would convene a Loya Jirga, the body authorized to amend the constitution. That Loya Jirga would consider whether to create the position of "executive prime minister," settling the issue at least for the immediate future. The conditions for convening such a Constitutional Loya Jirga are demanding, however. The government would have to hold parliamentary and district council elections so that the requisite office holders were in place to constitute a quorum. Preparations would also have included drafting a proposal for the constitutional amendment to be considered by the Loya Jirga.

Is Afghanistan a democracy?

In today's Islamic Republic of Afghanistan, the president and lower house of parliament are elected by popular vote. The country has relatively free media by comparison with its neighbors, and the restrictions on expression derive more from social pressure and antigovernment armed groups than from official censorship. These are significant achievements, which many in Afghanistan appreciate.

Nonetheless, these democratic characteristics fall short of most of the content of democracy. There are two main reasons for the weakness of the system:

- The electoral institutions are so weak that every presidential election result has been disputed. The 2009 and 2014 presidential elections were settled only through mediation by the US, which had thousands of troops in the country. At this writing there are contradictory claims of victory in the 2019 elections, and disputes are growing about the anticipated results that will be announced.
- Because nearly all state bodies, including all of security forces, are paid for by foreign assistance, elected officials have little oversight or influence over public expenditure. Most public expenditure comes out of the budgets of the United States or other aid donors and is not even reported to parliament. While the constitution requires parliamentary approval of the budget, this applies only to what Afghans call the "core" budget, that of the state itself, not to the "external" budget, a hypothetical account much larger than the core budget and almost impossible to estimate, composed of the disbursements of all aid donors and international financial institutions in Afghanistan. (See chapter 7.)

To be elected president, a candidate must get a majority of the valid votes cast. But what are the valid votes? There has never been a complete census in Afghanistan. Nobody knows how many people there are in the country, let alone how many citizens or eligible voters. There are no birth or death certificates. Nobody knows how many eligible voters there are in each province or in each district. Biometric devices helped identify voters in the 2019 presidential election, but interpreting their readings depends on algorithms known only to the German manufacturer.

The weakness of the concept of "nation" or "citizen" in Afghanistan is not cultural, as if people "identify" as members of tribes or clans rather than as citizens of the state. People everywhere identify with whatever identity works in a given situation. In order to have citizens, however, a state must possess information about people: place of birth and residence, entry to and exit from the country. Such institutions require investment of resources in administration and training. Afghanistan has not had such resources. There are no certificates to register births or deaths with the state or mosque. There are, however, passports and identity cards for those who enter educational institutions, who have a formal job, or who travel abroad through official border posts.

Furthermore, over decades of war approximately half of the population has been displaced, some internally, some internationally as refugees, some permanently, some temporarily, some multiple times. The citizenship status of many such people has never been determined. Plus, parts of the country's territory and population are inaccessible to the state, because they are controlled or contested by armed insurgents or terrorists. Those Afghan citizens living in such areas, who are mostly Pashtuns, may be deprived of the franchise. It is also very easy for political leaders to carry out electoral fraud in areas to which the state and media have little access.

The extreme aid dependency of the Afghan state also deprives its institutions of democratic content. Many important policies of the Afghan state are not made by elected officials of Afghanistan. The defense and security budget of Afghanistan is allocated primarily by the Congress of the United States, and it is the Congress of the United States that reviews its performance and decides whether to renew it. And this is the reason that Washington think tanks and especially the Defense Department's Special Inpector General for Afghanistan Reconstruction (SIGAR) produce the most authoritative reports on the performance of the Afghan state and security forces.

In any country the geographical distribution of expenditures is a major subject of debate in the national legislature. Representatives try to assure that their constituents receive their fair share. The belief that one section of the nation is unfairly benefitting from public expenditure corrodes national unity and a sense of justice.

The geographic distribution of aid is a very sensitive political issue in Afghanistan, but the lack of transparency about the basic facts makes it even more of a flashpoint. No one in the Afghan government decides how much aid goes where. Before they were closed at the end of 2014, PRTs were responsible for much of the aid disbursement at the provincial level. The size of the aid budget available to each province was determined by the lead country of the PRT, rather than by any Afghan political process. Since the American PRTs were located in areas with more intense fighting, those provinces received much more aid that did, say, Ghor province, one of the poorest provinces in Afghanistan, where the PRT was headed by Lithuania. While there might be a reason to allocate aid on the basis of what is needed to counter security threats rather than what is needed to address poverty, there is no forum for Afghans to discuss that issue. The distribution of aid results from the way the international donors have organized their presence, not from any political debate or decision by Afghans. (See chapter 7.)

What does it mean that Afghanistan is an Islamic republic?

An "Islamic republic" is a form of government based on popular sovereignty (and is therefore a republic, rather than a kingdom or emirate), but where the exercise of that sovereignty must comply with Islamic laws. Iran, Pakistan, Afghanistan, and Mauritania all describe themselves as Islamic republics but have very different institutions.

Iran differs from the others because the Shi'a doctrine developed by Ruhollah Khomeini institutionalizes executive power of the clergy through the position of the Supreme Leader and the councils of guardianship and of experts. This provides a degree of direct clerical supervision of the republican institutions that does not exist in Pakistan or Afghanistan. In Afghanistan, proposed laws and executive decrees are reviewed a priori for compliance with Article 3 by the drafting department (*riyasat-i taqnin*) of the Ministry of Justice. After the promulgation or enactment of decrees or laws, the Supreme Court has the authority to challenge their conformity to the constitution, including the requirement that laws may not contradict the beliefs and provisions of Islam.

What is possibly more important than the authority of formal institutions, however, is the general belief in Afghanistan that government is legitimate only if it is based on Islam, and in particular, on implementation of Sharia. Cases where human rights were threatened in the name of Islam have been more likely to result from public opinion. For instance, there was a case of an Afghan who had converted to Christianity and emigrated to Germany. In 2006 he came back to Afghanistan to try to gain custody of his child. The police arrested him for having converted to Christianity from Islam, and there was strong sentiment among the public, Islamic clergy, and judiciary that he should be tried and executed on the grounds that apostasy is a criminal offense in Sharia. The constitution, however, states that no one can be tried and found guilty of any crime in Afghanistan, except according to the criminal code. The Afghan criminal code does not include any prohibition of apostasy. There is no legal basis to arrest anyone for apostasy in Afghanistan, but that is contrary to the popular conception of law in Afghanistan. This question could not be resolved through the judicial system. Instead President Karzai arranged for the suspect to be declared mentally unstable and sent to Europe for treatment.

7

RECONSTRUCTION AND DEVELOPMENT

PRINCIPAL AUTHOR, NEMATULLAH BIZHAN

What was the economic and social condition
of Afghanistan at the start of the interim government?

When Hamid Karzai became the chairman of the interim government, Afghanistan was so poor and ungoverned that it could not produce data about its economic and social conditions. The treasury was empty, and the government was hardly able to pay its employees' wages or provide public services. It hardly collected US$131 million in taxes from domestic sources in 2002–03.[1] A few years earlier, the UN had managed to make rough estimates of humanitarian conditions, which showed that Afghanistan was one of the poorest countries in the world, the poorest country in Asia, and the poorest country in the world outside of Africa. On every social or economic indicator Afghanistan resembled the most impoverished and war-ravaged countries of Africa (Table 7.1). It scored at the bottom of every social or economic indicator, with extraordinary gender gaps: only 21 percent of school-age children were enrolled in primary school, and almost none were girls, as the Taliban banned women from work and access to education. Infant mortality was 115 per 1,000 live births; child (under five)

1. Nematullah Bizhan, *Aid Paradoxes in Afghanistan: Building and Undermining the State* (Abingdon: Routledge, 2017), 108.

Table 7.1 The same table is used in Barnett R. Rubin, "The Political Economy of War and Peace in Afghanistan," *World Development*, Vol. 28, Issue 10 (October 2000), 1789–1803. Table 7.1. Measures of humanitarian emergency in Afghanistan[a]

Indicators	Afghanistan	South Asia	Developing countries	Industrial countries
Human development index rank (out of 174)[b]	169	N/A	N/A	N/A
Population % with access to healthcare (1985–93)[b] Safe water (1990–95)[c]	29 12 (rural 5, urban 39)	7 77	79 69	100 100
Daily calorie supply per capita	1,523	2,356	2,546	3,108
Infant mortality per 1,000 live births (1993)[c]	165	85	70	N/A
Under five mortality per 1,000 live births (1993)[d]	257	122	101	N/A
Maternal mortality per 100,000 live births (1992)	1,700[e] or 640[f]	469	351	10
Life expectancy at birth in years (1993)[b]	44	60	62	76
Adult literacy rate (%, 1993)[b,c]	28 (men 45, women 14)	48	68	98

[a]*Sources:* All comparative data from other regions are from source (b). One indicator of humanitarian emergency in Afghanistan is the collapse of institutions able to produce such statistics. Unlike such presumably better-governed countries as Sierra Leona and Burundi, Afghanistan has not been listed in the standard source for such data, UNDP's *Human Development Report* 1996.

[b]UNOCHA (1996, p. 4); citing UNDP, *Human Development Report* 1996.

[c]UNOCHA (1997, p. 4); citing UNDP, *Human Development Report* 1997.

[d]UNOCHA (1997); citing UNICEF, *State of the World's Children Report* 1996.

[e]UNOCHA (1997); citing Study by UNICEF/World Health Organization, 1996.

[f]UNDP (1997).

mortality was 172 per 1,000 live births; and maternal mortality was estimated at 1,600 per 100,000 live births. On the Human Development Index, a composite of basic education and health indicators, very rough estimates placed Afghanistan 169 out of 174 countries. It was also one of the most heavily armed countries in the world and had a large population of disabled people due to both war injuries and the prevalence of preventable diseases, notably polio.

It took fully four years after the inauguration of the new Afghan government, until September 2004, for the World Bank to publish its "first Economic Report on Afghanistan in a quarter-century."[2] The bank summarized the situation:

> The starting point—in late 2001 at the fall of the Taliban—for recent developments in Afghanistan was dire. The Afghan economy was reeling from protracted conflict and severe drought, with cereal grain production down by half, livestock herds decimated, orchards and vineyards destroyed by war and drought, more than five million people displaced as refugees in neighboring countries, and remaining economic activities steered in an informal or illicit direction by insecurity and lack of support services.[3]

International financial institutions estimated macroeconomic statistics for the first time in decades. According to the International Monetary Fund, Afghanistan in 2002 ranked 183 out of 192 countries in per capita income as estimated by purchasing power parity. The only countries poorer than Afghanistan were Burundi, the Central African Republic, the Democratic Republic of the Congo, Ethiopia, Liberia, Malawi, Mozambique, Niger, and Rwanda. Afghanistan was the poorest country in Asia, with a per capita GDP only 81 percent of Tajikistan, the next poorest Asian state. It was even further behind Cambodia, Nepal, and Myanmar. Afghanistan had

2. World Bank, Poverty Reduction and Economic Management Sector Unit, South Asia Region, *Afghanistan: State Building, Sustaining Growth, and Reducing Poverty, A Country Economic Report* (Report no. 29551-AF), September 9, 2004.
3. Ibid., p. x.

38 percent of the GDP per capita of India and 30 percent of Pakistan.

Afghanistan also lagged far behind in telecommunications coverage: there were a few hundred landlines in the major cities, many of them connected to Pakistani area codes during Taliban rule, and no mobile telephone providers. There were single state-owned television and radio channels.

This poverty and lack of development resulted from both the direct and indirect effects of armed conflict since 1978. The World Bank summarized the direct effects as: (1) less labor power, with 30 percent of the population displaced and many males in their most productive years joining or fleeing the conflict; (2) "lower quality of human capital" due to the destruction of education; (3) destruction of physical capital such as irrigation systems, roads, and livestock; (4) contraction of available land due to mines and unexploded ordinance; and (5) special difficulties imposed on women.

Perhaps the biggest indirect effect was the isolation of Afghanistan from the global community. As the World Bank argued, Afghanistan lost the opportunity "to participate in the last twenty-five years of global development and to catch up" with other countries.[4] Figure 7.1 shows how Afghanistan lagged behind in advances in GDP per capita and life expectancy.

In addition, external intervention had implications for the economy, changing it qualitatively. British imperialism had made Afghanistan into an isolated buffer state, rather than a colony exploited for economic gain, and imposed major social and economic costs through the three Anglo-Afghan wars (1839–42, 1878–80, and 1919). In colonies under direct rule the imperial power introduced commercial farming for the international market of products such as tea, coffee, rubber, indigo, cotton, tobacco, sugar, and cacao, or extractive industries producing minerals or petroleum. Peasants lost land to such

4. Ibid., p. 2.

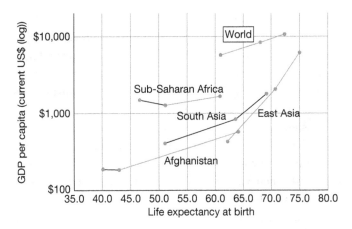

Figure 7.1 Development Trajectories: 1975-2002-2017

Source: World Bank, Poverty Reduction and Economic Management Sector Unit, South Asia Region, *Afghanistan: State Building, Sustaining Growth, and Reducing Poverty, A Country Economic Report* (Report no. 29551-AF), September 9, 2004; World Bank Open Data, https:// data.worldbank.org/.

enterprises and became subject to coercive labor systems ranging from slavery to debt peonage. Populations became dependent on cash and imported food. In Afghanistan, the 1980s war, rather than nineteenth-century colonization, brought global commercial agriculture and extractive industries on a massive scale. The main commercial crop, opium poppy, was illegal according to international treaties. The industry moved its cultivation to Afghanistan from Pakistan, Iran, Myanmar, and Turkey, not because Afghanistan had better physical conditions to grow poppy but because it had better conditions than elsewhere for producing and protecting illegality. The influx of cash to finance the war and opium production brought severe inflation, especially of the price of food.

Such a poor economy could not support a functioning government. A weak state could hardly collect revenue in the face of economic regression and pervasive insecurity. In 1975, before the start of the armed conflict, the Afghan government's tax revenue was estimated at only 7.1 percent of GDP. By the time the economy had recovered enough to yield estimates again, in 2003, it was barely a third of that, at 2.4 percent. Figure 7.2 compares the share of tax revenues to GDP from 2001 to the present for the world, South Asia (including Afghanistan), and Afghanistan. Even in 2013, Afghanistan was still below the South Asian average, which was quite low in global perspective. Afghanistan had the lowest ratio of tax revenue to GDP of any non-oil-exporting country that reported data. Since then revenue has increased, reaching an estimated 12.3 percent in 2017, according to a World Bank report.[5]

With such low tax revenue and without foreign aid other than a tiny flow of humanitarian assistance, it was no wonder that the level of public services such as education and healthcare was so low, leading to the outcomes in Table 7.1.

How did the economic and social conditions change after 2001?

Fifteen years later, the socioeconomic conditions in Afghanistan had improved significantly. However, the huge international expenditures on Afghanistan showed mixed results. In GNI per capita (PPP), in 2016 Afghanistan ranked 196 out of 216 countries, ahead of nineteen African states and Haiti. In addition to the nine countries whose average income Afghanistan had exceeded in 2002, it had also overtaken Uganda, Haiti, South Sudan (which did not exist at the time), Burkina Faso, The Gambia, Guinea-Bissau, Comoros, Togo, Sierra Leone, and Guinea. It was still the poorest country in Asia, with average income only 75 percent that of Nepal and about 55 percent that of Cambodia, Tajikistan, and the Kyrgyz Republic.

From 2003 to 2016, Afghanistan's GDP per capita (PPP constant dollars) excluding narcotics grew by an average of

5. World Bank, *Afghanistan Development Update* (Washington, DC: World Bank, 2019), 10.

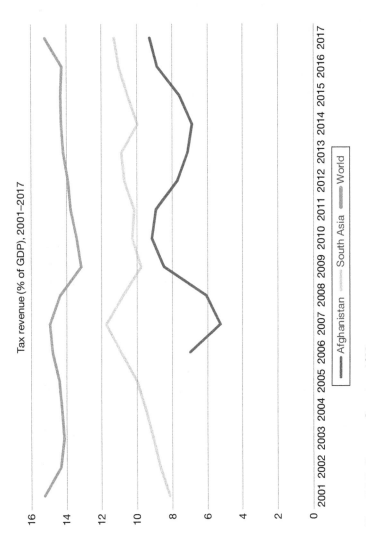

Figure 7.2 Tax Revenue as Percentage of GDP

Table 7.2 Improvement in Humanitarian Indicators, Afghanistan

Indicator	1990s, various	2015–16
HDI rank	169/174	169/188
Population percent with access to:		
Healthcare	29	90
Safe water	12	65
Calories/capita	1523	2090
Infant mortality per 1,000 live births	257	91
Maternal mortality per 100,000 live births	1,700/640	396
Life expectancy at birth	44	61
Adult literacy	28	38

3.7 percent per year, and by 5.7 percent per year from 2001 through 2012, before the withdrawal of most foreign troops. This performance was an improvement over previous decades, but it was insufficient to outdistance its neighbors. The Afghan average growth rate of 3.7 percent per year compares with an average for South Asia as a whole of 5.7 percent per year, though it is greater than the average during those years for sub-Saharan Africa, 2.3 percent per year.

Despite the continued moderate pace of growth, direct foreign aid to public services raised the level of humanitarian indicators (Table 7.2). Afghanistan still remained near the bottom of the HDI listings, ranking 169 as in 1996 but out of a larger number of countries (188 rather than 174). Nineteen countries, all in sub-Saharan Africa, ranked lower than Afghanistan in HDI.

In all indicators of health, life expectancy, child and maternal mortality, nutrition, and literacy, Afghanistan had made progress, as shown in Table 7.2. The cost of this progress was such an extreme level of dependency on aid that it is nearly impossible to envisage a transition toward self-sufficiency in the foreseeable future. Over half of aid from 2002 to 2010 was spent on security and the rest largely followed security priorities. As Table 7.3 shows in 2015 Afghanistan ranked eighth

Table 7.3 Ten Most Aid-Dependent Countries, 2015

Country	ODA as percent GNI
Tuvalu	89.2
Liberia	62.4
Central African Republic	30.6
Marshall Islands	24.0
Somalia	23.0
Sierra Leone	22.6
Micronesia, Fed. Sts.	22.0
Afghanistan	21.3
South Sudan	21.1
Kiribati	19.1

in the world in the percentage of gross national income (GNI) coming from overseas development assistance (ODA). Of the seven more aid-dependent countries, three were island microstates with populations ranging from 11,000 to 105,000, and the other four were Somalia, Sierra Leone, Liberia, and the Central African Republic. None of these states were called upon to bear the burden of being the front line in the global war on terror.

What were the development frameworks used by the Afghan government and its international supporters?

One of the early initiatives by the Afghan government was to write a document called the National Development Framework. This document attempted to outline national priorities and policy directions. The Board of the Afghanistan Assistance Coordination Authority (AACA), chaired by the chairman of the interim administration, and individual consultations carried out by the Ministry of Planning, the Ministry of Reconstruction, and the AACA contributed to this document, but its main author was AACA director Ashraf Ghani. Subsequently, the government prepared three more comprehensive strategies and plans: Securing Afghanistan's Future, which was presented by Minister of Finance Ashraf Ghani at the Berlin international conference in 2004; the Interim Afghanistan National Development Strategy (I-ANDS) in 2006; and the Afghanistan National Development Strategy (ANDS), which was presented at the Paris Conference on Afghanistan in 2008. Later, the National Unity Government also developed a five-year development strategy from 2017 to 2022, referred to as the Afghanistan National Peace and Development Framework (ANPDF).

These strategies and plans aimed to identify national priorities and allocate foreign aid and domestic revenue to realize them. These documents also helped the Afghan government to meet the conditions required by aid programs under some schemes. For example, ANDS served as a Poverty Reduction Strategy Paper (PRSP), something that the World Bank member countries prepare describing the country's macroeconomic, structural, and social policies, and programs to promote broad-based growth and reduce poverty. The PRSP was a condition for eligibility for debt relief within the Heavily Indebted Poor Countries initiative and access to aid from major donors and lenders.[6]

These strategies aimed to create a liberal market economy in Afghanistan by establishing rule of law, trade, and good relations with neighbors, and eventually transitioning out of illegal drug production into licit products. However, the National Development Framework was prepared more for the international donor community than the Afghan government or people. Most of the government departments were not fully functioning. While the planning process became

---

6. See ANDS Islamic Republic of Afghanistan, "Afghanistan National Development Strategy (ANDS), 1387–1391 (2008–13)" (Kabul: ANDS Secretariat, n.d.).

more inclusive and consultative, there remained a gap between donors' interests and those of the Afghan government. Donors prepared their own country programs and strategies. This was, in particular, the case with major bilateral donors, such as the US, the UK, and Japan. Those projects that donors directly funded were sometimes poorly aligned with Afghan government priorities and often not tailored to the context.[7]

Was there a plan for the reconstruction of Afghanistan? How was the aid coordinated?

International engagement in post-2001 Afghanistan was a reaction to the 9/11 attacks. There was no reconstruction plan or needs assessment available. The plans, such as they were, were prepared in the subsequent years. Major obstacles were the lack of reliable data, shortage of country expertise, and weak capacity in the government. The government purchased capacity by recruiting foreign and expatriate national advisors, who were recruited mostly through projects funded outside the budget. Bilateral donors, such as the US, the UK, and Japan, had their own country strategies for Afghanistan.

Donors used three methods to deliver aid: on-budget aid delivered directly to the government; on-budget aid delivered through trust funds jointly managed by the government, donors, and international organizations; and off-budget aid directly managed by donors and implemented by their own contractors or partners, bypassing the government budget and procurement system. The lion's share of aid was allocated to the security sector (51 percent from 2002 to 2011—see Figure 7.3). Both aid delivery and allocation were in part a response to weakness and corruption in the public sector as well as the presence of an urgent need to deliver basic services, such as

7. See, for instance, SIGAR, "Quarterly Report to the United States Congress" (Arlington, VA, July 30, 2014).

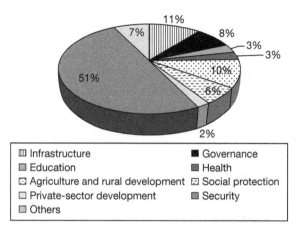

Figure 7.3 Foreign Aid Commitment by Sectors, 2002–11
Source: Ministry of Finance of Afghanistan, 2011.

health and education. Corruption was at least as prevalent in donor's off-budget projects as in the government.

The number of foreign donors and multilateral institutions operating in Afghanistan rapidly increased after 2001. Sixty governmental donors, including forty-seven countries that contributed military forces, many international organizations, and NGOs operated in Afghanistan. Coordination of aid became a major problem, exacerbated by the extensive use of off-budget mechanisms.

Many overlapping systems emerged. Each donor country sponsored particular sectors and programs, as in the lead-donor system for SSR. The United Nations Children Fund (UNICEF) was engaged in technically supporting primary and secondary education after NATO took the lead in ISAF in 2003. Provincial Reconstruction Teams (PRTs) funded by the troop-contributing countries tried to support their military presence in the provinces by delivering construction projects such as bridges, schools, and clinics for local communities. The World Bank and IMF worked closely with the Ministry of Finance and the Central Bank of Afghanistan (Da Afghanistan

Bank), focusing on public financial management and macroeconomic issues. UNAMA was supposedly responsible for coordinating but had no authority over bilateral donors. The US remained the single most important foreign military and economic actor as it contributed about two-thirds of the total aid to Afghanistan between 2002 and 2010 (see Table 7.4).

The government and foreign donors established multiple coordination mechanisms, with no sense of irony. In 2006, in addition to internal government and donor coordination structures, at least six types of coordination structures existed. There were twelve Consultative Groups, six Crosscutting Consultative Groups and forty-five Working Groups (at the technical level), and a Consultative Groups Standing Committee, (until 2005)—as well as, an External Advisory Group, three Standing Committees under the Joint Coordination and Monitoring Board (established in 2008), and the Joint Coordination and Monitoring Board (established in 2006) at the policy level. The government and donors would call JCMB meetings on a quarterly basis. The government would organize up to 128 meetings of these bodies annually. Government officials, members of aid agencies, international institutions, and civil society organizations would attend the meetings.

A major dilemma was how to balance building the capacity of the state institutions with delivering basic public services. This dilemma of aid delivery was not unique to Afghanistan, as in weak states there is always a tradeoff in aid provision between strengthening existing institutions and trying to deliver projects as efficiently as possible.[8] To overcome the shortage of capacity and ensure fiduciary control over aid spending, multilateral donors largely bypassed the state and spent above

---

8. See Nematullah Bizhan, "Aid and State-Building, Part I: South Korea and Taiwan," *Third World Quarterly* 39, no. 5 (2018); "Aid and State-Building, Part II: Afghanistan and Iraq," *Third World Quarterly* 39, no. 5 (2018).

Table 7.4 Top 30 Donors to Afghanistan (in US$ million), 2002–10

		2002–13	2002–11	2002–10			2002–10	
		Pledge	Commitment	Total Disbursement	On-budget Disbursement	Off-budget Disbursement	On-budget Disbursement (as percentage)	Off-budget Disbursement (as percentage)
1	United States of America	56,100	44,356	37,118	2,455	34,663	7	93
2	Japan	7,200	3,152	3,152	900	2,252	29	71
3	Germany	5,029	2,130	762	287	475	38	62
4	European Union/European Commission	3,068	2,883	2,594	774	1,820	30	70
5	United Kingdom	2,897	2,222	2,222	861	1,361	39	61
6	World Bank	2,800	2,137	1,700	1,700	0	100	0
7	Asian Development Bank	2,200	2,269	1,005	955	50	95	5
8	Canada	1,769	1,256	1,256	491	765	39	61
9	India	1,200	1,516	759	0	759	0	100
10	Norway	938	775	636	232	404	36	64
11	Netherlands	864	1,015	1,015	426	589	42	58
12	Italy	753	645	540	212	328	39	61
13	Iran	673	399	377	0	377	0	100
14	Denmark	533	438	438	252	186	58	42

15	Sweden	515	635	171	464	27	73
16	Australia	369	744	112	544	17	83
17	Spain	308	220	84	110	43	57
18	United Nations	305	446	2	180	1	99
19	Pakistan	289	5	0	0	0	0
20	Saudi Arabia	268	140	25	78	24	76
21	China	252	139	0	58	0	100
22	Russian Federation	239	151	4	143	3	97
23	Switzerland	197	118	7	95	7	93
24	Agha Khan Development Network	190	140	0	140	0	100
25	Finland	152	160	48	112	30	70
26	Turkey	143	213	0	180	0	100
27	France	134	323	62	112	36	64
28	United Arab Emirates	97	134	0.4	117	0	100
29	Islamic Development Bank	87	70	17	0	100	0
30	South Korea	85	116	6	77	7	93
31	Others	327	305	59	224	21	79
	Total	89,981	69,252	10,142	46,663	18	3

Source: Ministry of Finance of Afghanistan, 2010, and calculation by Bizhan.

two-thirds of their aid, including military aid, outside the Afghan government budget and national procurement system from 2002 to 2010 (see Table 7.4).

This method of aid delivery had adverse implications for building state capacity and the cost effectiveness of reconstruction. Reliance on off-budget aid mechanisms exacerbated aid fragmentation and fragmented the public financial management system.

Two budgets therefore emerged. The first was the state budget, which included public expenditure funded through domestic revenue or through aid provided to the government treasury either directly or through trust funds. The World Bank managed the largest trust fund, the Afghanistan Reconstruction Trust Fund (ARTF).

The second budget was the "external budget," for expenditures outside the government. This type of expenditure was funded by aid that bypassed the Afghan government budget and national mechanisms (e.g., for procurement). The government did not control and could not account for these expenditures. While reliance on off-budget aid mechanisms seemed plausible to deliver aid in the short term, it had adverse effects on institution building. It raised the cost of reconstruction and diverted political and financial resources away from reforming and building permanent state institutions.

Off-budget aid spending had a limited role in building the domestic economy. A study by the World Bank estimated that each dollar spent off-budget had only 10–25 percent domestic content, meaning using local products and services, in comparison to 70–95 percent of on-budget aid spending.[9] Preference to contractors from donor countries, as well as the different ways that each external actor delivered projects, inflated cost.

9. World Bank, "Afghanistan in Transition: Looking Beyond 2014" (May 2012), 2.

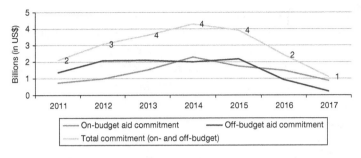

Figure 7.4 Total Aid Commitment and Aid Delivery Methods, 2012–17
Source: Ministry of Finance of Afghanistan, Kabul, 2018.

The construction of the national ring road in Afghanistan is one such example. Different donors financed it and implemented construction through different companies. As a result, "[s]tandards for different components of the ring road also differ[ed] from each other, and there [were] major variations in costs."[10] Additionally, projects were often subcontracted multiple times, with each subcontractor taking a percentage of the funds for overhead costs, lowering the benefit to direct beneficiaries. Technical assistance projects also suffered from poor coordination. In 2007, the World Bank found that "the widespread use of uncoordinated and non-strategically targeted technical assistance is neither fiscally nor politically sustainable."[11]

From 2002 to 2010, donors disbursed $57 billion in development and military aid to Afghanistan. While each donor used a different approach, as Figure 7.4 shows, a large portion of aid was spent off-budget. The World Bank, Asian Development

10. Ashraf Ghani and Clare Lockhart, *Fixing Failed States: A Framework for Rebuilding a Fractured World* (New York: Oxford University Press, 2008), 218.
11. World Bank, "Review of Technical Assistance and Capacity Building in Afghanistan: Discussion Paper for the Afghanistan Development Forum" (April 26, 2007), 2.

Bank, and International Monetary Fund channeled their aid through on-budget mechanisms, while major bilateral donors mostly relied on off-budget funding mechanisms.

The delivery of aid outside the state system did not strengthen the legitimacy of state institutions, though delivery of aid through corrupt or ineffective state institutions might not have done so either. People would go directly to donors to seek funding. Provincial Reconstruction Teams (PRTs), which spent $867 million from 2005 to 2008, used such a mechanism. Other types of off-budget spending also adversely affected government legitimacy. The bulk of finance for the twenty-six PRTs was concentrated in insecure areas. PRTs consulted with communities to identify and finance their needs, sometimes seeking the advice of government, but projects were then implemented under the auspice of PRTs. The government increasingly demanded that donors should channel more aid through the government budget and trust funds. Finance Minister Ashraf Ghani (2002–04), in particular, advocated such a policy. The World Bank also supported this policy.

There were some changes in approach in the upcoming years. At the Kabul International Conference in 2010, donors agreed to increase their share of on-budget development aid to Afghanistan:

> Conference Participants supported the ambition of the Government of Afghanistan whereby donors increase the proportion of development aid delivered through the Government of Afghanistan to 50 percent in the next two years, including through multi-donor trust funds that support the Government budget, e.g., the Afghanistan Reconstruction Trust Fund and the Law and Order Trust Fund for Afghanistan. But this support is conditional on the Government's progress in further strengthening public financial management systems, reducing

corruption, improving budget execution, developing a financing strategy and Government capacity towards the goal.[12]

Despite some increase in the share of on-budget contributions, by 2014 around 50 percent of international aid continued to bypass the state and national mechanisms. While this situation further improved over time, a significant portion of aid continued to flow outside the government budget. For instance, in 2017, 21 percent of total aid was off-budget (Figure 7.4). However, this figure does not include off-budget military expenditure.

Has the aid strengthened Afghan institutions?

Since 2001, Afghanistan has experienced major economic and political transformation. The country has made important progress in building state institutions such as the ministry of finance and expanding access to basic services such as education and health care. Since the state suffered from an acute deficit of capacity, it was crucial to devise ways to both provide public goods and build the state's capacity. Three strategies were adopted. The first strategy was to buy capacity from outside the public sector and country by hiring consultants, including expatriate Afghans, and by outsourcing some of the government's core functions to contractors. The second entailed bypassing the Afghan state and national mechanisms to deliver donors' projects directly through the private sector. The third focused on building the capacity of government departments through reforms, training, and new hiring.

12. Islamic Republic of Afganistan, "Kabul International Conference on Afghanistan: Communique" (July 20, 2010).

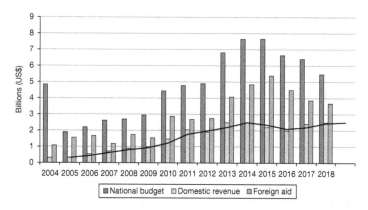

Figure 7.5 Public Expenditure, Aid, and Domestic Revenue, 2002–09

Note: Public expenditure is calculated based on annual aid disbursement and domestic revenue allocation. This method provides more precise information than the total budget of a year because often donors' commitments based on formulation of the annual budget were not disbursed and translated into real implementation of projects.

Source: Ministry of Finance of Afghanistan, 2018.

The capacity of state institutions has improved significantly since 2001. Despite these improvements, however, the state has remained weak; the state's fiscal, legal, and coercive capacities remain very low as evidenced by the low extraction and distribution capacities of the state. While tax revenue as a total share of GDP increased from 4 percent in 2004 to 14 percent in 2018, on average, it remained at 7 percent between 2003 and 2015.[13] The government development budget execution rate also remained low, 43 percent between 2002 and 2010 and 20 percent in the first six months of fiscal year 2017–2018.[14] The government's huge budget deficit was funded by foreign aid (Figure 7.5).

The second strategy for overcoming challenges of corruption and state weakness was to bypass the state by delivering

13. Bizhan, *Aid Paradoxes in Afghanistan: Building and Undermining the State.*
14. Ibid., 79.

aid through private companies and nongovernmental organizations (NGOs). This method of aid delivery created a parallel public sector, which delivered aid independently of the Afghan state. The problem with the parallel mechanisms and processes was not that non-state actors implemented projects, but that the much larger amount of aid provided through this mechanism rather than on budget was poorly aligned with local priorities. It also unintentionally induced institutional rivalry and fragmentation and strengthened non-state power holders on whom donors relied for logistics and security. A common form of such patronage was the employment of private security companies led by former warlords.

Both the bypass tactic and buying capacity had short time horizons. Even though these strategies helped to deliver aid, in some areas they led to the fragmentation of administration, created islands of efficiency, and increased transaction costs. Bypass tactics had adverse implications for capacity building. They made the government's permanent institutions less attractive for competent job candidates and diverted much of the financial and political resources from building and reforming the permanent state institutions.

The third strategy included direct intervention in building state capacity. Those government departments and ministries that had exposure to donors improved significantly. The Finance Ministry is a notable example. But even the capacity within the ministry varied and was less sustainable because of dependence on aid and technical assistance. The General Directorate of Budget of the ministry has significantly improved and reformed. Line ministries and departments, however, had to execute the national budget. The low budget execution rate, as noted earlier, does not result from a lack of capacity at the General Directorate of Budget. The General Directorate of the Treasury also demonstrated increasing capacity. But this was not the case with the Directorates of Revenue and Customs, as corruption and nepotism have damaged their reputations. The capacities of the Ministries of Health and Rural Reconstruction and Development also increased significantly.[15]

How has aid dependence shaped Afghan politics?

On-budget and off-budget aid had distinct impacts on state institutions, social actors, and the economy. Aid not only had profound effects on state-building processes but also influenced state-society relations, as major donors funded and engaged with social actors. Supporting the government budget and donors' direct spending through projects were two important mechanisms for donors' fiscal intervention. The on-budget aid mechanism assisted in financing the government operating budget and development projects. By contrast, off-budget aid sustained so-called civil society activities, funded the delivery of services by NGOs, empowered individual powerbrokers to deliver security services to international security forces or aid projects, and financed projects outside of government systems.

Off-budget aid established a direct relationship between donor and beneficiaries. Individuals and organizations had to bargain directly with the donors for funding. Neither the Afghan government nor the legislature had discretion to discontinue or appropriate off-budget aid, and the recipients of this type of aid depended on donors.

The availability of such aid and the demand for particular services encouraged social actors to refocus their activities. Those who formed NGOs invested in building skills in project proposal writing and reporting. Some specialized in a particular sector that could yield high returns through aid. While local NGOs were in the process of formation to meet global standards and requirements, international NGOs and companies were in a more privileged position to implement

15. "Building Legitimacy and State Capacity in Protracted Fragility: The Case of Afghanistan" (London: LSE-Oxford Commission on State Fragility, Growth and Development, 2018).

projects and used local NGOs and companies as subcontractors. They knew how the international system worked, especially the donors' procurement systems.[16]

The former anti-Taliban commanders who aligned with the US to overthrow the Taliban regime saw their powers confirmed and sometimes augmented by key positions in the new government. These commanders combined formal and informal sources of power, including networks of armed men. Their accommodation within state institutions further expanded their influence among the local population. They mostly relied on patronage funded by aid and contracting with the international presence while retaining capacities for violence and coercion. They in turn distributed government positions, access to contracts, and land to their supporters. Their expertise in warfare in Afghanistan put them in a privileged position to provide security services independent of the state and thus access military aid, especially from the US.[17]

The US and other NATO troop contributors who operated in the south and east of Afghanistan relied on commanders to provide security for their forward operations and protect their convoys. This was arranged through bilateral contractual agreements without the participation of the central government. This arrangement in some cases allied the Afghan expatriates who had returned, mainly from the US, with the militia commanders to form logistic and security companies. The expatriates dealt with donors on funding and contractual management, and the commanders and their militias managed operations and projects. The security companies and the commanders safeguarded the convoys by offering protection fees to the Taliban and other militias that were able to ambush the trucks. The cost per truck depended on the value of goods, ranging between US$800 and US$1,500. Many power holders

16. Bizhan, *Aid Paradoxes in Afghanistan: Building and Undermining the State*, 149.
17. Ibid., 150.

had brothers, cousins, uncles, or other male relatives with such profitable contracts with foreigners, and they used the profits to fund their political activities.

Off-budget projects required periodic reports in different formats to multiple oversight agencies to meet donor requirements. Hundreds of missions monitored and evaluated some of these projects annually, while each mission expected to meet at least with a minister or a deputy minister to obtain feedback. This process required and encouraged both the government and the off-budget project implementers, be they NGOs or societal actors, to bargain and work with donors.

Between 2002 and 2010, as shown in Figure 7.3, more than half of total aid was disbursed to the security sector, and the rest largely followed military priorities, in particular where donors also had a military presence. A mismatch, however, existed between development needs and aid allocation. A 2010 joint study by the World Bank and the Ministry of Economy of Afghanistan found that between 2002 and 2010 among the ten provinces receiving the most aid (Kabul, Helmand, Kandahar, Nangarhar, Herat, Kunar, Ghazni, Paktika, Paktya, and Balkh), only Balkh and Paktika suffered from high poverty rates. Other provinces with high poverty rates (Wardak, Badakhshan, Laghman, and Logar) received less assistance.[18]

The militarization of aid created perverse incentives. Efforts by people in more stable areas to improve local security seemed to deprive them of donor assistance. Some perceived that for projects to be funded it was imperative to create an atmosphere of insecurity.

Post-2001, the state-society relationship formed between a fragmented society dominated by its historical cleavages and a broken aid system orchestrated by an uncoordinated international community. Donors forged their relationships with the Afghan state and society using on- and off-budget mechanisms.

18. Ibid., 155.

This fiscal approach facilitated a divergence in state-society relations by encouraging and requiring state and social actors to be preoccupied with donors' priorities and perceptions. The donors boosted Afghan state capacity by financing its operational and development expenditures through on-budget mechanisms.

However, by funding projects off budget, which deprived the government and legislature of the ability to allocate and oversee projects and encouraged societal actors to prioritize their relations with donors instead of the state. Aid largely followed international military priorities, and initially four-fifths bypassed the state. While off-budget aid was largely justified because of the low government capacity and corruption, this aid reinforced the disconnection of the state from social actors.[19]

What is the role of Afghanistan's neighbors in reconstruction and development?

Aid from Afghanistan's mostly poor neighbors, except India, has been low in comparison to major Western development partners. As Figure 7.6 shows, India has supplied nearly 70 percent of all aid from neighbors and Iran nearly half of the rest, though aid from China has increased since 2012.[20]

China's efforts to expand bilateral trade and investment have significantly increased. In 2008, two state-owned Chinese companies secured the contract worth about $3 billion for Mes Aynak copper mine in Logar province, the world's second-largest undeveloped copper deposit. This project is, however, stagnant with three factors hindering its development: a deteriorating security situation, the existence of an archaeological site in the area, and a drop in prices of copper and other

19. Ibid., 160–61.
20. Islamic Republic of Afghanistan, "Development Cooperation Report" (Kabul: Ministry of Finance, 2010).

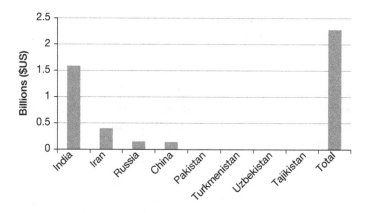

Figure 7.6 Flow of Aid from the Region to Afghanistan, 2002–11
Source: Ministry of Finance of Afghanistan, 2010.

metal.[21] Delays in this project have deprived the government of an expected $390 million in annual revenue. For the Afghan government, Chinese involvement in this project was essential both for implementation of the project and stability in the long run. The Afghan government expected that China, as a major economic power and close ally of Pakistan, would press Pakistan to relinquish or moderate its support to the Taliban.

India is involved in economic development as both a donor and contractor and has focused on infrastructure projects. Some notable projects include the Salma Dam in Herat province, a strategic highway from Delaram to Zaranj (linking the ring road to the Iranian port of Chabahar), a Khost–Gardez road, reaching the borders of Pakistan's former South Waziristan tribal agency, and the installation of an electricity line from Uzbekistan to Kabul. An Indian consortium won the second-largest mining contract in Afghanistan for the Hajigak iron mine in central

21. Islamic Republic of Afghanistan, Mining Contract for the Aynak Copper Deposit between the Government of Afghanistan and MCC-Jiangxi Copper Consortium (MCC) (Kabul: Ministry of Mines and Petroleum, 2008).

Bamyan province. However, the status of the final contract and actual exploitation have been stalled because of concerns about lack of security and low world mineral prices.

As one of the most important neighbors economically and politically, Pakistan has played a dual role in Afghanistan. Karachi, the southern port city in Pakistan, has provided landlocked Afghanistan with its main access to global and regional shipping. Pakistan has not only provided safe havens to Taliban insurgents, but it has also been criticized for predatory economic practices, such as product dumping and nontariff obstacles to trade. In addition, it has periodically closed its borders or imposed restrictions on the transport of goods to or from Afghanistan, which has adversely affected the relationship between the two countries.

Iran has also been the source of some investment for Western Afghanistan, but so far, the neighbors have been more beneficiaries from Afghanistan's aid. Pakistan in particular has benefited, because aid has led to growth in trade and transport through Pakistan. Afghanistan has also invested in diversifying its access to international markets, such as by using the Chabahar port in Iran that connects India to Afghanistan and Central Asia through Iran (see chapter 10).

Has aid decreased since 2014? What has been the economic effect of withdrawal of most foreign troops by 2014?

The flow of aid to Afghanistan has been volatile. It started from a very low base in the early years after the fall of the Taliban regime and then increased. However, since 2014 the flow of military and development aid to Afghanistan declined. This situation resulted in economic recession and unemployment, which was exacerbated by two other types of transition, namely political and military.

The economic shocks arising from a decline in the flow of development and military aid to the country increased the likelihood of a financial collapse of the state. The flow of overseas development assistance and official aid to Afghanistan decreased from US$6.3 billion in 2010 to US$4.6 billion in 2014 and to US$3.7 billion in 2016.[22] Some analysts compared a worst-case scenario of this situation if aid to Afghanistan was terminated with the collapse of the Najibullah government in 1992, in which the termination of Soviet aid provoked the collapse of the regime. Some short-term measures were therefore adopted. Afghanistan's major development partners committed to maintain a moderate level of aid and military support to mitigate the risk of a fiscal collapse.

While these measures were helpful, uncertainty had lasting effects on both the economy and political stability. The private sector suffered. Foreign direct investment sharply declined as the security situation deteriorated. GDP growth fell from 14 percent in 2011 to 1 percent in 2014, the lowest since the beginning of the last decade. Foreign direct investment (FDI) also fell to less than 1 percent of GDP in 2014 from 5 percent in 2005 and 2 percent in 2009 (see Figure 7.7).

The unemployment rate has also increased. With an estimated four hundred thousand youth entering the labor market each year, efforts have fallen short to support legal channels for skilled migration abroad and labor-intensive economic programs inside the country. In 2013–14, close to two million eligible people were unemployed, about half a million of them young males. The service sector collapsed in rural areas, due to decline in military and development aid. The unemployment rate increased from 25 percent in 2015 to 40 percent in 2016.[23] This trend was also associated with an increase in the poverty rate from 36 percent in 2011–12 to 39 percent in 2013–14. This

22. World Development Indicators, Washington, DC: The World Bank. Accessed July 17, 2019, http://datatopics.worldbank.org/world-development-indicators/.
23. Tolo News, "Unemployment Rate Spikes in Afghanistan," October 2016, https://www.tolonews.com/afghanistan/unemployment-rate-spikes-afghanistan.

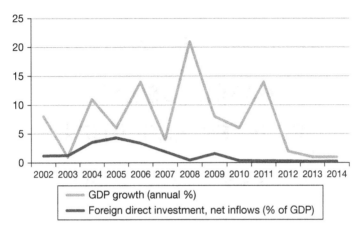

Figure 7.7 GDP Growth and Foreign Direct Investment Net Inflows (as Percentage of GDP)
Source: World Bank, 2017.

situation led to resentment and a sense of uncertainty, especially among young males. Not only did the return of Afghan
refugees slow down, but insecurity and uncertainty sparked a
new wave of migration from the country.[24]

Aid played an important role in the reconstruction and development processes in post-2001 Afghanistan. However, the
outcomes were largely affected by factors such as state weakness, donors' interests, aid modalities, and the preexisting institutional and sociopolitical conditions. While Afghanistan
inherited conditions that were not favorable for effective development and institution building, the types of interventions that
occurred—including an aid architecture that largely bypassed
the state, the subordination of state building to the war on
terror, and the short horizon policy choices of donors and the
Afghan government—reduced the effectiveness of the aid and
undermined effective development and institution building.

24. Nematullah Bizhan, "The Effects of Afghanistan's Political Evolution
on Migration and Displacement," *Migration Policy and Practice* 6,
no. 3 (2016), 4–9..

8

NARCOTICS AND COUNTER-NARCOTICS

PRINCIPAL AUTHOR, DAVID MANSFIELD

*How did narcotics become the largest industry
in Afghanistan?*

When the war started in late 1970s, most of the opium and heroin production in the world was in the Golden Triangle—Myanmar, Thailand, and Laos—with smaller levels of production in the Golden Crescent—Pakistan, Iran, and Afghanistan. Until the late 1980s and 1990s, opium poppy was grown in Afghanistan on a relatively limited scale and was largely confined to the hinterlands, places like the remote and mountainous areas of Badakhshan and the southern districts of Nangarhar bordering Pakistan. According to the US (the only country monitoring levels at the time), cultivation in Afghanistan rarely exceeded 18,000 hectares (44,479 ac) during the 1980s. At the same time Myanmar was cultivating more than 140,000 hectares (368,186 ac).

The rise in opium production in Afghanistan compensated for reductions elsewhere due to the revolution in Iran, counternarcotics efforts in Pakistan, and a drought in Myanmar. With the breakdown of state structures and authority in Afghanistan following the Soviet invasion, the conditions were in place for opium production to rise. The crop met a variety of local needs: the need of commanders to have autonomous sources of money, so as not to be totally dependent on the US, Pakistan,

Iran, and other regional powers, and the need of the population for cash incomes at a time of rising inflation and growing violence and insecurity.

The climate in several regions of Afghanistan was also ideal for opium poppy: not too cold during the planting season, enough precipitation in the winter and spring, along with warm clear days and cool nights during the harvest period. The final product is durable and can be easily transported along damaged roads, across borders, and through mountain passes, or stored to wait for prices to rise. Opium was the perfect cash crop for the political and environmental conditions in Afghanistan.

In the late 1980s and the 1990s, opium production began to spread from the mountains and the borders of Afghanistan to the more accessible river valleys. Its expansion was facilitated by the different microclimates in Afghanistan, a growing rural population, and a relatively skilled workforce that was able to move from area to area working the crop. By the late 1990s, when the Taliban had control of all but Panjshir valley and Takhar and Badakhshan provinces in the northeast, it was estimated that there were more than 90,000 cultivated hectares (222,395 ac) of opium poppy. Small-scale laboratories processing morphine and heroin could be found in most of the provinces where the crop was grown.

At that stage, the drug economy produced a limited amount of money. The price of opiates in Afghanistan was low—around $30 a kilogram for raw opium purchased at the farmgate—and the trade was not subject to any harsh measures of control. It was a fairly competitive industry, without huge profit margins.

It became much more profitable, first, when the Taliban banned the production of opium poppy, which created shortages, and then when the new government with its foreign backers implemented counter-narcotics policies. Those policies failed to eliminate or even reduce the narcotics economy, but they required producers and traders to seek political protection. What had been a fairly competitive, decentralized industry now began to become more concentrated, and the main actors depended on their relationships with officials in the government and neighboring countries. The search for protection from counter-narcotics policies became a chief motor of corruption.

Who benefits from the narcotics industry?

The real profit is in the trafficking of opiates outside Afghanistan. The price of opium in Afghanistan in the spring of 2018 was around US$60 to US$80 per kilogram, and the price of the best-quality heroin was US$2,000. In Iran the heroin price would nearly triple to US$5,800. By the time it got to Istanbul, that same kilogram would be worth around US$15,000, and across the Black Sea in Romania US$22,000. By the time the heroin was smuggled into Germany, it would be worth US$35,000, and once in the UK, as much as US$40,000. Diluted and sold on the streets of London, that heroin might sell for the equivalent of $74,000 per kilogram.

Those who control the market from production to retail— as did the Colombian cocaine cartels of the 1980s and early 1990s—can gain riches and power that can threaten the state. In Afghanistan, however, there is no equivalent. Afghan traders and traffickers typically transport opiates across the border, where they are sold on to other foreign or transnational criminal organizations. Inside the country, the profits on heroin production can be as little as US$70 per kilogram, and where poor-quality opium is combined with an inexperienced "cook," losses will be made.

Therefore the greatest profit in Afghanistan lies in bulk production and transporting opiates across the border. Armed groups that protect the trade, whether in the government, the Taliban, or a criminal group, receive payments or "taxes." These are typically negotiated and leveled at a rate that is not punitive—often less than 2 percent, since many of these armed groups do not wield absolute power and may require the support of traders at a later date.

The farmer benefits least from opium. Those with sufficient land and labor in a well-irrigated area of central Helmand earned a profit of up to $1,125 per jerib (one-fifth of a hectare) of opium poppy in 2016. Those who were landless and worked on the land of others for a share of the final crop earned only US$350 per jerib. Net earnings from opium poppy were less than $1 for each day worked for those without land, and just over $3 per day for the landed.

Do farmers make more from opium poppy than they could from other crops?

There are other crops potentially more profitable than poppy. Saffron, apricots, pomegranates, grapes, and in some years, even wheat can generate a higher net return than opium poppy. Opium poppy is an input-intensive crop that requires land preparation, fertilizers, and water—a lot if the farmer is to obtain a good yield—as well as considerably more labor than any other crop. These inputs, particularly the labor, can be expensive and cut deep into profits. If farmers cannot obtain these inputs at a low cost, they can end up losing money, especially if they are also compelled to pay local officials to avoid the destruction of their opium crop.

But it is important to look beyond crop-by-crop comparisons. Where they can, Afghan farmers engage in a number of activities, including sending someone from the family to work on other people's farms or in the city. A mix of crops—particularly a combination of short-season vegetables and fruits—can also yield higher income to a farmer than one poppy crop. When combined with a member of the family running a shop, working for the army or police, or working in a skilled job such as construction—things they would not have the time to do if they were busy in their poppy fields—incomes can be much higher than were the family to continue with opium production.

The challenge is that this mix of opportunities is a function of location, wealth, and family size and composition. Those located close to a city or district center who have land and sons of working age will find it much easier to find work and sell licit produce. They are also more vulnerable to losing their opium crop to law enforcement based in the city and district centers. Farther away from the centers of the state and market, particularly in the mountains or deserts, there is neither the risk of eradication, the opportunities to sell other crops and find work, nor the government services—like healthcare—that can reduce the high costs a family incurs when a member is sick.

In such areas, opium is an economic lifeline. It is less susceptible to crop failure during drought—a relatively common phenomenon in Afghanistan; it can still yield usable product when struck by disease; it has an almost guaranteed demand in local, regional, and international markets; traders will purchase the crop at the farmgate, mitigating against the costs and risks of transporting it along insecure, unmaintained roads; and it is subject to an international prohibition regime and domestic counter-narcotics policies that, although ineffective, inflate its value.

How did the Taliban suppress poppy cultivation in 2001?

The Taliban suppressed poppy cultivation in 2001 using a combination of threats, rewards, and promises of future assistance. Previous attempts by the Taliban to ban opium had come to nothing. Prohibition was successfully implemented only when the Taliban had consolidated their position in the countryside and cities, some five-and-a-half years after they had taken the southern region including the province of Helmand, the country's most prolific opium producer. They also implemented the ban when opium prices were particularly low, in the midst of a drought, and while wheat prices were rising.

Imposing a ban on opium without provoking rural unrest required planning and a steady hand. It needed the support of key tribes, such as the Shinwaris in Nangarhar, who lived in the areas that are among the first to plant. Leaders of these tribes were convinced to cooperate through gifts, threats, and the offer of future international development assistance. Their compliance sent a message to those in lower-lying areas where resistance to the Taliban's ban would be more difficult.

The ban proved short-lived, lasting only one year. Where Western powers saw strength and the projection of power, the local population saw a Taliban that negotiated with the more influential tribes and imposed a ban contingent on future development support that they could not deliver.

The ban imposed significant costs on the rural population. Opium prices went up more than tenfold in the year that opium was banned. Many farmers had debts that were denominated in opium, so that a debt of one kilogram of opium worth $40 at the beginning of that year amounted to $400 at the end of that year. Some repaid by selling their livestock, their possessions, and their land, or by agreeing to marry daughters as young as eight to the family of their creditors. Others were saddled with debts for years to come. The ongoing drought, the failing economy, and the absence of meaningful donor response to the ban increased tensions in those rural areas most affected by the Taliban's suppression of opium.

Even if there had not been any September 11 and the international intervention, it seems unlikely that the Taliban would have been able to continue to enforce a ban on poppy. It was not a good model for a long-term, successful counter-narcotics policy.

By increasing rural poverty and resentment against the authorities, the ban also played a part in the Taliban's downfall. It was easier for the US and Western powers to gain popular support to drive the Taliban from power following the ban than had there been a buoyant economy, something the governments that have followed have been very much aware of when making their policy choices in counter-narcotics.

What is the goal of counter-narcotics policy?

Counter-narcotics is a particularly complex area of policy, in that there is a goal that policy makers desire to achieve, as defined by various United Nations treaties, but there is no set of agreed and delineated counter-narcotics interventions by which to achieve it. The challenge in counter-narcotics policy is not just an issue of disagreements over the different means by which an end might be met; it is also a function of a much broader conceptual debate about how societies and institutions respond to complex social phenomena that are beyond the reach, resources, and mandate of a single institution.

For example, if we were to take the legal interpretation of counter-narcotics policy, then the end state would be to reduce the supply and consumption of illegal narcotic drugs. Yet, in most countries there is considerable debate about how this might best be done, or indeed whether this is the right goal, and whether a more realistic one is to reduce the harm that drug production, trafficking, and consumption do to individuals, communities, and the wider society.

In Afghanistan, the debate over counter-narcotics was all the more complicated by the other pressing policy priorities that the country faced. These included countering the insurgency, strengthening the legitimacy of the government, reducing endemic corruption, and mitigating the levels of poverty experienced by the population. There continue to be genuine concerns as to whether counter-narcotics efforts will support these priorities or undermine them.

Moreover, the tools at the disposal of what is referred to as the counter-narcotics community—international bodies such as the United Nations Office on Drugs and Crime (UNODC), US institutions such as the Bureau of International Narcotics and Law Enforcement Affairs (INL) of the Department of

State, and the Drug Enforcement Administration (DEA); as well as Afghan organizations, such as the Ministry of Counter Narcotics (MCN), and the Counter Narcotics Police Agency (CNPA) in the Ministry of the Interior—were very limited. The levers by which to achieve the kind of wider social change required to address the widespread production, trade, and use of drugs lay with an array of other institutions, with far greater reach and resources, the most important being the institutions responsible for security within the country and on its borders, as well as those charged with Afghanistan's economic and social development.

Many institutions from several countries involved in both security and development efforts did not want to engage in counter-narcotics, let alone factor it into their own policies and planning. The most important organization responsible for security policy was the US Department of Defense, which for many years resisted efforts to include counter-narcotics objectives in its mission, believing it would undermine military goals. The pursuit of al-Qaeda and the Taliban required alliances with power brokers who had a long-standing involvement with the drug trade. Some of these individuals were armed allies in the "war on terror," became officials of the new government, and/or were local partners in counterinsurgency efforts. Their involvement in drugs was tolerated in pursuit of military and political objectives, much to the frustration of those pursuing counter-narcotics goals in Afghanistan.

This was not Colombia, where the US Department of Defense was in the backseat to the Department of State, and was keen to support counter-narcotics efforts as a way of maintaining resources and relevance following the end of the Cold War. Afghanistan was and continues to be DoD's lead and in the words of General David Barno, commander of Combined Forces Afghanistan between 2003 and 2005, after an empty drug lab was destroyed in January 2004: "I don't want counter-narcotics getting in the way of things."

While this reluctance to engage in counter-narcotics dissipated at the most senior level with the departure of Secretary of Defense Donald Rumsfeld in 2006, the aversion that combat commanders felt could still be found well into the surge of 2010–14, where the DEA and other law enforcement officials would often have to convince an ever-changing military leadership in the Regional Commands of the efficacy of counter-narcotics efforts. The Afghan Ministry of Defense mirrored its colleagues in DoD, showing an unwillingness to provide support to annual eradication efforts, despite instruction from the highest levels of the Afghan government.

Development donors were almost as reluctant as the military to see their missions compromised by counter-narcotics. From the start USAID, the largest single bilateral development donor, was averse to pursuing the kind of alternative development projects that it had undertaken in Latin America, which it believed had shown little evidence of success. Ultimately the agency had to fall in line following the rise in cultivation in 2004 and pressure from US Department of State and the US ambassador to Kabul at the time. However, it did so reluctantly and never fully engaged in operationalizing policies and programs that integrated an understanding of the causes of opium poppy cultivation.

Instead, USAID focused on efforts to support growth in the legal agricultural economy, not recognizing that the legal economy might not always crowd out the illegal economy, and that both economies might grow in parallel. Some of the programs USAID supported served to increase cultivation by providing improved irrigation or as in the case of the Helmand Food Zone—wheat seed and fertilizer mixed with a threat of eradication—led to farmers relocating to former desert areas and cultivating even more poppy there. This response to the Helmand Food Zone was entirely foreseeable by those with an understanding of land tenure in central

Helmand and the different labor inputs required for wheat and poppy.

USAID's national partners within the Afghan government, the development ministries, were also averse to counter-narcotics. They saw counter-narcotics as a deeply contested policy area where even the donors could not agree on how it should best be addressed or what priority drug control should be given. There were also fundamental disagreements over attempts by agencies like INL and UNODC to make development assistance to communities contingent on reductions in opium poppy cultivation. For MRRD (the Ministry of Rural Rehabilitation and Development) and its international donors in the World Bank, DFID (UK Department for International Development), and the EC (European Commission), "conditionality" was counterproductive: weakening the social contract between a state and its population, not strengthening it. Development agencies were not in a position to withdraw aid from impoverished rural communities because some or all of them persisted with poppy—this was not their mandate and in some cases would not even have been legal.

To avoid being drawn into these discussions, many development agencies followed the lead of USAID and focused on efforts to expand the licit economy regardless of what might happen to the cultivation, trade, and consumption of opium and its derivatives. They left so-called alternative development efforts—rural interventions directly aimed at reducing poppy cultivation—to drug control organizations like INL and UNODC.

The post-2001 policy environment in Afghanistan was crowded. It was full of many agencies each with different mandates, resources, and understandings of the international efforts. Those responsible for delivering on counter-narcotics were not only not in the lead in Afghanistan but were also relatively minor players with few resources, particularly when

compared with those responsible for development and security. Counter-narcotics agencies such as UNODC and INL required the resources and the political and operational support
of far more powerful and better-resourced agencies, but their
failure to present a convincing picture of how countering the
illicit drug economy in Afghanistan could be effectively integrated into the mandates of other agencies in order to support
the overall mission in Afghanistan, as well as an unwillingness
to compromise on their goal of reducing cultivation, did little
to build the kind of partnership required.

**What policies did the international community and Afghan
government pursue against narcotics, and what has been
the result?**

Counter-narcotics policy includes programs in four areas: (1) alternative development: rural development projects designed to
reduce production by providing alternative sources of farm income; (2) eradication: the destruction of the standing crop; (3) interdiction: the arrest and prosecution of those involved in the
production and trafficking of drugs and the money associated
with it; and finally, (4) demand reduction: efforts to raise aware-
ness of the harm of drug use and provide treatment in order to
reduce the demand for illicit drugs.

Afghanistan, however, was no typical drug-producing
country. Around 90 percent of the world's illicit opium production was grown in Afghanistan, and narcotics was (and is) the
country's largest industry except for the war. Moreover, the crop
was not grown only in the boondocks as in other drug crop-
producing nations, but just outside cities and alongside highways. By 2004 it was found in each of the country's thirty-four
provinces.

In 2002 there were no functioning law enforcement institutions to work with. As an international law enforcement expert
with long-term experience in the region noted, while reviewing
the then Counter-narcotics Department of the National Police,

"the Police stations were gutted, there was nothing in the provinces at all." In Kabul officers "had no equipment, no radios and used their own vehicles."[1]

This was not an environment for the kind of discrete area-based alternative development projects used in countries like Colombia, Peru, or Pakistan, nor could the DEA run programs with national partners as in Latin America and Pakistan. As Rand Beers, assistant secretary of state for INL, argued at a donors' conference in Brussels in December 2001, there was a need to emphasize reconstruction and development rather than drug control per se.

Implementing counter-narcotics policies in Afghanistan was also quite different than in other drug-producing nations. This was a multilateral mission under the auspices of the United Nations and, from 2003, NATO. While the US was by far the biggest contributor of military might and funding, policy also required the support of allies and the new government. This was not a bilateral mission like Colombia where the US could dictate terms and press aerial eradication upon the government. It needed to get others on board.

The development architecture was also very different. Counter-narcotics was one of several sector-based interventions in which Western nations and multilateral institutions supported reform across entire areas of government delivery. Sectoral assistance often took the form of both technical support to central ministries in Kabul and funding delivery of national development programs. While the UK had been designated lead nation for counter-narcotics as part of the Security Sector Reform program (see chapter 6), much of the assistance went through the World Bank, which took the lead in the design and oversight of the National Priority Programs (NPPs) and was administered the Afghan Reconstruction Trust Fund (ARTF; see chapter 7). Many rural areas in Afghanistan were

1. SIGAR, "Counter-Narcotics Lessons from the US Experience in Afghanistan," 40n234.

also congested with multiple agencies and initiatives. Drug control organizations like UNODC could not set apart areas where they could implement sectoral programs tied to reductions in opium production as they had done formerly in Afghanistan and other source countries. The debate over the sequencing of crop destruction and development dominated discussions for more than a decade. Both INL and UNODC wanted to destroy the crop, regardless of the development conditions on the ground, and had little time for those who talked of poverty and gender. They saw development advocates as apologists for poppy cultivators. Explaining that a campaign of widespread crop destruction without changing the conditions that led to cultivation was counterproductive fueled the antagonism of INL officials. They lived in a black-and-white world of legality and illegality, and had little tolerance for analyzing the causes of production or waiting for development programs to deliver. They—and their bosses in Washington—wanted dramatic reductions in cultivation quickly and believed alternative development programs could come in later to deal with the consequences.

Nor did the military escape the scorn of those driving the drug control effort; they dismissed the legal constraints on the use of military force in law enforcement operations. It became an aim of INL to bring the military on board, at least to provide the air support required. By 2006, Gen. Dan McNeill, commander of US forces and NATO in Afghanistan, directly linked poppy cultivation with insurgency funding. By 2008 NATO's Operations Plan was changed to include support for counter-narcotics law enforcement efforts if the targets were tied to the insurgency.

It had been a long time coming. Those in DoD who were tasked since 2003 with building drug-control capacity in Afghanistan (the Office of Counter-narcotics and Global Threats, CNGT), had become adept at finding opportunities to work in Afghanistan, despite senior leadership concerns. With far greater flexibility than the Department of State, they had helped fund the establishment of specialist units in the Counter Narcotics Police of Afghanistan (CNPA) as well as a Special Mission Wing. With the inputs of the DEA, and alongside parallel specialist counter-narcotics units established by the UK, the interdiction capacity of the Afghan authorities increased.

Conscious that the corrupt and politicized Afghan judicial system often failed to follow up arrests of major traders with effective prosecution, the UK and US also funded the Criminal Justice Task Force (CJTF) and Counter Narcotics Justice Center (CNJC). To bypass the judicial system entirely. The DEA also established Foreign-deployed Advisory and Support Teams (FAST) which, along with the UK's Afghanistan Special Narcotics Force, or Task Force-333, undertook paramilitary-style raids on drug labs and traders, with the intent of disruption rather than collecting evidence and intelligence that would lead to prosecutions. In 2010, as Obama's surge increased resources for interdiction, seizures increased from 79 metric tons in 2009 to 98 metric tons in 2011.

This did not last for long. Transition reduced the availability of military support that these special units needed to operate. Furthermore, some of the investigations touched on political actors within the Afghan state, leading to recriminations from President Karzai. Some of the infrastructure required for investigations such as wiretaps, polygraphs, and foreign mentoring were curtailed by the president while growing insecurity in Kabul and the provinces also prevented their deployment.

In a bid to avoid the military and development community's concerns about eradication, parts of the US, the UK, and Afghan governments tried to deter planting, as had the Taliban in 2001. Despite talk of incentives and compensation for losses that farmers experienced by forgoing poppy cultivation, in reality farmers were coerced not to plant as they had been by the Taliban authorities in the fall of 2000. While political elites at the provincial, district, and local level were given favors and the promise of future assistance, farmers were threatened with arrest and crop destruction.

Such campaigns were launched in Nangarhar twice, in late 2004 and 2007, in Balkh in the fall of 2006, and in late 2008 in Helmand, under the title of the Helmand Food Zone. Provincial governors oversaw implementation. Governors would travel to the far reaches of the province to tell villagers that planting would lead to arrest, and restraint would be rewarded with development assistance.

In each province, cultivation fell dramatically in the initial years of these campaigns, reducing levels of production, for which both the governors and the PRTs claimed credit in Helmand and Nangarhar. Balkh was poppy free from 2007 until 2013, Nangarhar achieved the same in 2008 and persisted with low levels of cultivation until 2011. In Helmand cultivation fell from 103,000 ha (254,518 ac) in 2008 to 63,000 ha (155,676 ac) in 2011.

Each of these campaigns benefited—as had the Taliban ban—from being launched when opium prices were low and wheat prices rising. Increasing the perceived risk of cultivation in the minds of farmers was also common. In Nangarhar and Helmand there was significant gain from the increase in foreign and national military presence and their involvement in getting the message out about farmer restraint. Governor Atta in Balkh succeeded in exerting his influence over the Afghan Army and local political structures, and in later years gained considerable influence over the local police; all of which served to reinforce the message that the threat of arrest and eradication was real. Crop destruction was used with restraint, often done early after planting, to allow farmers to plant something else, and targeted in areas where elders had already been co-opted through gifts, the promise of assistance, and the odd threat.

An uptick in economic activity often accompanied these campaigns. In Nangarhar and Helmand an increase in the foreign military presence was accompanied by an inflow of development assistance. The problem was it was never enough. It is impossible to simply replace the opium economy of a province where cultivation is in the tens of thousands of hectares in a single year. While those farmers who have the resources move on to other things—send a son to work in the bazaar, grow other crops, sell some livestock and start a business—others cannot. These farmers grow wheat, become hungry, and grow resentful that they received only a couple of bags of wheat seed and some fertilizer. They watch as the village elder, who had agreed to the ban in the first place and received gifts and kudos from the governor, receives more than his share of agricultural inputs, alongside other projects, like a new well, a flood protection wall around his land, a tube well, some saplings for an orchard, and help in starting a tailor shop.

As the ban goes on, and the development assistance fails to improve the standard of living of many of those who have shown restraint, each year more coercion is required to sustain low levels of cultivation. Initially the crop returns to remote areas. Sometimes the provincial leadership forgets the negotiated nature of its power and the history of resistance in these communities and goes in heavy-handedly to eradicate the crop. They forget that rural communities are political actors capable of shaping their own terrain.

When the authorities do forget—as in the district of Sherzad in Nangarhar in 2010—they can lose the fragile hold they have over some of the remote rural areas. Solders were injured and killed and had to retreat in the face of armed revolt. Yet, a more measured response, one fearful of violent backlash, that allows poppy to continue but perhaps with some eradication just for the cameras, also exposes the weakness of state power. With the routing of the state, the perceived risk of cultivation begins to lessen. The elders who agreed to the ban change their position or leave the village, and more farmers return to growing poppy.

In this situation there is very little that can be done. Political commitment—a common criticism leveled at the Afghan leadership by the drug-control community—means little when political power rests more on consensus and argument than military might. As then-president Karzai told a consultative jirga observed by Western diplomats and others (including Rubin) in April 2005, "Do not expect that I can go again in front of the people of Afghanistan and tell them not to grow poppies—they will either laugh at me or shoot me."[2]

Why not just buy all the opium from the farmers?

There were often suggestions either to buy the opium crop and burn it or legalize it for medicinal purposes. Ultimately, however, as long as there are no viable economic alternatives to opium for the farmer, and the Afghan state cannot guarantee a monopoly over the purchase of the crop, buying up the crop—for whatever purpose—would increase the demand for opium, and hence the farmgate price, leading to higher levels of cultivation in following years. The Afghan state, NATO, or the US could never guarantee that they could purchase the entire opium crop; without this guarantee farmers could grow it for sale to both authorized buyers and illegal traffickers.

Purchasing the crop would boost the illicit opium economy rather than other crops and sources of income. The next year the cost of buying the crop would rise dramatically, making the entire exercise a huge waste of public resources.

By way of comparison, India is the fourth-largest producer of illicit opiates in the world, after Afghanistan, Myanmar, and Laos. Most of India's illicit production is leaked from licensed cultivation. If the Indian government cannot guarantee it is the sole purchaser of the licit opium crop there, and as much as 30 percent of the crop leaks into the illegal market, what level of diversion would take place in Afghanistan?

2. US Embassy Kabul, "Security Sector Reform Coordination Committee Meeting on Counternarcotics," Cable Kabul 001419, April 19, 2005.

What crop can substitute for poppy?

Crop substitution is very much "old school," but it permeates policy discussions to this day. How about apricots, saffron, grapes, pomegranates, canola, even cannabis? These crops and so many more, including wheat, have been suggested as substitutes to opium since 2001.

Some of these crops can generate more net income than opium poppy, but most of those that can do so on a consistent basis require investments in inputs such as trellising, pesticides, and herbicides, and require several years before they mature and yield an income, raising concerns over what a farmer will earn in the interim. Some crops may be fragile and require improved roads, packaging, or cold storage. Other crops may require extension and market support to improve quality and hygiene standards so they can be exported—which takes even more time and the support of regulation in consumer markets in the region and beyond.

Many of these crops will provide an income to the landed but offer little to no income to the numerous sharecroppers or tenants on farms growing opium poppy. When the landowner starts to grow pomegranates, grapes, or wheat, the land-poor will have to look for land elsewhere to grow opium. This happened in Helmand, where reductions in poppy cultivation in the Helmand Food Zone were more than matched by growth in former desert areas irrigated by the land-poor. The Helmand Food Zone increased the capacity of the province to grow opium to the point where 144,000 ha (355,832 ac) were grown in 2017, up from 104,000 ha (256,990 ac) in 2008, the year before the Helmand Food Zone began.

Supporting the cultivation of crops cited as possible alternatives to opium has a role in encouraging farmers to move away from poppy cultivation, but it is not sufficient. There is a need for a much broader economic strategy, which includes improving job opportunities and access to land for the poor. All of this has to take place within a secure environment where the population is confident that it will benefit from long-term agricultural investments, where it can travel to and from markets in cities and towns without being subject to predation and violence from the government or other armed actors, and where investments in social infrastructure, such as health and education, can reduce vulnerabilities to chronic illness and death.

Do drugs support terrorism in Afghanistan?

The ideological construct of "narcoterrorism" relies on the belief that drugs and terrorism are symbiotic and inherently related. Much of the debate on narcoterrorism focuses on the potential revenue that terrorist groups earn from the drug trade to purchase weapons and pursue their political objectives.

Official narratives, especially those of the drug-control community, argue that over time and increased exposure to the drug trade, many of these groups lose any political ideology that they may have had and become criminal organizations. This was the narrative associated with Khun Sa and his secessionist Shan United Army (later Mong Tai Army) in Myanmar in the 1980s, and with the FARC in Colombia in the 1990s and early twenty-first century.

We can see the same argument at work in the words of officials and in the media covering Afghanistan: the Taliban and the drug trade are viewed as synonymous. This was never more so than in November 2017 when the United States Forces Afghanistan (USFOR-A) began a bombing campaign targeting drug labs. At the time General Nicholson, the commander of USFOR-A and NATO's Resolute Support, argued that the Taliban had "evolved into a narco-insurgency," suggesting they had "increasingly lost whatever ideological anchor they once had." This was only weeks after William Brownfield, the assistant secretary of state for INL, had stated, "I pretty firmly feel [the Taliban] are processing all the [opium] harvest," and after UNODC had reported a truly unprecedented level of cultivation of 328,000 hectares (810,506 ac).[3]

Despite the claims of General Nicholson, the relationship between the Taliban and the drug economy is more nuanced and localized; it always was, even in the 1990s when the Taliban were in Kabul and dominated 90 percent of the country's territory.

Insurgent groups like the Taliban often rely on local sources of revenue. In the 1990s much was made of the collection of the agricultural tithe known as 'ushr. This is a traditional tax paid on all agricultural produce, at a rate of 10 percent of gross production. In the 1990s this was typically paid to the village mullah. Payments could be made in kind as a proportion of the yield of the different crops that households grew, including opium, or this amount could be converted into cash. The claim was that once an area came under the Taliban's control, it was they who collected the 'ushr, not the mullah, and in doing so the Taliban collected 10 percent of the entire opium crop in any given year. We have heard the very same claims since the Taliban resurgence in 2005-6.

However, the idea that an armed and often disparate grouping like the Taliban can run a uniform tax policy across the country appears rather naïve. The Taliban did not achieve this in the 1990s, when efforts to absorb the agricultural tithe were rejected by mullahs in the southern provinces, and to no surprise they still did not have a formalized national system in place by 2018.

In practice, payments at the farmgate were rarely more than 2 percent of the value of the crop and often as low as 1 percent. Punitive tax rates would do little to win the support of a rural population. Moreover, as many from the Taliban were local fighters, they had to tread carefully with their relatives

3. Andrew Cockburn, "Mobbed Up: How America Boosts the Afghan Opium Trade," *Harpers*, April 2018.

and neighbors were they to find themselves on the losing side in the future and in need of succor. The same relatively low rates of tax could be seen on the production and trade of drugs. Furthermore, rates on both opium and heroin were fixed, regardless of price.

The relationship between the Taliban and the drug trade is not intrinsically any different from that with other goods and services, except that the drug trade is Afghanistan's most valuable export and can therefore generate greater revenues.

What does make the opium economy stand out from other goods and services is its illegality and consequently the obligation on the Afghan government to act. It is here that the Taliban succeeded in exploiting resentment among the rural population toward an Afghan government that was seen to press for crop destruction at the behest of foreign powers, in particular the US, while ignoring the economic conditions of the people. This sense of betrayal was exacerbated by the threat to spray the crop.

When combined with the failure to improve licit livelihoods, the rural population in provinces like Helmand, Farah, Kandahar, and Nangarhar began to look at the Afghan government as a threat to their welfare. They saw the government placing the interests of foreign powers ahead of the Afghan population.

Some Taliban commanders have been directly involved in the drug business, as they have also engaged in the trade of other commodities, such as gemstones and marble. It is however quite different to argue that a movement of multiple commanders actually controls the drug trade and has purely criminal intent. It is this narrative of a centralized and criminal Taliban, compounded by what is seen as a selective representation of the Afghan government as merely corrupt, which is so often out of sync with what the rural population sees.

Farmers see government officials extract payments from them in exchange for not destroying their crop, and offer protection to some of those most involved in the drug trade, by arranging their shipments in police vehicles, obstructing prosecutions, and offering them amnesty, or having them moved to provincial prisons so that they can bribe their way out. The population has seen international military forces and diplomatic staff show deference and support to provincial and national officials who farmers see deeply entrenched in the drug trade. It should perhaps be no surprise that to be told that these are the "good guys," and that it is the insurgents who are criminals and the masterminds of the drug trade arouses deep suspicions among the population.

What is the relationship of the narcotics industry to the Afghan government?

The narcotics industry could not survive without protection from parts of the Afghan government, and some power holders in the Afghan government could not function without the money and patronage from the narcotics industry. Accusations of government involvement are widespread, and as noted earlier, it is a widely held belief among the rural population that the government is more deeply involved in the drug trade than the Taliban.

Allegations have been made against a wide range of government officials, most notably the late brother of the former president Karzai, Ahmad Wali Karzai. Similar claims were made about Gul Aga Sherzai, former governor of Kandahar and Nangarhar; the late Marshal Fahim Khan, once minister of defense and vice president; Atta Mohammed Noor, former governor of Balkh; Sher Mohammed Akhundzada, senator for Helmand and former governor of the province; Haji Abdul Zahir Qadir, former deputy speaker of parliament and border police commander for Takhar; as well as the late Abdul Raziq Achakzai, security chief of Kandahar.

Such claims are hard to verify. Other than a few individuals within the government who have been caught red-handed, what we are often left with is supposition; for officials not to patronize the largest local industry would be political suicide.

What are the most important areas of cultivation?

Cultivation is heavily concentrated in the south and south-west of the country, but as of 2018, poppy was grown in all but nine of Afghanistan's thirty-four provinces. The province of Helmand has consistently been the most prolific producer of opium. Typically the province has grown almost the same amount of opium poppy as the rest of the country. In 2018, for example, 144,000 hectares of opium were grown in Helmand out of a total of 328,000 hectares for the country as a whole.

Since 2001, Helmand has consistently been followed in rankings by neighboring Kandahar and the other southern provinces of Uruzgan and Nimroz. The province of Farah in the southwest has also been a major producer of opium in recent years and, like its neighbors, has been a popular location for processing. These four provinces combined were often responsible for around 80 percent of total cultivation in any given year since 2005.

A new entrant into the ranks of the top opium producing provinces was the northern province of Badghis, ranking third after Helmand and Kandahar in 2016. Explanations for such a meteoric rise could be found in the growing insecurity in the districts of Bala Murgab and Ghormach, and also in tribal links to the southern provinces of Uruzgan, Helmand, and Kandahar. Many inhabitants of Badghis are Ishaqzais and other Pashtuns from Helmand resettled in the north by Amir Abdul Rahman Khan and his successors. Farmers from those tribes in Badghis sought refuge back in Helmand during the drought that hit the province in the late 1990s and subsequently in 2008. As share-croppers and laborers in the south they learned about opium poppy cultivation, bringing the seeds, the knowledge, and the harvesting tools back to Badghis.

Nangarhar province in the east has a strong tradition of production, but cultivation and processing have waxed and waned since 2004. As a major entrepot for trade between Pakistan and Afghanistan, and in particular for NATO supplies, it was of key interest to US military forces. It was also the route by which al-Qaeda and the Taliban escaped from US forces in November 2001 and therefore where the US focused its military efforts in the early part of the war.

By 2004 the US had established one of the country's first PRTs in Nangarhar. When opium cultivation began to rise dramatically during the initial years of the campaign, the US and other donors put pressure on the government of Afghanistan and the provincial authorities in Nangarhar to deter poppy planting in late 2004. As with the Taliban ban of 2001 they succeeded in the short term, but cultivation soon rose again. By 2007 there were more than 18,000 hectares of poppy (44,479 ac) cultivated in the province.

Between 2008 and 2010 the US military and development effort, economic growth, and the governor Sherzai's political ambition kept the poppy at bay. Cultivation crept back into the hills of the southern borderlands, but it was kept out of the lower valleys, where landholdings were larger and cultivation could be more extensive.

There is only so much coercion that a relatively cohesive population with a long history of resisting state intrusion will tolerate, particularly in the absence of a viable alternative to opium. What started as acts of resistance to eradication soon become rebellion, and by 2012 the Taliban were entrenched in the southern districts. By 2014 and the departure of US forces, cultivation had once again risen to around 18,000 hectares. By 2017 it was found in all but six of the provinces, twenty-two districts, and adjacent to the Jalalabad-Torkham highway.

Most recently the province saw another downward turn in cultivation, this time at the behest of Islamic State Khorasan Province (ISKP), which kept cultivation at bay for two years, imposing a total ban on opium and cannabis production when it wrested control of some mountainous districts from the Taliban in the summer of 2015. It achieved this by driving the local population out of the valleys through acts of brutality. Ultimately it is far easier to impose a ban on poppy cultivation when neither the movement nor the population depend on the crop for a livelihood, and when those controlling the valley are not trying to gain favor, food, or fighters from the local population. Given past experiences with prohibition, the ban on opium in the upper reaches of Achin by the ISKP said much about the foreign nature of the movement and its external sources of finance.

Why is Afghanistan the center of world heroin production, and how can this change?

Afghanistan has the ideal conditions: the climate is perfect for opium production; there is an abundance of relatively cheap labor to work the crop; there are few other legal economic opportunities for a burgeoning rural population; the international intervention has improved the country's access to new technologies such as solar panels, mobile phones, and transportation; the government has little control over its territory and is viewed by many with antipathy; government institutions are weak, and corruption is endemic; and, finally, there is an ongoing insurgency that needs support from the rural population and funding for its fight against the government and international forces.

What will change this? The answer does not come in the form of saffron, apricots, grapes, or pomegranates. Nor does it come with buying the crop to burn it or turn it into medicine. Massive eradication will not fix it. The answer lies with the long, hard slog of building a stable Afghan government that can secure its territory and borders and provide an economic environment where the population can diversify its agricultural base and move into nonfarm income. This is not a counter-narcotics strategy but a development strategy in a drug environment. It does not fit neatly into the mandate of drug control budgets, mandates, and institutions, and it requires collective ownership, and a deep understanding of the operational space and trade-offs. It may be too much to ask, given how governments operate.

What are the main sources of corruption in Afghanistan other than narcotics?

There is one ingredient that is required by all forms of corruption, and that is money. Without money, you cannot corrupt people. Hence the biggest source of corruption in Afghanistan is the money spent by international actors. The way that one prevents money from causing corruption is by spending it through institutions and procedures that are understood, monitored, and transparent. The way that the US and other foreign aid donors and troop contributors have spent money has included throwing around large amounts of cash without knowing exactly how it is spent or by whom.

One way to reduce corruption is to put money in banks and pay salaries and bills via checks or credit cards. In that case, every time you have an expense, there's a record of it. Cash transactions are much less transparent, but in Afghanistan, in 2001, there were only cash transactions, even for transactions of hundreds of millions of dollars. That is still the case for many transactions in Afghanistan.

Such huge expenses on the ground create inflation, so people's salaries soon are worthless. Trying to put huge amounts of money into a system not designed to handle them, where no normative system or institutions can restrain the pressures to profit from a windfall on people whose past sources of livelihood are vanishing, creates corruption. War, insecurity, and corruption go together. Only peace and security will create conditions to marginalize corruption.

9

MORE WAR, INSURGENCY, AND COUNTERINSURGENCY

PRINCIPAL AUTHOR, ANTONIO GIUSTOZZI

How did the insurgency against the Afghan government
and international presence in Afghanistan start?

The Taliban were utterly defeated in 2001 and dispersed among remote villages in Afghanistan and Pakistan; some even sought refuge in Iran. Attempts to negotiate deals with some of the leaders in the north and in the south by leaders of the anti-Taliban coalition (Gen. Dostum and Hamid Karzai) were sabotaged by the American authorities, who refused to recognize such deals. Those Taliban who chose to return to their villages in Afghanistan still hoped that the amnesty promised by President Karzai would be respected. Between late 2001 and the first half of 2002, the Taliban movement had effectively imploded. It had no functioning leadership, and only some sparse groups were still carrying out acts of resistance in isolated pockets, with no external support.

From around mid-2002 the Taliban started gradually coming back together as a result of a number of developments. Initially the main factor was that the amnesty promised by Karzai was only partially applied. Since the new Afghan government could not consolidate its power by taking control of a functioning state, which did not exist, it initially allied with local armed groups funded by the US to fight the Taliban and al-Qaeda. In doing so it was following in the path of most previous Afghan governments, since they too did not possess an administration powerful enough to control the country without alliances with local strongmen. Emboldened by the support of the Americans, the new officials appointed by Karzai indulged in revenge taking against former Taliban, often tipping off US forces intent on seeking remnants of Taliban and al-Qaeda. That prompted a growing number of former Taliban either to move to Pakistan, where most of their leaders already were, or to organize locally to resist.

The new Afghan officials came predominantly from the tribes and communities of the leading figures in the anti-Taliban coalition, and they worked to exclude rival communities to monopolize power and resources. As each favored commander sought to use the money he received to form armed groups and take control of local administration, the strongmen transformed the kinship networks of their tribes into instruments of power. In the south, for instance, the dominance of the Barakzais, Popalzais, Achakzais (a Barakzai branch), and Alokozais meant that other tribes lost out on patronage and could be punished by telling the Americans they were Taliban. These included the Alizai, Nurzai, and Ishaqzai tribes as well as the Ghilzai tribes such as Hotak and Tokhi, from which much of the Taliban leadership was drawn. Mullah Omar, for instance, was Hotak. His successor, Mansur, was Ishaqzai. His successor, Haibatullah, is Nurzai. The one-time military commander Abdul Qayum Zakir is Alizai.

In Pakistan, Taliban leaders started reconnecting to each other, while al-Qaeda and groups of Pakistani Taliban sympathizers were beginning to carry out raids into Afghanistan from Pakistani territory. Resources were scarce at this time, and there was no overall leadership in charge. Gradually some private donors, mostly linked to al-Qaeda initially, and some intelligence agencies (initially Saudi and Pakistani) started offering some support. The Haqqani network was the first to benefit from some external funding already during 2002, while a cluster of Taliban leaders based around Quetta managed to raise some funding from 2003 on. Around these leaders and this funding, the Quetta Shura started shaping up.

As the Taliban leaders started reconnecting, and resources became available, the emerging Quetta Shura tried to reconnect to local Taliban groups throughout Afghanistan and Pakistan. The abuses of the new officials drove local dissidents toward Quetta, which could offer weapons and funds to organize resistance. It took a few years for Quetta to reach out to all of them; by 2007–08 most of them had joined the Quetta Shura, including the Haqqani network, and had recognized it as the leadership of the Taliban. Mullah Omar endorsed the Quetta group early on, even if he never took an active part in running the insurgency and served as a figurehead for only a few years, before falling seriously ill. As the Taliban leadership consolidated, the dominant feeling that drove their actions was anger at their exclusion from the new political settlement in Afghanistan, and the determination to force their own inclusion into it.

Some of the leaders, such as Mullah Dadullah, seem to have believed that a military victory could be achievable. Others, however, saw that the only realistic aim was forcing Kabul to accept a settlement with the Taliban. The Taliban made several other attempts to reach out to the Afghan government. In 2004, a group of Taliban leaders was close to reaching an agreement with Kabul, and the Taliban's demands were quite modest, but the effort collapsed as the Americans refused to offer security guarantees.

The Taliban of 2002–5 could be described as representing the interests of Taliban veterans, seeking inclusion in the political and social life of Afghanistan. There was an ideological influence of al-Qaeda and allied jihadist groups, which were providing considerable help to the Taliban in certain areas, and particularly in the east and southeast, but on the whole global jihadist ideas had little currency within the Taliban of these years. The Taliban at this stage did not have a substantial base of local support anywhere in Afghanistan, except some remote tribal communities in the south (mostly Zabul) and in the southeast (mostly Paktika).

The year 2005 was a turning point for the Taliban. Disappointment with the new government was building up in some parts of the south, and, most importantly, funding from external patrons started building up into tens of millions of dollars. The increase in funding from Pakistan and from the Arab countries of the Persian Gulf might be related to the completion of the Bonn Agreement and the end of the political transition in Afghanistan. As the political system consolidated, negotiating the inclusion of the Taliban seemed to require an increase in pressure. It was also clear that there was little interest in Kabul to consider what Pakistan believed were its national interests. By 2006 the Taliban insurgency was escalating dramatically in the south, helped by the deployment of Western troops (British and Canadians mainly) there. The communities alienated by the central government saw in the deployment a direct threat to their interests (smuggling and drug trade). As a result, for the first time the Taliban gained extensive community support in large tracts of Afghanistan, especially Helmand and Kandahar.

Taliban attempts to expel the British and the Canadians from the south in alliance with local tribes failed, but they still left the Taliban with a massively expanded influence there. At this point the Taliban had reached the critical mass where they could be seen by a whole range of disenfranchised and disgruntled Afghans as a viable opposition movement. The more remote rural communities, for example, were beginning to see the post-2001 setup as not very advantageous for them. Urban Afghans and communities located closer to the cities and more exposed to modern education in the past were benefiting massively, while marginal and remote villages felt increasingly left behind, not least because the better-connected communities were monopolizing investment and aid. The mullahs were a social category who mostly felt it was losing out after 2001, as their influence in society was declining. Some smuggling gangs that were poorly connected with the authorities, often because some rival gangs had preceded them in making deals with government officials, also turned to the revitalized Taliban for protection. The alliance was sanctioned by a fatwa of Mullah Omar, suspending his earlier prohibition of the drug trade.

What are the main centers of the insurgent leadership?

The Taliban leadership and many members went into Pakistan, following the routes of migration and trade that Pashtuns and Baloch have used for centuries. From the south they went into Balochistan Province and then into the port city of Karachi, which has a larger Pashtun population than any city in the world. Pashtun tribes with strong links to Southern Afghanistan predominate in the Quetta area of Balochistan, which became one of the main Taliban hubs inside Pakistan. By 2004 this hub was becoming popularly known as the Quetta Shura, which is a series of structures around the Leadership Council (Rahbari Shura) set up by a handful of Taliban leaders, led by Mullah Baradar.

In parallel and in fact slightly sooner, another hub formed around Miran Shah in North Waziristan, and started being known among Taliban as Miran Shah Shura and more widely as the Haqqani network.

By 2005 a third hub was forming in Peshawar, where Taliban from Eastern Afghanistan had gathered after 2001. This hub was initially weak, because the Taliban emirate had never recruited much there, but by 2008 several Hizb-i Islami networks had decided to join the jihad and become part of the Taliban.

A fourth hub developed in the city of Karachi, closely linked to Quetta, which turned into the rear of the Taliban military machine, partly because it was more secure. Smaller hubs developed gradually anywhere Afghan communities existed, such as throughout Pakistan; in the end there might well have been more than two hundred local shuras of the Taliban.

In later years a new hub formed in Iran, after the Iranian Revolutionary Guards gradually developed closer and closer relations with the Taliban from 2005 on. Initially seeking to obtain intelligence about American activities, the Revolutionary Guards realized that many Taliban commanders and even leaders were not averse to establishing relations with the Iranians, especially if that translated into substantial support. By 2007 the Revolutionary Guards were helping the Taliban develop networks in Western Afghanistan, presumably in order to be able to control and monitor closely Taliban activities there, as well as to use the Taliban for putting pressure on the Americans, whose presence in Afghanistan was becoming more of an irritant to Teheran after President Bush's "axis of evil speech," the declaration of US-Afghan Strategic Partnership in 2005, and the election to the presidency of Mahmoud Ahmadinejad. The relationship intensified year on year, as the Revolutionary Guards worked hard to identify Taliban figures they could work with, mostly in the west but then also in the south and elsewhere. Eventually in 2013 what the Taliban initially knew as the Mashhad Office was established as an extension of the Quetta Shura.

What is the Haqqani network?

The Haqqanis are a family and clan, the historic leader of which was the late Jalaluddin Haqqani. The family is from the Zadran tribe in Khost province, right across the border from North Waziristan. They are named Haqqani because they attended the Haqqania madrasa in Akora Khattak in Pakistan, which is on the grand trunk road between Peshawar and Islamabad and is one of the main centers of Deobandi instruction in Pakistan. Haqqania madrasa in Akora Khattak, and the Darul 'Uloom in Binori Town in Karachi, are the two madrasas that produced most of the Taliban leadership. In fact many Taliban are named Haqqani, and also some non-Taliban, even if they have nothing to do with the network.

Jalaluddin Haqqani started fighting against President Daud of Afghanistan in about 1975. He became, in the course of the war against the Soviets, one of ten commanders whom the United States supplied directly, rather than going through Pakistan, and was very popular with the CIA and other supporters of the war as an effective and ruthless commander. He developed links with al-Qaeda and other global jihadists early on and became a major recipient of their support. In early 1995 the Haqqanis agreed to swear loyalty to Mullah Omar. After the Islamic Emirate established a government based in Kabul, Jalaluddin became the minister of tribes and frontiers. At that time he was not seen as an ally of global jihadists. In 2001, when the ISI was trying to propose moderate Taliban for the leadership, they brought him to Islamabad to talk to the Americans.

After 2001 the Haqqanis became the dominant Taliban group in Southeastern Afghanistan and excelled in asymmetric warfare, an art with which most other Taliban were struggling. In 2006 the Haqqanis took responsibility for opening the Kabul front by carrying out terrorist attacks in the city. They became the main practitioners of suicide bombing within the Taliban. From 2007 on, the Haqqanis started expanding operations beyond the Southeast, especially in Wardak and Ghazni. Soon they were deploying special operations teams to almost everywhere in Afghanistan, essentially taking responsibility for most terrorist and complex attacks carried out by the Taliban.

Jalaluddin's son, Serajuddin, took operational control of the network in 2007; he has closer relations with Arab jihadists than his father. As Serajuddin took over, relations with the Quetta Shura started deteriorating. The Quetta was partially funding the Haqqanis but did not agree to appoint members of the Haqqanis to the leadership structures of the Quetta Shura. Serajuddin demanded a proportional representation in the Leadership Council and in other structures but was offered only token concessions. Serajuddin demanded to take part in any meeting considering important decisions for the Taliban.

This limited "autonomy" may be the reason that the US government has sometimes identified the Haqqanis as a separate insurgent group, which is not accurate.

The partial autonomy of the Haqqanis formally ended in August 2015, when then leader of the Taliban Akhtar Mohammad Mansur appointed Serajuddin as one of his deputies and integrated many other members of the Haqqanis in the structures of the Quetta Shura.

Does the insurgency consist of a small number of extremist leaders allied to al-Qaeda, and a large mass of fighters without ideological motivation?

For a long time American policy makers rejected the idea of reconciliation with Taliban leaders, on the ground that they were connected to al-Qaeda. What was considered to be feasible was to reconcile instead the fighters, who were seen as lacking ideological motivation. In fact some Taliban leaders had close ties to al-Qaeda, and others did not. Among those who had ties, some were being pragmatic and were accepting any help they could get, and others had ideological sympathy for al-Qaeda. No Taliban leader is in any case known to have actively participated in global jihad operations until the Syrian war, but some, like Dost Mohammad (Eastern Afghanistan) and Serajuddin Haqqani helped by providing shelter for the fighters of al-Qaeda and allied organizations.

It is obvious that Taliban leaders tend to be more ideological motivated than their rank-and-file, but what really matters is the quality and commitment of the Taliban's officer corps, that is, the commanders of the combat groups, the shadow governors, and others who lead the insurgency on the ground. The fighters are primarily loyal to the commanders, as became evident during efforts to reconcile them in 2009–14. It is nearly impossible to separate them from the Taliban if their commanders do not quit as well.

While evaluating the loyalty of the Taliban's officer corps to the organization is hard, as a general rule it can be said that the mature Taliban insurgency of post-2009 included two main components: a local insurgency based in the villages and tied to local communities, and mobile insurgent groups with no ties to any specific locality—the so-called out-of area Taliban. This is the same structure that Massoud adopted in Panjshir, and it seems well adapted to the needs of guerrilla warfare in Afghanistan. The mobile units are much more likely to be ideologically motivated, especially their commanders. Often they come from Taliban families, which have already sacrificed for the cause.

The few Taliban who have reconciled with Kabul came by and large from the local Taliban. They often defected as their areas were falling under government control and they were faced with the option of leaving their properties and homes or being detained by the authorities. The local Taliban are likely to tolerate NGOs and even government projects that bring employment and money to the area. Their commanders have to be approved by the Taliban structure, but they too are usually local people.

Before 2001, the Taliban sought US recognition and support and did not support anti-American campaigns or global jihad. The Taliban identify the beginning of their misfortunes with the arrival of the international coalition led by the Americans in 2001. Unsurprisingly, therefore, expelling the "invaders" has always been a major recruitment driver into the Taliban. Cultural friction, abuses, and civilian casualties caused by Western troops fueled resentment, especially within the most conservative quarters of Afghan society where the feeling was widespread that the Westerners were trying to reshape the country in their image. These local factors rather than global Islamist ideology are the main source of Taliban ideology among both leaders and followers.

How important has al-Qaeda been in the insurgency?

After 2001 the relationship between al-Qaeda and the Taliban was initially quite solid, if for no other reason than that al-Qaeda had nowhere else to go, and the Taliban needed any help they could get. Around 2010, however, this relationship started fraying, as al-Qaeda and allied organizations like the IMU got wind of efforts by senior Taliban figures to open talks with the US. Al-Qaeda was not in a position to break with the Taliban, but it started focusing its support on figures and leaders it believed could help stem the tide of reconciliation. These efforts were not fruitful: one of the leaders supported by al-Qaeda for some time was Akhtar Mohammad Mansur, who subsequently became the main promoter of reconciliation.

The death of bin Laden in 2011 changed little. The presence of al-Qaeda has been fluctuating over the years but was always marginal in terms of numbers—a few hundred cadres, tasked to set up a few training camps and to advise some groups of Taliban. Mostly al-Qaeda's influence was exercised through the targeted distribution of funds, and that fluctuated widely depending on what donors to al-Qaeda were willing to pay and what other theaters of operations of al-Qaeda were demanding.

Al-Qaeda had hoped that the NATO transition and US withdrawal in 2014 would allow it to expand its influence and operations in Afghanistan again, helping the Taliban drive to victory and then using Afghanistan as a jumping pad for exporting jihad to the region. Funding to the organization was resurgent because of the Syrian civil war, where al-Qaeda was very active. Instead in 2015 the appearance of the Islamic State in Afghanistan undermined al-Qaeda's plans, turning into a direct challenge to its long-standing bases in the east, and co-opting some long-term allies of the organization, like many Central Asian fighters based in Afghanistan, the front of Dost Mohammed in the east, and eventually even some of the Haqqanis.

Overall al-Qaeda left some ideological legacy in Afghanistan, but it was mostly the Islamic State that reaped the benefits of it. At present al-Qaeda is as weak as ever in Afghanistan, especially in the east where it has had to weather US assaults for many years.

What international support does the insurgency have?

No government has ever admitted publicly to supporting the Taliban after 2001, for obvious reasons. It is also obvious that the Taliban have enjoyed safe haven in Pakistan from 2002 on and more recently in Iran too. There is evidence of Chinese-made weapons being transferred to the Taliban through Pakistan, especially in the east, or of Iranian weapons reaching the Taliban, especially in the west. There is also evidence of Pakistani and Iranian assistance and training. Taliban sources openly talk of large-scale funding (tens of millions of dollars per year) accruing from sources in Pakistan, Iran, and Saudi Arabia, though some of this talk may be boasting. The Taliban's bomb-making expertise was entirely imported from Pakistan, while the Iranians provided more advanced tactical training than the Pakistanis. The extent to which Pakistan committed its own funding to supporting the Taliban is unclear, as it reportedly channeled funding from other sources (chiefly Saudi Arabia).

What are the local sources of funding for the insurgency?

Apart from external support discussed above, the Taliban mounted efforts to raise funds locally, through a system of taxation and of "voluntary contributions." The Taliban tax any economic activity in areas under their influence or control, except when related to education or health. Farmers pay a percentage of their harvest in kind to Taliban, who then use it for their local expenses. Even businesses working for the Afghan government or for Western-funded projects are required to pay taxes to the Taliban. In practice most of the local revenue accruing to the Taliban has come from the drug trade. Part of it was taxes, but mostly it was money contributed by drug smugglers to the Taliban in order to secure their protection, or sometimes to weaken government presence in specific areas. As in any taxation system, preventing massive leakage of funds on their way from the bottom, where they are collected, to the top has always been a problem for the Taliban, as for the government. Whereas external funding tends to accrue directly to the leadership and in particular to the finance commission, taxes change hands several times before they reach the finance commission. Contributions agreed upon behind closed doors between drug smugglers and the Taliban are the most likely to be at least in part embezzled, because their amounts cannot be estimated by the finance commission and therefore leakage is hard to assess. Taliban sources in the finance commission have long been reporting the embezzlement of funds at all levels of the Taliban structure. In practice, most of the contributions raised by the Taliban do not reach the coffers of the central organization. Some of the cash might be used by Taliban commanders and leaders to fund their own groups or fronts, while some others might simply be embezzled for personal benefit. Akhtar Mohammad Mansur was widely criticized within the Taliban for his "investments" in Dubai, estimated before his death at $2 billion by ISAF intelligence. Clearly, these were not savings accruing from his salary as deputy and then successor of the Amir al-Muminin.

What are the objectives of the insurgency. Is negotiation or political settlement possible?

The Taliban do not have today, and perhaps never had, a unified aim. Their polycentric character accentuated as they expanded and incorporated new networks, like the aforementioned Hizb-i Islami groups in the east, and former mujahidin in the west and in the north. They also started recruiting in state schools, as opposed to focusing on religious seminaries (madrasas). As the Taliban movement started becoming more heterogeneous, so did views, perceptions, and aims within it.

The Taliban as a result do not have any clear idea of what a peace settlement should look like, except that they need the exit of foreign troops, an injection of Islam into Afghanistan's institutions, some form of power sharing, and resources to allow them to compete on a par with other political groups.

The majority of the political leaders of the Taliban (those sitting in the Rahbari Shura) have tended to be favorable to some kind of reconciliation talks, even if the character of such reconciliation would probably not resemble what US or Afghan government policy makers are seeking to achieve. Political leaders have a vested interest in aiming for reconciliation, because without it the only possible outcomes are a disintegration of the Afghan state, a defeat of the Taliban, or a military victory of the Taliban. None of these options is very appealing to the Taliban's political leaders, even the third one, because in order to achieve it the political leaders would have to empower some of the Taliban's most capable military minds, individuals like Abdul Qayum Zakir, Qari Baryal, or Serajuddin Haqqani. These individuals have demonstrated Bonapartist tendencies in the past, and the political leaders rightly fear that in the event of a military victory, the Taliban's conqueror of Kabul would take power and marginalize them. These fears have been growing as Mullah Omar, whose personal legitimacy was never questioned within the Taliban, fell sick and eventually died in 2013.

The military leaders, on the other hand, have a vested interest in working against reconciliation, which is what Zakir was doing when he was at the top of the Taliban's Central Military Commission. Typically, his views moderated after he was sacked from the job. After Zakir's departure, the Quetta

Shura's political leadership has tried to ensure that the person in charge of the Taliban's military structure (which means also the bulk of the Taliban's budget) would not be too charismatic or capable.

In practice, keeping the charismatic military commanders away from the driver's seat of the Taliban war machine has been hard. After Akhtar Mansur's efforts to start negotiation with President Ghani collapsed during the summer and autumn of 2015, under Pakistani pressure the Quetta Shura decided to relaunch military operations in spring 2016. To prepare for that, Mansur's deputy Serajuddin Haqqani was given extensive powers to supervise the Taliban's campaigns to capture Afghanistan's cities. Within months Mansur was so fearful of a takeover by Serajuddin that he sought refuge in Iran and negotiated a resumption of Iranian support, to counterbalance Serajuddin's power (bankrolled by Saudi and Pakistani money). Even after Mansur's killing by the US on his return from Iran in May 2016, Serajuddin continued to concentrate massive power within the Quetta Shura's military structure, until he was relieved of his task in spring 2018.

The "jihadism" of the military leaders can therefore be described as being driven by self-interest. It is their way to power, much the same as the political leaders' way to power is negotiations. The dilemma of the political leaders is that if they marginalize the most capable (and dangerous) military leaders, they ensure their power within the Taliban but also lose the military leverage to force the US and Kabul to make the kind of concessions that the Taliban need to accept a peace settlement. If they empower those military leaders, they risk losing control of the Taliban to them. Zakir tried to oust Mansur from the top of the Quetta Shura in 2010–14 (when Mansur was deputy but de facto leader, because Omar was first ailing and then died). Hence there has been a constant pattern within the Taliban of charismatic military leaders being appointed and then sacked: Zakir was fired twice, the second time for good. When then military leader Dadullah was killed in 2007, his followers suspected political leader Mullah Baradar of having a hand in his death—since sacking him might not have been possible because of his power.

In the effort to build a military organization capable of withstanding the American armed forces, however, the Taliban has been using ideological indoctrination extensively to strengthen the motivation of the fighters. It might well end with their mobile units, discussed earlier, becoming an obstacle to reconciliation because of their increasingly strong jihadist leanings. Removing these leanings is likely to be much harder than removing a rogue military leader.

The Taliban say that their goal is the withdrawal of all foreign troops from Afghanistan and the establishment of an Islamic order. However, they have not defined what they mean by an Islamic order. It is noteworthy that they almost always talk of Islamic order, rather of reestablishing the Islamic emirate, because the suggestion is that there might be some scope for incorporating other groups and parties, as long as the Islamic character of government is preserved. Invitations to the old mujahidin to join the jihad have in fact been repeatedly issued by the Taliban, not without some tactical success. In a nutshell the Taliban seem to have been inclined toward some kind of reconciliation with parties and groups that at least support the aim of Islamizing the Afghan government. That would make reconciliation acceptable even to the Taliban hardliners, although perhaps not to the Americans and Western-leaning Afghans.

By 2018 the Taliban's leaders were aware of the risk that Kabul's offers to negotiate might be aimed at splitting and weakening them, rather than to achieve genuine reconciliation. Mullah Haibatullah was Mansur's deputy when the latter's efforts to reach out to Ghani (under Pakistani pressure) damaged the Taliban's morale. Haibatullah has been trying to consolidate his leadership, reunify the Taliban, and gain legitimacy as a leader with military victories and then negotiate from a position of strength, perhaps also trying to lure to his side some of the parties and factions that make up the NUG.

While the Americans have been trying to pressure Pakistan to push the Taliban toward the negotiating table and compel them to make a deal, the Pakistanis have to take into account the possible reaction of their own internal jihadist constituencies. At this point, they are not hostile to the Pakistani authorities, but that could change if Islamabad was perceived to be betraying the cause of Afghan jihad. The Pakistanis also have to take into account the role of Iran, which is not as well placed as Pakistan to support the Taliban throughout Afghanistan but can offer considerable reach now, well beyond Western Afghanistan, also thanks to cooperation with Russia in the north. The Iranians would want to sabotage any peace settlement that does not take their interests into account and especially one with a significant role for Saudi Arabia.

How have the Taliban fared on the battlefield since the major reduction of US coalition troops that began in 2011?

The Taliban's best chance of overthrowing the Afghan government was probably in 2015, as the few American forces still in country were bound to tight rules of engagement, and the Afghan security forces were going through a crisis, having lost the support provided by ISAF. President Ghani's strategy of engaging diplomatically with China, Saudi Arabia, and Pakistan succeeded in convincing the Pakistanis that Ghani was ready for the deal that they had been waiting for, and they halted the planned Taliban onslaught. Then the internal controversies of the Taliban over Akhtar Mansur's efforts to succeed Mullah Omar paralyzed the Taliban for some months. It was only in autumn that year that a desperate effort by Mansur to save some credibility and strike back at Ghani resulted in the Taliban taking Kunduz. Although that was a media success, it was too late. Winter was coming, and the fighting season was over. The Taliban would resume their campaign on a large scale in 2016, attacking Kunduz again, almost taking Tarin Kot and trying several times to take Lashkargah. But they had lost their chance: the Americans relaxed their rules of engagement after Kunduz and sent in reinforcements. There was no way the Taliban could take and keep a city under American watch. In mid-2016 they were close to entering Lashkargah after the Afghan security forces' outer ring of defense collapsed, but their forces were caught on open ground just outside Lashkargah and slaughtered by the US Air Force.

Tactically the Taliban clearly had the upper hand over the Afghan security forces, but their internal divisions, their indecision over the strategy to follow (negotiations or war?), and the resumption of US intervention in the conflict prevented them from achieving strategic successes. In 2017, divisions among the Taliban worsened, with Haibatullah at odds with Serajuddin Haqqani, and the campaign against the cities was called off. The Taliban reverted to attrition warfare, inflicting growing casualties on the Afghan security forces and further eroding their presence in the rural areas, but not getting close to any strategic success.

The Taliban have in the meanwhile been building a new capacity to capture cities: they are developing "special forces" called Red Units, which are meant to infiltrate cities and then strike behind Afghan government lines. The Taliban started deploying these units in attacks against cities in 2018, scoring a tactical success in Ghazni in August. The Taliban kept developing these tactics, but the political leadership imposed a freeze on assault against cities in February 2019, which was only lifted at the end of August 2019. In early September the Taliban resumed raids against cities, entering Kunduz and Pul-i Khumri, but the 2019 fighting season was already approaching its end and the Taliban elite units did not have the several weeks they needed to stockpile ammunition and weapons for large assaults on cities.

The Taliban do not need to take every Afghan city on the way to Kabul to cause the collapse of the Afghan government. A string of victories would probably shake the government and either paralyze it or make it collapse. The August

2018 battle of Ghazni mentioned earlier, for example, led to immediate recriminations between Hazara politicians and Ghani's supporters, due to the decision of the Independent Election Commission (IEC) to suspend parliamentary elections in Ghazni because of the security situation. Hazara candidates expected to sweep the board as in 2010, thanks to the suppression of Pashtun participation in Taliban-controlled and -contested districts. Leading Hazara politicians started threatening to resign from government positions.

Some within the Taliban, like the Haqqanis, argued that the same could be achieved with a string of bloody terrorist attacks in Kabul, at much lower costs to the Taliban, but Haibatullah vetoed this idea, fearful that it would damage the image of the Taliban irreparably. Then in early 2019 Haibatullah managed to impose the suspension of large terrorist attacks in urban areas, to avoid civilian casualties. UN Assistance Mission in Afghanistan (UNAMA) documented a decrease in civilian casualties caused by Taliban attacks at that time. In the first six months of 2019, no major attacks took place in Kabul. Following increasingly tense negotiations in Doha, however, the Taliban's leadership decided to resume attacks in Kabul on July 1; what followed was the most intense campaign of bombings in the capital yet.

What has happened to the Taliban since the death of Mullah Omar?

Since 2001, Mullah Omar was mainly a figurehead who legitimized the decisions of a leadership group in which until 2010 the main figure was his deputy Mullah Baradar. Omar stopped appearing at Taliban meetings sometime between 2006 and 2009. The arrangement worked well as long as the leader in charge day to day enjoyed a consensus of support within the leadership. With Baradar's detention in Karachi in 2010, disputes over who should take his place started. Mullah Omar did not intervene in the debate, a sign that he was probably already too sick. Akhtar Mohammad Mansur took Baradar's job against serious opposition, headed by Abdul Qayum Zakir. The two never agreed whether they had been coequal deputies of the absent Mullah Omar or whether Mansur, as he claimed, was first deputy with authority over both civilian and the military matters headed by second deputy Zakir. The revelation in 2011 that Mansur had sent Tayyib Agha to negotiate with the US in Germany and Qatar without informing Zakir caused serious friction in the organization.

Many Taliban were already wondering why Mullah Omar was not doing anything. They feared he might be sick or that the Pakistanis might have detained him. After the detention of Baradar, this kind of speculation was not science fiction. Consequently when Omar died, almost no one noticed except the family and Mansur. Later some other Taliban leaders were told by the ISI but ordered to keep quiet about it, lest the Taliban disintegrate under the shock.

In 2015, when some Taliban leaders met with Kabul government representatives in Murree, Pakistan, in apparent violation of a policy set by Mullah Omar, Taliban leaders in Quetta clamored for a justification from Mullah Omar, and the NDS (National Directorate of Security) spokesman in Kabul revealed that he had died two years earlier. Mansur decided to go for the top job to consolidate his de facto control of the Quetta Shura. Mansur's power grab combined with the obvious fact that he had kept Mullah Omar's death secret, damaged the organization. At one point some members of the leadership, including Zakir and the family of Mullah Omar, refused to acknowledge Mansur's leadership. Eventually Pakistani threats and the failure of the splitting group to secure sufficient funding led most to go back to the fold of the Quetta Shura, and others still to turn to Iran. What was left of the opposition became known at the end of 2015 as the Rasul Shura, which with NDS support fought a low-intensity intra-Taliban civil war against the Quetta leadership throughout 2016 and much of 2017.

Who are the Pakistani Taliban? Are they the same as the Afghan Taliban?

The Pakistani Taliban are organizationally distinct from the Afghan Taliban. They arose as a result of events after 2001. Al-Qaeda fled from Afghanistan into Pakistan with a lot of money and started paying people in the tribal territories and elsewhere to lodge and protect them. The US then put pressure on General Musharraf to root out al-Qaeda by sending the Pakistani Army into the tribal agencies for the first time since 1947, when the withdrawal of the army was an essential component of the agreement under which the tribal agencies agreed to join the new state of Pakistan. When Musharraf sent troops into FATA, local militants started organizing to resist, with some initial popular support for the defense of traditional autonomy. The militants did not originally call themselves Taliban, and in fact they are less "clerical" than the Afghan Taliban, with fewer genuine madrasa students and more young tribesmen radicalized by the situation in FATA and contact with al-Qaeda. Unlike the Afghan Taliban they often mobilized along tribal lines.

The leading group originally came from the Mehsud tribe of South Waziristan. In December 2007 Baitullah Mehsud managed to convene the majority of these disparate groups under his leadership and established the Tehrik-i-Taliban of Pakistan (TTP), the Taliban Movement of Pakistan. The TTP is a loose umbrella organization and has known several splits, mergers, and de-mergers, especially after American drones killed Baitullah and his Mehsud successor, leading to tribal struggles over the leadership.

Despite having adopted the name Taliban, the TTP was more heavily influenced by al-Qaeda and its jihadist allies and was born in order to fight the Pakistani Army primarily, even if it also helped the Afghan Taliban by dispatching some fighters to Afghanistan. The relationship with the TTP was sometimes a source of embarrassment for the Afghan Taliban, dependent as they were on support from the Pakistani military. Quetta in particular avoided them. The Haqqanis, whose base was in North Waziristan, established relations with TTP. The ISI in turn used the Haqqanis as their intermediaries in dealing with the Pakistani Taliban. The Pakistani Army tried to establish truces with TTP, encouraging them to turn their attention toward Afghanistan, but it only worked for short periods of time. Eventually the Afghan Taliban had to cut relations with TTP, a development that later contributed to pushing several TTP commanders toward the Islamic State in 2015.

The TTP was never very proficient militarily, and perhaps for that reason turned to terrorism in Pakistan's cities as a more effective tool of pressure against the Pakistani authorities. The purpose appears to have been to blackmail them into tolerating a more extensive presence of al-Qaeda and allied groups, especially Central Asians, in the tribal areas.

The 2014 Pakistan military offensive against TTP called "Zarb-e Azb" (cutting strike) managed to reduce the TTP's territorial control inside Pakistan, forcing many of its active members into the cities, such as Karachi and Peshawar, and into Afghanistan, from where they carry out occasional raids into Pakistan. Some of those who fled to Afghanistan helped found the so-called Islamic State in that country. The Islamic State is commonly called "Daesh" in the area, using the Arabic acronym for "Islamic State in Iraq and Shams (Syria)." The Islamic state itself, however, called its Afghan units the Islamic State in "Khorasan Province" (Vilayat-i Khurasan), abbreviated in English as ISKP.

What effect did the rise of the Islamic State have on Afghanistan?

ISKP was largely the creation of dissident Afghan Taliban leaders who had adopted radical Salafi jihadism from their Arab comrades in Guantanamo, former TTP members of the Orakzai tribe who fled to eastern Nangarhar province in the wake of the TTP 2014 leadership struggle, and erstwhile al-Qaeda allies from the IMU and other Central Asian groups. Between 2014 and 2017, some thousands of members of these organizations went over to the Islamic State, weakening their original organizations as a result. Dissidents from both the Pakistani and Afghan Taliban won recognition from IS headquarters in January 2015 after exchanges of visits between Afghanistan/Pakistan and Syria/Iraq. Benefiting from a flow of funds from Raqqa, where IS still had access to tax revenues and oil rents, the new group managed to gain control of several districts in Nangarhar province along the Pakistan border. The IS also established an underground terrorist network, which carried out mass-casualty attacks on civilians, mainly Shi'a, in Kabul. The IS was trying to replicate the strategy used by its founder in Iraq, Abu Musab al-Zarqawi, of setting off sectarian conflict that would weaken the government supported by the US. ISKP seriously weakened the Afghan Taliban in Eastern Afghanistan (Nangarhar and Kunar), where most of the defections to the Islamic State were concentrated. It has largely moved into more remote areas of Kunar but retained a position in about three districts of Nangarhar as well until combined though uncoordinated offensives by the Taliban and the Afghan government ousted them in November 2019.

The US and the Afghan government have focused their attention on IS in Nangarhar, which is of particular importance to those two governments, because their main ground lines of communication (GLOCs) run from Karachi to Peshawar through Khyber Agency to Nangarhar and then on to Kabul via Jalalabad. Russia and Iran, however, have been focused on Northern Afghanistan, where a small group of former Taliban, former pro-government militia fighters, and Central Asians had established a pocket of IS control in Darzab district of Jawzjan province, less than 100 kilometers from the largely unmonitored border with Turkmenistan, the only Afghanistan–Central Asia border that is not demarcated by a river. These fighters included members or affiliates of the Islamic Movement of Uzbekistan (IMU), as well as some Uighurs from the East Turkestan Islamic Movement (ETIM), who had been expelled from Waziristan during the Pakistan Army's *zarb-e-azb* offensive in the summer of 2014. They were joined by Uzbeks and other Central Asians who had fought with IS in Syria and Iraq. These fighters allied with dissident ethnic Uzbek groups in the fragmented society of Northwestern Afghanistan to establish heterogeneous Islamic State–Khorasan Province (ISKP) units composed of former Taliban, former government militias, and Central Asian Islamic State veterans who had fought in the Middle East. Russia and Iran accused the US of bringing these fighters from Syria into Afghanistan to threaten them, a charge the US denied. Chinese officials stated that they shared Russian and Iranian concerns, but not their "conspiracy theories." Estimates of the number of these foreign fighters ranged from a few hundred to more than five thousand. Russia was a principal source of the largest estimates.

The Taliban denounced the attempt by outsiders to bring Afghanistan under the authority of the IS caliphate, rather than of the Taliban's Islamic Emirate. The emergence of the Islamic State turned into an additional source of infighting and acrimony within the Taliban. Taliban leader Akhtar Mansur had hesitated vis-à-vis the IS, but his successor Haibatullah Akhund took a line of determined confrontation. He has seen IS as a direct threat to the Taliban. Haibatullah receives substantial funding from the Iranian Revolutionary Guards, who insist on pushing the Taliban toward fighting ISKP. Haibatullah struggled to mobilize the Taliban for a thorough campaign against the Islamic State, while at the same time keeping the campaign against Kabul going. His main successes were in Zabul in 2015, where his forces inflicted serious casualties on ISKP and its Central Asian allies, and in Darzab district of Jawzjan province in Northwestern

Afghanistan in 2018, where the base of mainly Uzbek ISKP fighters was destroyed. But even successes like the Zabul offensive of 2015 proved costly for Haibatullah: several family members of Central Asian fighters were massacred, and Haibatullah came under strong criticism in the Rahbari Shura. The idea of fighting against another jihadist group was not popular among the Taliban rank and file, nor among many of the Taliban's Arab donors.

ISKP presented the Taliban with a diplomatic opportunity. The Taliban had conducted a low-key diplomatic offensive in the region for years, trying to convince the US, Russia, Iran, and others that they had no political or military ambitions beyond Afghanistan and could be relied upon not to allow Afghanistan to be used as a base for international terrorism. Their reluctance to break publicly with their longtime supporters in al-Qaeda, undermined this message, but IS gave them a new talking point to reinforce it: Taliban would be the sword point of the international effort against IS in Afghanistan. The Taliban reportedly agreed both to fight ISKP and to include al-Qaeda by name in the list of organizations to be kept out of Afghanistan in the draft agreement initialed with the U.S. at the end of August 2019. President Trump's decision to suspend the process prevented that agreement from being signed and implemented before this book went to the printer.

Despite having very weak roots in Afghanistan, the Islamic State has demonstrated resilience and military proficiency. Fortunately for the Taliban, the collapse of the Caliphate in Iraq and Syria has taken steam away from ISKP in Afghanistan. The future evolution of ISKP and the degree to which it might represent a threat will depend on the ability of the former to raise sufficient funds to sustain its operations. Expecting external support to remain at modest levels for some time to come, ISKP has concentrated its energy on seizing control over mining assets in Afghanistan.

Can the Afghan Taliban return to power?

Most of the Taliban's political leaders do not believe they can return to monopolizing power in Afghanistan, nor desire such an outcome, aware that in such a case different Taliban factions and groups would start fighting each other. None of the main donors to the Taliban (Iran, Pakistan, Saudis) want them to reestablish the emirate either. The preferred option for all players involved on the Taliban side would be a negotiated settlement that protects the interests of each of them. This is not as simple as it might sound, considering that the interests of Iran and Saudi Arabia are seemingly irreconcilable. Each of the sponsors of the Taliban has other clients in Afghanistan, whose interests they will also want to protect: for example, the Saudis have Hizb-i Islami, the Iranians have a range of Hazara and Tajik groups and even some Pashtun strongmen. The real challenge is therefore reconciling these multiple and often contrasting interests, and then selling the package to a sponsor who will agree to pay for the cost of peace, while being an actor acceptable to all those involved. In recent years China has been hinting that it might be available to play such as role, and more recently even Russia has been cautiously advancing its candidacy.

What has been the relationship of the Taliban to Pakistan, especially the ISI?

The Pakistani ISI has been one of the main sources of funds and supplies to the Taliban since its founding in 1994, and the most influential external "partner" of the Taliban. To a large extent the influence of the ISI is the reason that the Taliban leadership is based in Pakistan; the ISI has been able to pressure the Taliban leaders and even threaten them, thanks to this. Several Taliban leaders have been detained by the ISI, and a few died in detention (such as Obaidullah).

However, as the Taliban diversified their sources of funding and supplies, the leverage exercised by the ISI has been reduced. The availability of bases, funds, and supplies in Iran has been a major source of leverage over Pakistan. Both Akhtar Mansur (2016) and his successor Haibatullah (2017) sought temporary refuge in Iran when relations with the ISI were deteriorating. From 2017, if not earlier, the Taliban has also enjoyed some support from Russia, through Tajikistan, which has improved their capabilities in Northern Afghanistan. Russian sources claim that this assistance goes to Northern "warlords," not genuine Taliban.

The ISI has increasingly been accepting that it cannot coerce the Taliban into doing what they resolutely do not want to do. Occasionally it will still detain prominent Taliban for short periods of time, in order to warn them. But mostly the ISI has been using more sophisticated influencing techniques, such as shifting funding and support between Taliban leaders, based on the willingness of each one of them to follow ISI "advice." For example, Abdul Qayum Zakir was a favorite when the aim was to maximize military pressure on Kabul, but he was cut off from funding in 2015 when the ISI wanted the Taliban to try negotiations with Kabul. The new favorite was the leading "moderate," Akhtar Mohammad Mansur. Once the ISI determined that a new military push was necessary, it shifted funding again to Serajuddin Haqqani (early 2016). The ISI threw its weight behind Haibatullah in 2018, when it saw that US Special Envoy Khalilzad was interested in framing a deal that took Pakistani demands into account.

The ISI has provided extensive training to the Taliban, but it has capped the quality of training and military supplies at rather low levels. The Taliban received modest engineering skills and technologically backward equipment only. The Taliban, for example, had to obtain night vision equipment elsewhere, and never received significant numbers of antiaircraft missiles or advanced mines.

10

PEACE OR MORE WAR?

The 2014–19 term of President Ghani and the National Unity Government (NUG) overlapped with that of President Donald Trump. Trump struggled to reconcile his America-first impulses with the global hegemonic national security commitments and ideologies of Republican Party elites from whom he originally recruited his administration. Acquiescing to those people, he first appeared to grant Ghani the time and support he wanted to implement his theories of building the Afghan state. The effort that both Ghani and Trump touted to turn the tide against the Taliban so that they would sue for peace on Kabul's terms failed, however. The Taliban continued to refuse direct negotiations with the Afghan government until reaching agreement with the United States. The division of territorial control remained stalemated, and casualties mounted on all sides, especially among civilians.

In the fall of 2018 Trump changed course to seek a quick political settlement to facilitate American troop withdrawal. He appointed veteran Afghan American diplomat ambassador Zalmay Khalilzad to lead the effort as Special Representative for Afghan Reconciliation (SRAR). The consequent decision to accept the Taliban demand for direct negotiations with the US broke the stalemate over talks. The US-Taliban talks, held in Doha, where the Taliban had established their political office during the Obama administration, eventually produced a draft agreement on Taliban counterterrorism guarantees and a US troop withdrawal initialed by both sides at the end of August 2019. The agreement also provided for intra-Afghan negotiations including the Afghan government, a cease-fire between the Taliban and the US, and negotiations over a comprehensive ceasefire. Only intra-Afghan negotiations could establish a government capable of implementing the agreement on counterterrorism, and a comprehensive ceasefire would be necessary for those negotiations to succeed.

Faced with increasing discord in his administration over the nearly complete peace deal and failing to coax the Taliban to meet him and President Ghani to sign the agreement at Camp David, President Trump abruptly suspended the negotiations by Tweet on September 7, 2019. Trump's suspension of the process upended plans to convene the Intra-Afghan negotiations in Oslo at the end of September.

After extensive consultations by Khalilzad, on November 12 President Ghani announced that Kabul would release three members of the Haqqani network of the Taliban from detention. In return the Taliban would release ten detained Afghan soldiers as well as two professors from the American University of Afghanistan, and American and an Australian, who had been held hostage since 2016. The exchange was finally implemented on November 20. The Taliban had kidnapped the professors precisely to be exchanged for the Haqqani members. The agreement was supposed to serve as a confidence-building measure, and Khalilzad returned to Doha to discuss how to resume the negotiations. During a surprise Thanksgiving visit to US troops at Bagram Air Base in Afghanistan on November 28, 2019, President Trump announced the resumption of the peace process, based on the ambiguous claim that the Taliban had accepted the demand of the Afghan and US governments for a ceasefire. The Taliban confirmed they had agreed to a ceasefire with the US only to facilitate its troop withdrawal, and to negotiate a comprehensive ceasefire at the Intra-Afghan Negotiations. They denied any change in their position. Khalilzad nonetheless prepared to resume his work.

The state's continued inability to extend its administrative reach and curb violence also made meeting constitutional requirements for elections impossible. After repeatedly postponed Wolesi Jirga elections that finally took place in October 2018, parliament was partially seated in May 2019, four years after the constitutionally required date. The opening session degenerated into a brawl over election of the speaker.

Ghani extended his presidential term by decree after it expired on May 22, 2019, the constitutionally specified date of the first of the Afghan month of Jawza in the fifth year of his mandate. He scheduled elections instead for September 28, five years to the day after his inauguration as president, the last day on which he could claim to have served no more than the mandated five years. His determination to oversee his own reelection put him at odds with a US administration focused on withdrawal and a political settlement.

The elections took place as scheduled with a low turnout. Despite the use of biometric devices to verify voters, ballot stuffing was still rampant. Extended operations to eliminate fake ballots by painstaking comparison of ballots to biometric records meant that as this book went to press, the Independent Election Commission (IEC) had still not announced results over two months after the election. Both CEO Abdullah and some supporters of President Ghani claimed to be headed for a first-round victory. Abdullah supporters mounted growing demonstrations charging that the IEC would hand Ghani a victory by certifying over one hundred thousand votes with inadequate biometric verification. The prospect of another electoral crisis loomed.

What reforms did President Ghani enact?

Ghani counted on his reform program and diplomatic efforts to transform the state without having to compromise with internal forces he viewed as corrupt, as outlined in his book, *Fixing Failed States,* co-authored with Clare Lockhart.[1] His reforms paid off in increased domestic revenue, a rise in Afghanistan's exports and the diversification of foreign trade away from Pakistan, and, by some indicators, improved performance of the security forces, whose leadership he sought to purge of incompetents and patronage beneficiaries. Public perception of his efforts to combat corruption, however, was largely swamped by massive changes he could not control. The withdrawal of the bulk of the international forces by the end of 2014 triggered an economic crisis manifest in the loss of jobs by educated youth, leading to mass migration to Europe. In 2015–16, Afghans were second only to Syrians among those whose migration into Europe triggered multiple crises and bolstered support for populist and even racist nationalism. The Afghan economy continued its slowdown. The estimated proportion of the population living below the official poverty line exceeded 50 percent in 2019.

Ghani's efforts to reform the revenue system, part of his overall plan to make Afghanistan more self-sufficient, turned around a decline in the proportion of GDP collected in taxes. Throughout Karzai's second elected presidency (2010 to 2014), tax revenue as a share of GDP fell from 9.2 to 6.9 percent. Under Ghani, revenues rebounded to 9.3 percent of GDP in 2017. The absolute quantity of revenue collected also accelerated, growing by an average of 19 percent per year during 2014–17, as compared to 5.4 percent per year during 2010–14.

Ghani accelerated efforts to improve Afghanistan's connectivity to markets and increase exports, also key to gains in self-reliance. Most of the efforts would have only long-term effects, but some results were visible. His efforts to open Afghanistan-India overland trade via Pakistan in return for granting Pakistan

---

1. Ashraf Ghani and Clare Lockhart, *Fixing Failed States: A Framework for Rebuilding a Fractured World* (New York: Oxford University Press, 2008).

land access to Central Asia through Afghanistan remained unsuccessful, hostage to the Pakistan Army's security paradigm. He signed agreements that finally made it possible to start the construction of the Turkmenistan-Afghanistan-Pakistan-India (TAPI) pipeline and the development of Chabahar port in Iran and its linkage by road and rail to Afghanistan. The former would eventually guarantee Afghanistan transit fees from gas from Turkmenistan, while the latter connects Afghanistan to India by sea and land transit through Iran. US sanctions against Iran have slowed the development of Chabahar, despite an official exemption for investments of benefit to Afghanistan. The government also reached agreement with Turkmenistan, Azerbaijan, Georgia, and Turkey over a "Lapis Lazuli corridor" from Northeast Afghanistan to Turkey and then Europe by way of Turkmenistan, across the Caspian Sea, and then via the Caucasus to Turkey. The first convoy reached Turkey from Herat by that route on December 28, 2018, after nineteen days of travel. Afghanistan signed a Memorandum of Understanding (MoU) with China about cooperation with its Belt and Road Initiative (BRI) as well. China started a rail connection from eastern China to Hairatan via Central Asia, through which Afghanistan exported a thousand tons of talc to China in September 2019.[2] The opening of Uzbekistan after the death of President Islam Karimov in September 2016 also presented Afghanistan with expanded opportunities for trade with Central Asia.

Under the leadership of Ghani's economic advisor Ajmal Ahmady, the government developed subsidized air corridors for exporters, initially to India but then expanding to Turkey, China, Russia, Saudi Arabia, the European Union, Kazakhstan, and the UAE. From 2016 to 2017 Afghanistan's exports shot up by nearly 40 percent. Exports to Pakistan held steady, but

2. Xinhuanet, "First Cargo Train from Afghanistan to China via Uzbekistan, Kazakhstan Departs," September 6, 2019, http://www.xinhuanet.com/english/2019-09/06/c_138371401.htm.

exports to India nearly doubled, to near par with Pakistan. Even more important, Afghanistan decreased its dependence on Pakistan for imports, including transit. Imports from both Iran and China each reached approximate parity with Pakistan at 15–17 percent of total imports in 2018. These changes are nowhere near the magnitude needed to reduce Afghanistan's external dependence, however.

Afghanistan remains poor, and it is not yet on a path out of that poverty and dependence. Since the NATO withdrawal and election of President Ghani, yearly GDP growth has been estimated at under 3 percent. Per capita growth was estimated as negative for most of this period. Surveys indicated an increase in poverty, so that by mid-2019 more than 50 percent of the population was living below the very modest official poverty line.

Ghani's efforts against corruption increased the proportion of revenue collected that actually reached the state, but given the decline in foreign aid, more revenue did not translate into enhanced public services. He presided over arrests of high-level officials involved in corrupt fuel sales to the Ministry of Defense and dismissed several thousand military officers, some of whom may have been corrupt, but many of whom were simply patronage appointees. It was not until 2019, however, that Ghani was able to appoint Khoshal Sadat, a dynamic, reform-minded thirty-five-year-old as head of the national police, a major focus of corruption in the country. In the runup to the 2019 presidential elections, the US suspended aid to Ghani's signature National Procurement Agency, citing evidence of corruption.

Ghani accelerated a generational change already underway in the administration. Just as the school system established by Daud Khan in the 1950s produced the leftist and Islamic radicals who battled each other in the 1970s and 1980s, and as madrasas supported by Persian Gulf and Pakistani donors during the 1980s produced the Taliban, the post-2001 educational system—reestablished with US support—also produced new elites. These came of age under Ghani, who appointed many of this group to senior positions in the palace, the officer corps, the cabinet, and elsewhere in the bureaucracy, including as ambassadors. More than three hundred Afghans who studied in the US on the Fulbright program, together with two hundred more who studied in the UK on Chevening scholarships, formed the core of this new elite.

Was the National Unity Government agreement implemented?

Ghani made no effort to resolve the ethno-political issues over the structure of the state and its relationship to society by implementing the NUG agreement's provisions for constitutional change. Dr. Abdullah Abdullah retained a role in making appointments but did little to press for the constitutional reform at the heart of the NUG agreement. The NUG became a Ghani presidency in which Dr. Abdullah was marginalized from decision making.

The core political content of the NUG agreement was in a sequence of events leading up to a Loya Jirga, which was to address ethno-political issues over power sharing and the structure of the state that both the Bonn Agreement and the constitutional process had left unresolved. Preparations for the Loya Jirga would have included drafting a proposal for the constitutional amendment to establish the office of "executive prime minister." The NUG agreement also stipulated that after inauguration the president would appoint a commission to draft such an amendment. President Ghani, who opposed any such amendment, never appointed the commission. Dr. Abdullah and his supporters also made little effort to implement this part of the agreement, which should have been of greatest importance to them.

By the end of the NUG's term in 2019, the government had not made any preparations for the Loya Jirga, and none of the basic political issues within the constitutional coalition had been addressed. As US efforts to negotiate with the Taliban gained traction from the fall of 2018, it became evident that any resolution of the conflict over the structure of the state and its relation to society would have to await a broader peace settlement.

Elections to parliament and district councils would have been needed to constitute the Loya Jirga. First came the appointment of a Special Electoral Reform Commission (SERC). Based on the SERC's recommendations, parliament would pass a new electoral law and the president would appoint a reformed Independent Electoral Commission (IEC). The distribution of electronic identity documents (e-Tazkiras) would for the first time create an electoral roll. The reformed IEC would then organize elections to the Wolesi Jirga (lower house of parliament) and district councils, which the government had not been able to hold. According to the constitution, Wolesi Jirga elections had been due thirty to sixty days before June 22, 2015, the legal end of the parliament's term.[3] Since then the parliament continued to sit extra-constitutionally by executive decree. With the election of a new parliament and district councils, the president would be able to convene a Loya Jirga, which includes all members of both houses of the National Assembly, chairs of the provincial councils, and chairs of district councils.

It proved impossible to hold the elections in October 2015, given the security situation, lack of international funding, and absence of preparation. Distribution of electronic IDs as provided by the NUG agreement proved more difficult than the government anticipated. Disputes over the language used for ethnic and national identities on identity documents escalated. The government also introduced biometric identification to avoid fraud, which caused further delays.

In the absence of progress toward implementation of the NUG agreement, former president Karzai was the most

3. Afghan Const., art. 83, 2004.

prominent of several leaders who claimed that the NUG has no mandate to govern past September 2016 unless it convened a Loya Jirga, which was based on the questionable hypothesis that the NUG agreement took legal precedence over the constitution. That protest movement petered out for lack of either domestic or international support.

When parliamentary elections were finally held in October 2018, however, many voters still had not received e-Tazkiras, there were allegations of fraud in their distribution, and the biometric systems in some cases failed to work or were not used properly. President Ghani dismissed the entire IEC in February 2019, leading to further delays. The Wolesi Jirga elections were so flawed that it took seven months, until May, to certify the results, and even then no results were certified from Ghazni, where a November 2018 Taliban attack on Hazara areas and a March 2019 assault on the provincial capital had made it impossible to hold elections or ascertain their results. District council elections had still not been scheduled.

Ghani campaigned for president in 2019 using a different strategy than in 2014. Having alienated his Uzbek vice president, Dostum, and the other former warlord powerholders who had backed Dr. Abdullah, he promised not to accept another unity government. Instead he gestured toward ethnic inclusion by recruiting former intelligence chief Amrullah Saleh as his first vice presidential candidate. Saleh had been a close aide to Ahmad Shah Massoud and enjoyed a passionate following among urban Tajik youth. Though Saleh had been an outspoken critic of what he charged were Ghani's Pashtun ethnic politics, he likewise positioned himself as a reformer aligned with the country's youth. The pair campaigned on a platform of trans-ethnic nationalism, firmness in negotiating with the Taliban on the basis of constitutional principles, and reliance on the youth.

Ghani's campaign benefited from the collapse of the ticket of his main challenger, former national security advisor Muhammad Hanif Atmar. Atmar, a UK-educated Mohmand

Pashtun from Laghman, had agreed to make Massoud's political deputy and former parliament speaker Yunus Qanuni his first vice presidential candidate and gained the provisional support of Balkh strongman Muhammad Atta. The basis of the alliance was an agreement to make Atta CEO under an NUG-like arrangement, but, fearing Pashtun backlash, Atmar ultimately balked at providing a written commitment to Atta listing the powers he would cede to him, leading Atta to withdraw support and Atmar to suspend his candidacy. Some reports claimed that Atta had been paid to withdraw, but as usual it was impossible to verify them. The ethno-political divide over the structure of state power persisted.

What effect did the NUG have on intra-ethnic relations?

In the absence of structural reforms to accommodate ethnic demands, tensions increased. In February 2016, senior presidential advisor Ahmad Zia Massoud, brother of Ahmad Shah Massoud and at least nominally part of Ghani's team, toured Northeastern Afghanistan commenting on the inability of Afghan government forces to provide security and urging "mujahidin" to take up arms.[4] In March, President Ghani welcomed Abdul Rashid Dostum (first vice president), the country's most prominent Uzbek leader, back to Kabul after he had spent much of the previous year leading fighters against the Taliban in his own region of Northern Afghanistan, outside the command and control of the Afghanistan National Defense and Security Forces (ANDSF). In October 2015, Dostum had visited Russia apparently on his own, stopping in Grozny, where he met Chechen president Ramzan Kadyrov,[5] a sign of

---

4. Interview with diplomat, Kabul, February 16, 2016.
5. Frud Bezhan, "Afghanistan's Dostum Turns to Old Ally Russia for Help," Radio Free Europe Radio Liberty, October 17, 2015, http://www.rferl.org/content/afghanistan-russia-dostum-seeks-military-help/27293696.html.

Russia hedging against the central government's instability and Ghani's perceived hostility to Russia.

In 2016, Hazara activists mounted three large public demonstrations against the Palace, one over the beheading of Hazara bus passengers by terrorists, and two over the change of the planned route of a power transmission line from Central Asia. The change in route bypassed Hazara areas. The government claimed it changed the route for technical reasons, but activists accused it of ethnic bias. The second demonstration against the transmission line route, on July 23, 2016, ended in carnage when suicide bombers (claimed by ISKP) blew themselves up in the midst of the largely Shi'a crowd, killing eighty and wounding more than two hundred. This was part of a series of anti-Shi'a massacres carried out by ISKP in a thus far unsuccessful attempt to replicate the sectarian strategy that had destabilized Iraq. The Taliban condemned the bombing as an attempt to divide the nation. First deputy CEO Muhammad Muhaqqiq, leader of the principal Shi'a party, expressed solidarity with the demonstrators and threatened to resign, calling the shift of the pipeline route "discriminatory."

Many observed that ethnic and tribal tensions of all sorts increased throughout the tenure of the NUG. The agreement to divvy up appointments between two leaders of different ethnic backgrounds led to intensified competition rather than compromise and coexistence. Opposition forces charged Ghani with Pashtun chauvinism; leaked government documents showed discrimination against non-Pashtuns by some officials. Ghani's supporters responded that warlords and corrupt powerholders were appealing to ethnic anxieties to derail the president's reform efforts. Ghani's recruitment of Saleh as his running mate helped neutralize ethnicity as a factor in the presidential campaign. The demonstrations by Abdullah supporters protesting fraudulent vote certification have been concentrated in the north but have not assumed an explicitly ethnic character, given the ethnically mixed composition of both leading presidential tickets.

How has the international context changed?

Just as the terrorist threat has changed since 2001, so has the region. The economic growth of China and India, and even of Russia and Pakistan has changed the stakes. Beyond combating terrorism, China, Russia, India, Pakistan, and Iran seek stability in Afghanistan and the areas around it for infrastructure to connect their economies to global markets. This need is acute for China, which cannot maintain its historic level of economic growth without opening up its central and western regions to international investment and trade. The growing antagonism of the US under the Trump administration to China's Belt and Road Initiative (BRI) and the escalating trade war between the two countries added another level of complexity to Afghanistan's regional balancing act.

In 2001, the interests of the US converged with Afghanistan's neighbors (Pakistan excepted); the relative weakness of the regional states left them little choice but to accept US leadership of the antiterrorism effort. Iran and Russia assisted the US, India applauded, China was hardly involved, and Pakistan was marginalized. As the balance of power in the region has changed, however, the neighbors moved toward balancing the US rather than bandwagoning with it. The neighbors came to view the American presence in Afghanistan as geostrategic and not aimed solely at terrorism. The US could instead use its presence against them, even if under the banner of counterterrorism. The US gave support for terrorism as one of the rationales for the invasion of Iraq, and it could do so to justify intervention in Iran, classified by the US as the leading state sponsor of terrorism, or Pakistan, where nuclear materials or weapons could fall into terrorist hands. Some Russians think that the US could use destabilization in Central Asia as an excuse to intervene there, with Russia as the ultimate target. Pakistan, Iran, and Russia all consider a long-term US military presence in Afghanistan as a threat as great, if not greater, than that posed by Salafi jihadists. China is relatively more concerned with the immediate impact of a US withdrawal on stability, though it too opposes a permanent US military presence.

Table 10.1 of the GDP of the US, Afghanistan, and its key neighbors in 2001 and 2016 shows the change in the balance of forces that makes it possible for the regional powers to attempt this effort. In 2001 the combined GDP of all the regional powers equaled 24 percent of the US economy, meaning that the US had over four times the resources of those states. In 2016 the regional economies produced 84 percent of the US economy, and the US preponderance was reduced to near parity—the US economy was only 20 percent larger than the combined economies of China, India, Russia, Iran, and Pakistan. The US relative advantage over the states of the region decreased by a factor of 3.5, calculated as the ratio of 4.1 to 1.2, with rounding error.

China and India's growth are the largest factor in the change, and though neither country is clamoring for a US exit, vital connectivity projects of both depend on Pakistan and Iran. President Xi Jinping of China has staked his ten-year term on the Belt and Road Initiative, the centerpiece of which is the China-Pakistan Economic Corridor. India has responded with its joint venture and transit agreement with Iran and Afghanistan to develop the Iranian port of Chabahar and link it by road and rail to Afghanistan and Central Asia. Japan joined the consortium in January 2017.

Iranian officials have been urging China and Pakistan to link the two megaprojects by building the Iran-Pakistan-India gas pipeline and linking BRI's projected Central Asia initiatives to the Chabahar project. India objects to CPEC, which crosses territory it claims as part of pre-1947 Jammu and Kashmir, but has expressed interest in cooperating with China in connecting Central Asia to Chabahar by rail, as long as the project is not labeled as part of the BRI. The abolition of the special status of Jammu and Kashmir by the Modi government on August 5 and the subsequent imposition of massive prohibitions of

Table 10.1 Change in GDP of US and Afghanistan's Neighbors, 2001–16

Measure	Year	US	Afghanistan	Pakistan	India	Iran	Russia	China	Regional Powers
GDP in billions US current dollars	2001	10,622	4	78	494	325	329	1,344	2,571
	2016	18,562	18[a]	288[b]	2,251	412	1,268	11,392	15,610
As percentage of US GDP	2001		0.0%	0.7%	4.6%	3.1%	3.1%	12.7%	24.2%
	2016		0.1%	1.5%	12.1%	2.2%	6.8%	61.4%	84.1%
As ratio of US to regional powers GDP	2001		2,432.3	136.3	21.5	32.6	32.2	7.9	4.1
	2016		1,009.1	64.5	8.2	45.0	14.6	1.6	1.2

a. Afghanistan's GDP is for 2002, not 2001, and 2016.

b. Pakistan's GDP is for 2001 and 2015, not 2016.

Source: IMF

movement and expression, however, limited the possibility of overcoming Indo-Pakistan hostility in Afghanistan and started to reverse India's positive image in the country.

How did US policy toward Afghanistan change with the Trump administration?

Donald Trump was elected president of the United States in November 2016, less than two months after the deadline set in the NUG agreement for convening the Loya Jirga to amend the Afghan constitution. President Obama had paused his troop withdrawal in 2014, and repeated efforts to draw the Taliban into negotiations ran into one obstacle after another, including the announcement of Mullah Omar's 2013 death in July 2015, and the assassination of his successor, Mullah Akhtar Muhammad Mansur, by a US military drone in Pakistan in May 2016.

The only successful negotiations were indirect talks between the US and the Taliban, mediated by Qatar, that led to the release of five Taliban leaders held in the Guantanamo detention center in exchange for the freeing of US Army Sergeant Bowe Bergdahl in May 2014. Talks on the subject had begun in 2011 as part of a discussion of confidence-building measures for a political settlement in Afghanistan, but they were concluded solely as a prisoner exchange.

Trump's intentions on Afghanistan were as obscure as the rest of his national security policy, other than a determination to reverse Obama's accomplishments. While Trump had intermittently denounced Afghanistan as a wasted effort, during the campaign he put forward no proposal to either end or win the war. His choice of retired Lieutenant-General Michael Flynn as national security advisor seemed to augur for continuity with the military's desire for long-term counterinsurgency, placing negotiations on hold, establishing a "generational" presence in Afghanistan, and halting attempts to negotiate with the Taliban.

Flynn's abrupt dismissal after a mere twenty-four days of service for lying about his conversations with Russian ambassador Sergei Kislov, and his replacement by Lieutenant-General H. R. McMaster, did not change the direction. Both Flynn and McMaster had served under Generals David Petraeus and Stanley McChrystal in Afghanistan and were associated with the doctrine of counterinsurgency (COIN). McMaster directed the Trump administration's review of Afghanistan policy, the result of which Trump announced in a speech from the White House on August 21, 2017.

The methodical review orchestrated by McMaster was disrupted by a proposal from Erik Prince, founder of the private "security" firm formerly known as Blackwater and brother of Trump's secretary of education, Betsy DeVos. Prince proposed replacing the US military in Afghanistan with private contractors who would train and mentor Afghan forces as the CIA and Special Forces had done in 2001, supposedly assuring a repeat of the successful defeat of the Taliban. Prince's plan disregarded any Afghan political considerations. It had the backing of presidential strategist and alt-right ideologist Steve Bannon, who argued that the US should wait out the result of an inevitable civil war in Afghanistan rather than try to stabilize the country. While the proposal appealed to Trump, even Prince's aggressive marketing attempts in both Washington and Kabul failed to win serious consideration for his plan. Its sole supporter in the administration was Bannon. Prince was barred from the meeting at Camp David where the interagency team approved the strategy, and Bannon was asked to resign.

Trump opened his discussion of Afghanistan policy in his August 17 speech by noting that his instinct was to withdraw, but that the generals had persuaded him it was too risky. He did follow his instinct to claim that everything he did aimed to reverse the policies of his predecessor: the rhetorical centerpiece of the speech was the claim that any US withdrawal from Afghanistan would be based not on "arbitrary timetables" but on "conditions." Trump read without conviction a text that stated the goal was to create conditions for a negotiated settlement:

> Someday, after an effective military effort, perhaps it will be possible to have a political settlement that includes elements of the Taliban in Afghanistan, but nobody knows if or when that will ever happen. America will continue its support for the Afghan government and the Afghan military as they confront the Taliban in the field.[6]

The US changed the rules of engagement to accept greater risk of causing civilian casualties and also to give US forces in Afghanistan, which the Obama administration had largely reserved for operations against al-Qaeda and other global terrorist groups, renewed authorities to target the Taliban. As a result in the first six months of 2019, according to UN reporting, the US and Afghan government for the first time were responsible for more civilian casualties than the Taliban. The Taliban regained their lead in the third quarter.

McMaster tried to frame the plan as a regional "South Asia Strategy," which in practice meant a rhetorical emphasis on pressuring Pakistan by terminating or imposing conditions on aid and threatening to designate it as a state sponsor of terrorism. The speech also linked support for greater involvement by India to attempts to pressure Pakistan. The "South Asia Strategy" made no mention of China, Russia, or Iran.

The military developed a pseudo-scientific argument to support the strategy: According to some dubious classified research on insurgencies in India and Colombia, insurgencies agree to negotiate when the government controlled at least 80 percent of the population, so that was set as a goal. Of course,

---

6. "Remarks by President Trump on the Strategy in Afghanistan and South Asia," https://www.whitehouse.gov/briefings-statements/remarks-president-trump-strategy-afghanistan-south-asia/.

the Taliban had long been willing to negotiate, but initially only with the US. The military hypothesized—or hoped—that control of 80 percent of the population would force the Taliban to agree to negotiate with the government. When the strategy made no progress toward the goal, however, it was set aside and disavowed. The military stopped reporting estimates of control of population and territory. Instead, military spokesmen reverted to the Vietnam-era practice of announcing "body counts," how many of the "enemy" had been killed, as a measure of military achievement. While Pakistan made some gestures toward pressing the Taliban to negotiate, its ability to compel the Taliban to do things they resisted was limited, and Pakistan refused as always to consider military action against the Afghan Taliban, or, as Pakistani spokesmen put it, to fight the Afghan war on Pakistani soil.

President Ghani's first act as president of Afghanistan was to instruct his national security advisor, Muhammad Hanif Atmar, to sign the Bilateral Security Agreement that Karzai had negotiated but never signed with the United States. Ghani saw the "South Asia Strategy" as a payoff from that decision—Trump appeared to promise the open-ended support that Ghani wanted to implement his reform strategy without pressure for quick results. Furthermore, Trump's speech never mentioned the NUG agreement, in effect giving Ghani license to continue to disregard its political requirements.

In principle a "conditions-based" approach meant that the US would maintain its military presence and support for the Afghan government indefinitely, or until the strategy succeeded (whichever came first). Generals compared the military presence in Afghanistan to the US presence in Japan, Germany, or South Korea, ignoring that these deployments all resulted from unconditional defeat of the enemy in World War II or an armistice in the Korean War.

American diplomacy on Afghanistan lacked focus. Secretary of State Rex Tillerson, who resigned on March 31, 2018, showed no interest in Afghanistan. Nearly three years into his term, Trump had not even nominated a candidate for assistant secretary of state for South and Central Asia.

A one-year review of the South Asia Strategy by the National Intelligence Council issued in August 2018 concluded (as such reviews always had) that US strategy in Afghanistan was not succeeding. Government control continued to erode, and the level of casualties suffered by the ANDSF was unsustainable. While Trump disregards any intelligence findings that contradict his predilections, he seized upon these, which reinforced his gut instincts, and, once again, began looking for the exit. He instructed his third national security advisor, John Bolton, to prepare a plan for the withdrawal of several thousand troops from Afghanistan. His new secretary of state, former congressman and CIA director Mike Pompeo, however, prevailed upon him to try for a diplomatic solution first.

In September 2018 Pompeo appointed Zalmay Khalilzad, the Afghan American former ambassador to Afghanistan, Iraq, and the United Nations, as Special Representative for Afghan Reconciliation (SRAR) with a mandate to negotiate directly with the Taliban as the latter had long demanded. Khalilzad's mandate contradicted President Ghani's plan for a political settlement led by his government over the course of his second five-year term as president (his reelection was part of his peace plan) in tandem with the implementation of his reforms of the Afghan state. It did, however, unblock the process.

Khalilzad operated under the omnipresent threat of what came to be known as the "Tweet of Damocles," the risk that President Trump might upend the negotiations at any moment by an abrupt plan for withdrawal or other Tweeted announcement. That was a metaphor for a real if unarticulated deadline imposed by the president, though when the Tweet of Damocles dropped in September 2019, it took a different form. On June 25, 2019, Secretary Pompeo stated in Kabul, "I hope we have a peace deal before September 1. That's certainly our mission set." Khalilzad had long hinted that he was operating under a deadline, though the time kept slipping, along with the date of the Afghan presidential election. By the summer of 2019, however, the date set for the Afghan presidential election coincided with the launch of Donald Trump's 2020 reelection campaign, for which the president presumably wanted to announce progress in extricating the US from Afghanistan. Khalilzad and Pompeo hoped to have enough elements of the deal agreed by September to justify postponement of Afghanistan's presidential elections until after the formation of a government as part of the political settlement. In any event, President Trump suspended the negotiations, and the Afghan presidential election went ahead as planned on September 28, 2019.

How did the Afghan peace process start? What did it consist of?

Efforts to end the war—or wars—in Afghanistan go back as far as the wars themselves. The Soviet-Afghan war ended with the Geneva Accords and the Soviet withdrawal but was soon transformed into a civil and regional proxy war. Early attempts to end the post-withdrawal proxy war led to the fall of the Najibullah government. The Taliban, with Pakistan's support, nearly won a reshaped proxy war. The US intervention ended that war. Efforts to transform that war termination into peace were frustrated by the US insistence on eliminating and punishing the Taliban for harboring al-Qaeda rather than integrating them into the Bonn process that formed the new government.

The peace process that seemed close to culmination in 2019 originated in 2007–08, when President Karzai asked King Abdullah of Saudi Arabia to mediate between the government and the Taliban. The Taliban also established their political commission in 2007. The commission was headed by Agha Jan Mu'tasim, a close associate of Mullah Abdul Ghani Beradar, Mullah Omar's deputy, who was then in charge of day-to-day leadership. Karzai wanted direct negotiations with the Taliban, while the Taliban had concluded that such talks were pointless without the support of the US. The Taliban also approached

Saudi Arabia, but as an intermediary with the US rather than with the Afghan government.

The Saudis tried to merge the two efforts in September 2008, when King Abdullah hosted an iftar dinner on the last Friday of Ramadan (the "night of power," or "Layl al-qadr"). Afghans close to the government and former Taliban living in Kabul attended, all of whom were Pashtuns. Mu'tasim was staying in a nearby hotel, where former Taliban from Kabul briefed him on the discussions. King Abdullah had asked Mu'tasim to bring a letter or audio recording from Mullah Omar stating that the Taliban:

1. Respected His Majesty King Abdullah as Guardian of the Two Holy Mosques (Khadim al Haramain);
2. Had no connection to al-Qaeda or international terrorism;
3. Requested King Abdullah to act as a mediator between them on the one hand and the US and Afghan government on the other.

The letter that Mu'tasim brought fell short of Abdullah's conditions. While Mullah Omar referred to the king respectfully— as he had not in June 1998 when Saudi intelligence chief Prince Turki al-Faisal came to Kandahar to demand the handover of Osama bin Laden—Omar did not meet the other two conditions. The Taliban wanted to settle matters first with the United States. Any break with al-Qaeda would result from negotiations that also led to the withdrawal of foreign troops from Afghanistan, and they would negotiate with other Afghans, including the government they did not recognize, only after agreement on the withdrawal of foreign troops.

The iftar led to months of negotiations involving Saudi intelligence chief Muqrin bin Abdul Aziz al-Saud (a younger brother of the king), Mu'tasim, Mullah Abdul Salam Zaeef, President Karzai's brother Qayum, and a Saudi lawyer and former mujahid in Afghanistan, Mansur bin Saleh al-Khonizan, from a family linked to the royal clan who undertook various assignments on behalf of Muqrin. During this period the Taliban formulated their demands for confidence-building measures from the US, including the lifting of sanctions, the release of their senior leaders from Guantanamo and Bagram, and the recognition of a political office for the Taliban, then to be established in Saudi Arabia. The political office would enable the Taliban to formulate their positions free of direct Pakistani control. Zaeef informed the US government of these positions through me during my visit to Kabul in April 2009. I was about to be appointed as senior advisor to US Special Representative for Afghanistan and Pakistan Richard Holbrooke.

The Taliban and the Saudis continued to differ on whether the Taliban break with al-Qaeda would be a precondition for or the result of talks. By spring 2009, tensions between Zaeef and Mu'tasim led to the latter's dismissal by Mullah Omar. Mu'tasim had been authorized to travel to Saudi Arabia by the ISI in order to raise funds, and the confusion of his two roles led to charges that he had embezzled funds given by Muqrin for the Taliban. Mullah Omar suspended Mu'tasim as head of the political commission and replaced him with his other close aide, Tayyib Agha, who was related to Zaeef by marriage (they were married to two sisters). The Taliban informed Mansur that Tayyib Agha was now the only authorized representative for political negotiations. Mansur informed Muqrin and King Abdullah, and the US through me.

When Zaeef introduced Tayyib Agha to Muqrin during Ramadan 2009, however, Muqrin challenged Tayyib's credentials, and the two disputed their positions on preconditions for and the sequence of talks. Muqrin refused to meet Tayyib Agha again and forbade him to enter the kingdom a few months later. About the time of Muqrin's first meeting with Tayyib Agha, Pakistan ISI chief Major General Shuja Ahmad Pasha visited Muqrin in Riyadh and remonstrated with him for undertaking Taliban outreach without consulting Pakistan. After Pasha's visit, Muqrin began to charge that Tayyib Agha was in the pay of the Iranian intelligence operations chief, General

Qasim Sulaimani. The intervention of Pakistan and the break with Tayyib Agha ended Saudi Arabia's role as an intermediary with the Taliban.

These events took place in 2009, as the Obama administration's efforts in Afghanistan focused on the presidential election and the policy review of the autumn of 2009, which led to Obama's surge, a time-limited effort at COIN meant to set conditions for a US withdrawal. Proposals for exploring a political settlement received no consideration in the interagency process, and the Afghan government was, of course, consumed with the elections. Karzai, however, ran on a plan of outreach to the Taliban, which fit well with Obama's intention to disengage. In the run-up to an official visit by Karzai to Washington in May 2010, which was intended to repair the damage to the bilateral relationship done by the fracas over the elections, the US reexamined its position on "reconciliation." The US rescinded a "blacklist" of Taliban "linked" to al-Qaeda with whom Karzai was not to engage. Knowing that a change in US policy was in the offing, ISI chief Pasha air-dashed to Kabul just before Karzai's departure to the US to offer him the prospect of a deal with the Taliban through Pakistan rather than the US.

During Karzai's visit to Washington, May 11–12, 2010, both President Obama and Secretary of State Clinton told him that the US now supported "Afghan-led" reconciliation with the Taliban. Karzai responded by asking what the US position on Pakistan might be. That was as important for him to know before talking to the Taliban as it was important for the Taliban to know the US position on troop withdrawal before talking to the government. He never received an answer he considered satisfactory: the US never took Afghanistan's side over the Durand Line or treated Pakistan, as Karzai and many Afghans wanted, as a state sponsor of terror. Both geography and broader counterterrorism objectives militated against such a position: the US depended on Pakistan for access to landlocked Afghanistan and relied on the ISI and the Pakistan army for intelligence and operations against al-Qaeda.

With the backing of the US for his outreach to the Taliban, Karzai went about building domestic support. Non-Pashtun members of the ruling coalition feared that a Karzai-Taliban deal would come at their expense, rebalancing the government in favor of Pashtuns, especially the southerners. The mainly urban beneficiaries of the government's internationally funded programs of education, health, and reconstruction feared a return to Taliban obscurantism as the price of a deal. To address these and other concerns, Karzai convened a "Consultative Peace Jirga" on June 2–4, 2010, under the chairmanship of former president Rabbani. The jirga endorsed the search for peace with the Taliban and established the High Peace Council, led by Rabbani.

The Taliban, however, continued their quest for dialogue with the US even as their leadership underwent a shakeup. Mu'tasim had started the Taliban's outreach on behalf of Mullah Beradar, whose authority on behalf of Mullah Omar was unquestioned. The arrest of Mullah Beradar in Karachi, Pakistan, in a joint CIA-ISI operation in January 2010 led to a struggle over who would represent Mullah Omar in daily administration of the movement.[7] Mullah Akhtar Muhammad Mansur and Mullah Abdul Qayyum Zakir became first and second deputy leaders, but it was always disputed whether Mansur exercised overall authority while Zakir was head of the military commission, or whether the two were peers reporting to Mullah Omar

7. The CIA insists that the arrest was a "counterterrorism" operation based on intelligence obtained by the United States. President Karzai and many others believed a story reported by the *New York Times* that the ISI manipulated the CIA into capturing Beradar in order to end his reconciliation contacts with Karzai. The CIA denied that Beradar was involved in reconciliation talks. Pakistani officials have taken a variety of positions, depending on circumstances. I was in the government at the time and tried to make sense out of what happened, but I still do not find either version of the story persuasive.

with respective authority over civil and military affairs. (See chapter 9.)

Mansur took over supervision of Tayyib Agha without telling Zakir about the reconciliation initiative. After the break with Saudi Arabia, the Taliban instead approached Germany, which cooperated with Qatar in starting a dialogue with Tayyib Agha. German SRAP Bernd Mützelburg told Holbrooke and me about the contact at a meeting in Abu Dhabi in January 2010, just as the US was reviewing its policy on reconciliation with the Taliban. By the end of summer 2010 the talks had advanced to the point that Mützelburg's successor, Michael Steiner, conveyed to the US a proposal for a direct meeting with Tayyib Agha. While this was not obviously consistent with "Afghan-led" reconciliation, it presented a channel for exploring the possibility of a political settlement. In the face of resistance and skepticism from much of the national security establishment, President Obama and Secretary Clinton authorized the contact, which took place in a safe house outside Munich on November 29, 2010. Present were Steiner and his assistant, two Americans including Holbrooke's deputy Frank Ruggiero and an intelligence aide from the NSC, Tayyib Agha, and a representative of the Emir of Qatar.

This meeting led to a year of direct talks interrupted by the death of Richard Holbrooke a mere two weeks after the talks began, press leaks, the killing of Osama bin Laden on May 2, 2011, the assassination of the High Peace Council chair and former president Rabbani by a Taliban envoy in September, and whipsawing positions taken by President Karzai, whose objection to talks in which he was not included was among the factors that led the Taliban to suspend them in March 2012. On the US side, the talks were led by Holbrooke's successor, Ambassador Marc Grossman, who was tasked with what Secretary Clinton called a "diplomatic surge" in a speech to the Asia Society in February 2011.

At the first meeting Tayyib Agha, operating on behalf of Mullah Omar and Mullah Mansur, presented the Taliban framework for a process. The US would have to withdraw, and the Taliban would give guarantees against al-Qaeda and other international terrorist groups; but first, the Taliban outlined a series of confidence-building measures between the US and the Taliban, after which the Taliban would negotiate with the Afghan government but without recognizing it as such. The US would free Taliban detainees from Guantanamo, relax sanctions, and recognize an official Taliban political office, now to be established in Qatar rather than Saudi Arabia. The Taliban would free Sergeant Bowe Bergdahl, the American soldier who had left his base in Eastern Afghanistan in May 2009 and ended up in the custody of the Haqqanis in Waziristan (Pakistan). They would also issue statements distancing themselves from international terrorism and committing to a political settlement with other Afghans. In the course of more than a year, the US supported the "delisting" of reconciled Taliban from the UN sanctions list and led a successful effort in the UN Security Council to place sanctions against the Taliban in a resolution separate from that against al-Qaeda and international terrorists. The Taliban were henceforward identified as threats to the peace and security of Afghanistan, not as international terrorists. The resolution provided for suspension of sanctions to facilitate peace negotiations.

The US, Taliban, and Qatar also agreed on the text of a memorandum of understanding (MoU) to be signed by Qatar and the Taliban on the rules of operation of the Taliban political office. The sequence of prisoner releases by each side, statements, and the opening of the office was not resolved. In November 2010, the US Senate Armed Services Committee led by Sen. John McCain (R-AZ) amended the Defense Appropriations Act to prohibit the president from releasing Guantanamo detainees without explicit and politically risky certification by the secretary of defense. This measure was part of the overall Republican strategy to prevent President Obama from carrying out his campaign promise to close Guantanamo, and it also blocked negotiations with the Taliban.

In the fall of 2011 Tayyib Agha provided the US with a video of Bergdahl, confirming his effective link to the organization, including the Haqqanis. The negotiators believed they were close to agreement, but in December, at a conference in Bonn commemorating the tenth anniversary of the Bonn Agreement, President Karzai demanded that the US tell the Taliban that the talks could continue *only* with the inclusion of the Afghan government and that Qatar could host a Taliban political office only by agreement with the Afghan government. By this time so much had leaked to the media about the negotiations that the Taliban had to issue a public statement clarifying to their fighters that they were indeed talking to the US, which they justified as necessary to gain the release of their detained leaders. The confirmation of secret talks with the enemy complicated mobilization for the 2012 Taliban spring offensive, while the March 11 massacre of sixteen civilians by US Sergeant Robert Bales in the Zharai district of Kandahar assured that the Taliban had no incentive to resolve the problem. On March 15, they announced suspension of the talks.

The US and Afghan government continued efforts to draw the Taliban into talks. President Karzai focused on secret contacts with the Taliban based in Pakistan, which the Taliban used several times as cover to carry out assassination attempts, such as the successful killing of the Afghan High Peace Council (HPC) chair President Rabbani in September 2011 and the explosion in October that left intelligence chief Asadullah Khalid badly wounded. The US concentrated on reactivating the existing negotiations, talking indirectly with the Taliban political office in Doha via Qatar and other intermediaries such as Norway and the UK. The idea was to find an acceptable agreed sequence of events for the exchange of prisoners, the Taliban statement and opening of the office, the resumption of US-Taliban talks, and the start of talks between the Taliban and the Afghan government.

In fall 2012 Qatar conveyed a proposal to change the sequence: the Taliban would make their statement and open their office, which would then be the site for reaching agreement on the prisoner exchange and the start of negotiations with the Afghan government through the HPC. Presidents Obama and Karzai made the proposal public in a joint statement capping the Afghan president's official visit to Washington in January 2013. On April 23, the Emir of Qatar, Tamim bin Hamad Al Thani, presented President Obama with a copy of the Taliban's proposed statement in the White House Oval Office, as Secretary of State John Kerry met with Karzai and Pakistan's Army Chief of Staff, General Ashfaq Pervez Kayani, at the residence of the US ambassador to NATO in Brussels. By a strange coincidence, this is the same day on which Mullah Omar reportedly died of tuberculosis, either in a hospital in Karachi or near a US military base in Zabul province of Afghanistan, according to two competing accounts. There is no indication that any of the participants in that day's diplomatic meetings knew of this event, which was not revealed until 2015.

In their statement, the Taliban distanced themselves from international terrorism by stating, as they had before, that "The Islamic Emirate never wants to pose harms to other countries from its soil, nor will it allow anyone to cause a threat to the security of countries from the soil of Afghanistan."[8] They also pledged "to support a political and peaceful solution which includes the end of the occupation of Afghanistan and the establishment of an independent Islamic system and true security . . . and . . . to hold meetings with Afghans as times may demand," meeting the second criterion set by the US, committing themselves to a political process.

All of this, as well as the subsequent negotiations leading to the official opening of the office on June 18, took place with no direct talks between the US and the Taliban. In December in Bonn, Karzai had objected to the plan for Qatar to sign an MoU

8. For the full text, see https://www.theguardian.com/world/2013/jun/18/taliban-peace-talks-us-afghanistan-full-text.

with the Taliban, a nongovernmental organization. He did not oppose the opening of the office but proposed instead that it be governed by an MoU between the governments of Qatar and Afghanistan. The Taliban said they would not accept the office as a "gift" from Karzai. In the subsequent diplomatic whirlwind, the Qataris included the MoU text in a diplomatic note about the office sent to the State Department, and President Obama sent a letter to President Karzai pledging that the office would not infringe on the sovereignty of Afghanistan. The US did not know and apparently did not want to know what communications about the office passed between the Qataris and the Taliban. On the weekend before the opening, the mid-level US team preparing the initiative (including me) left Qatar, except for an intelligence aide from the NSC. No senior official of the US government wanted to be associated with the event. No one sat down with all parties to be sure they understood the terms of the verbal non-agreement in the same way, and, sure enough, they did not.

The MoU stated that the name of the office would be the "Political Office of the Afghan Taliban," and that the Taliban would use no other name for the office in public communications. During the talks, there were informal exchanges saying that the Taliban could call themselves what they wanted, and others would call them what they wanted, and that the Taliban were free to use whatever language they liked inside the office. Qatar and the Taliban thought these informal exchanges justified calling the office the "Political Office of the Islamic Emirate of Afghanistan."

The opening of the office was broadcast live on Al-Jazeera. The Taliban and the Qatari foreign minister spoke in front of a banner of the "Islamic Emirate of Afghanistan." The office affixed a brass plaque with the same name to the outer wall, and the members of the political office raised the Emirate's white flag in what resembled a victory celebration. The US told Karzai it would close the office, and the signs and flag were down within two days. This was the effective end of reconciliation efforts during Karzai's presidency. Afghanistan-US relations focused instead on the bilateral security treaty that would govern the US military presence in Afghanistan after the end of the NATO mission in December 2014. With the agreement of the US, however, the members of the Taliban political commission remained in Doha, where they continued to meet international envoys and other Afghans.

Ashraf Ghani made the quest for peace one of the major themes of his presidential campaign. Upon taking office in accord with the NUG agreement, he clarified that for him, a peace process would first of all be with Pakistan. Like Karzai, he denied that the Taliban had sufficient autonomy to open their own political office, which he did not recognize, or conclude their own agreements. Thus began two years of vain efforts to negotiate peace through Pakistan. Ghani first visited Saudi Arabia and China to line up support from Pakistan's regional allies. In November 2014 he traveled to Pakistan, where he visited army chief General Raheel Sharif, who had taken over from Kayani in November 2013, at his headquarters in Rawalpindi. Ghani offered a framework for a complete settlement of the disputes between the two countries. There followed an exchange of visits with Sharif, kindling hopes that Pakistan would prevent the Taliban from launching a spring offensive in 2015.

The US and China also intensified cooperation for a political settlement in Afghanistan, meeting with Afghanistan and Pakistan in the Quadrilateral Coordination Group (QCG). These diplomatic efforts, backed up by Pakistan Army pressure on the Taliban leadership, led to a meeting between a delegation of the High Peace Council and ISI-sponsored Taliban figures in Muree, a resort outside of Islamabad, on July 7, 2015. The meeting was chaired by the Pakistani foreign secretary, flanked by generals, and included observer delegations from the US and China. Taliban leader Mullah Mansur, according to the Pakistani organizers, had authorized the participation by the Taliban figures present. The meeting met the Afghan government's demand for direct talks with the Taliban, and the Pakistani government demand for peace talks under Pakistani control. The problem was that it violated the conditions set for talks by the Taliban themselves, who had repeatedly stated that the location for talks was the political office in Doha, that talks could not take place in Pakistan, and that direct talks with other Afghans could occur only after agreement with the US on troop withdrawal and sanctions relief.

Although Mansur may well have approved the participation by individual Taliban leaders linked to the ISI, such individuals could not represent the movement. Instead, the meeting set off a protest within the Taliban leadership in Quetta and Karachi: direct talks with the Afghan government violated policy set by Mullah Omar, and he had not issued any statement authorizing the change. Where was Mullah Omar? Under the circumstances, it became impossible to continue to conceal that the Taliban leader had died more than two years before, and that Mansur had been exercising authority and issuing official statements in the name of a dead man. As a result, a planned second meeting was canceled. The first public revelation of Omar's death seems to have come from the NDS spokesman in Kabul, but it is disingenuous to charge, as some do in Pakistan, that NDS hardliners staged the announcement to undermine the talks: the rumors and reports of Omar's death were already circulating, and it was only a matter of time before someone confirmed the information.

Pakistani pressure on the Taliban extended only to pushing them into negotiations, not to reducing the Taliban's military and terrorist activities in Afghanistan. That pressure, however, was sufficient to drive members of the leadership to seek alternatives to Pakistani sanctuary. Some tried to establish themselves in areas of Southern Afghanistan under relatively stable Taliban control. Some went to Iran, where the Islamic Revolutionary Guard Corps (IRGC) welcomed the opportunity to gain a partner in pressuring the US but refused, as Pakistan did not, to permit nonstate militants to establish bases on its national territory.

Mullah Zakir, the former military commander who was emerging as the political leader of the Alizai tribe in Helmand, close to the Iranian border, visited Iran and spent more time in central Helmand. Together with Mansur, Zakir controlled much of the heroin trafficking coming out of Helmand, which, if it could not stop it, Iran at least wanted to keep out of the hands of Baloch separatists supported by Saudi Arabia. This may have been among the topics that Mansur discussed with his IRGC hosts during a two-month-long stay in spring 2016. Mansur's trip became public after the US military assassinated him on with a drone on May 21, 2016, while he was taking a taxi home to Kuchlak, Balochistan, after crossing from Iran into Pakistan. The passport with an assumed name he had used, suspiciously intact for having allegedly been found in the smoking ruins of Mansur's taxi, was posted on the internet, showing the date when he had crossed the border. The image of the intact passport, which may have been confiscated at the border, was among the pieces of evidence that led some to suspect that the ISI, concerned by Mansur's outreach to Iran, had provided the Americans with Mansur's coordinates.

In the remaining days of the Obama administration, the US State Department conducted a few rounds of talks with the Taliban in Doha aimed at opening the political office so that the expected administration of Hillary Clinton could support a peace process without having to take the risky step of opening the office in its first few months. These efforts foundered when the Taliban proved reluctant to respond, and Donald Trump won the election. The Trump administration abolished the office of the Special Representative for Afghanistan and Pakistan and left the position of assistant secretary of state for South and Central Asia vacant. It undertook no major diplomatic effort on Afghanistan until the appointment of Khalilzad.

Russia stepped into the gap. It had begun to reorient its regional policy to coordinate with China, Iran, and Pakistan, which shared similar concerns about a potential long-term US military presence in Afghanistan.

Russia and Iran also reevaluated their relations with the Taliban, who shared their opposition to both the US military presence and the Islamic State. In October 2015, the Russian presidential special envoy Zamir Kabulov obtained authorization to open political contacts with representatives of the Afghan Taliban. As a result, both Russia and Iran became proponents of a political settlement with the Taliban that would weaken the pro-American orientation of the Afghan government and lead to a complete US military withdrawal.

American officials charged Russia and Iran with providing material support to the Taliban. There is some evidence of Iranian support for commanders in Southwest Afghanistan and along their borders, especially to limit or eliminate US military and intelligence presence there. The evidence for Russian material support seems sketchier, and US military spokesmen were reluctant to go on the record about it. Neither Russia nor Iran was trying to use the Taliban to overthrow the Afghan government.

For the first time since the Soviet withdrawal from Afghanistan, in 2016 Russia launched a major initiative on Afghanistan, which became known as the "Moscow process." Defining the goal as a political settlement that would lead to the withdrawal of US troops from Afghanistan and the region, in a series of meetings, Kabulov set about building a consensus, starting with Russia, China, Iran, and Pakistan. Whereas in 2001 Russia had supported bringing in the Americans so to keep al-Qaeda out and the Taliban down, it now supported bringing the Taliban in to keep America out and IS down.

According to Kabulov, peace would come from the region, not from the US. The region would establish peace in Afghanistan together with the US if it could, but without the US if it must. When Russia invited the US to participate in the Moscow process in April 2017, the US declined. The Trump administration claimed to support an "Afghan-led,

Afghan-owned" peace process, meaning that it did not plan to make any efforts to start it. President Ghani tried to transform the Moscow process into a "Kabul process" at an international conference he convened in Kabul in June 2017. The Moscow process, however, continued to advance, as both the Taliban and most of Afghanistan's political opposition agreed to participate. Afghanistan's government might have sat at the table with the Taliban in Moscow in June 2018, as both sides initially accepted Russia's invitation. Under US pressure, however, President Ghani sent only High Peace Council rather than official representatives. This decision precipitated the resignation of National Security Advisor Hanif Atmar, who soon announced his candidacy for president.

The US national security strategy (NSS) issued in December 2017, as McMaster's last initiative before his March 2018 resignation, undermined the Afghanistan strategy of which the national security advisor had been the principal sponsor. The NSS said that henceforward the primary threat to the US was great power conflict with China and Russia, and, in a throwback to the Bush administration, the secondary threat was the old "Axis of Evil" without Iraq—the "rogue states" of Iran and North Korea. Terrorism was relegated to a tertiary status. The strategy did, however, allow for cooperation with China and Russia where they and the US had common interests.

From Russia's point of view, the most important change of US policy was a new and possibly genuine desire to withdraw from Afghanistan. Ambiguity remained around the question of a "residual" counterterrorist force, but this was now presented as a subject for discussion rather than a red line. Khalilzad for the first time authorized low-level US participation in the November 2018 session of the Moscow process, which included Taliban representatives. Kabulov regarded Khalilzad as one of the architects of the US permanent presence in Afghanistan and agreed to meet him with the greatest skepticism, but the two found common ground. Russia and the United States agreed for the first time that the goal of a peace process was to produce an agreement that would stabilize Afghanistan through an agreement with the Taliban and lead to the departure of US military forces.

Khalilzad started his attempt to open dialogue with the Taliban not only by meeting them in Doha but also by taking up offers from Saudi Arabia and the UAE to arrange meetings with "real" Taliban leaders. Under the influence of its Gulf Cooperation Council (GCC) allies, who did not want Qatar to succeed in anything, Khalilzad held some pointless meetings in Dubai and Abu Dhabi. The main result of these meetings was to humiliate the Afghan government, which was invited but with whom the Taliban would not meet, and to further alienate Iran, which was convinced that the process was aimed against it. The deterioration of US-Iran relations remain perhaps the greatest external threat to the process. Ironically, Saudi Arabia and the UAE proved less capable than Russia of brokering talks between the Taliban and the Afghan government.

In February 2019, when Russia used an association of Afghan expatriates in Russia to invite the Taliban, along with representatives of Afghanistan's "constitutional coalition," for discussions on a settlement, the US and Russia coordinated their response. Rather than back up the Ghani government's opposition to the meeting, the US remained silent. Russia did not force a US response by sending official representatives to the meeting—Foreign Minister Lavrov declined an invitation to speak, and it remained an Afghan meeting. The Afghans who participated, as well as their Russian sponsors, spoke of turning the Moscow format into the framework for the Intra-Afghan talks or negotiations that would result if the US-Taliban talks reached agreement on a timetable for troop withdrawal and counter-terrorist guarantees by the Taliban.

The remarkable consensus on how a political settlement would meet the common security needs of both Russia and the US was expressed in a joint statement issued by Russia, China, and the US after a consultation among their Afghanistan envoys in Moscow in April 2019. The eight agreed points laid out the new counterterrorism context of the agreement and presented a political roadmap more consistent with the Moscow format than with the Kabul process, in particular by distinguishing an "Afghan-led, Afghan-owned peace process," which they endorsed in principle, from one led by the Afghan government, the role of which was more circumscribed than in Ghani's proposals. The US agreed to an unprecedented joint statement with its two great-power rivals on the withdrawal of US troops from Afghanistan. While the language did not call for the withdrawal of "all" troops, neither did it exempt counter-terrorist forces from the withdrawal.

The three met again in Beijing on July 10–11 in a four-party format with Pakistan. Iran had been invited, but Iran objections to the U.S.-led process prevented it from attending. Their joint statement called for "relevant parties to . . . immediately start Intra-Afghan negotiations between the Taliban, Afghan government, and other Afghans," to produce a "framework" to "guarantee the orderly and responsible transition of the security situation and detail an agreement on a future inclusive political arrangement acceptable to all Afghans." The statement called on "all parties to take steps to reduce violence leading to a comprehensive and permanent ceasefire that starts with Intra-Afghan negotiations."[9]

What are the prospects for peace and stability in Afghanistan?

Trump's decision to suspend the peace process, Tweeted out on September 7, 2019, immediately followed by the resignation of National Security Advisor John Bolton, and then by the start of the impeachment process, introduced even greater uncertainty into the administration's national security policies. Trump's public rationale, anger at continuing Taliban violence,

9. "Four-Party Joint Statement on Afghan Peace Process," https://www.fmprc.gov.cn/mfa_eng/wjdt_665385/2649_665393/t1680481.shtml.

including the death of an American soldier and refusal of an immediate comprehensive ceasefire, most likely concealed his pique at being unable to stage manage a photo opportunity to bolster his slipping approval rating, which would shortly start to slip further after the revelations about Ukraine.

The cancellation of the plan to sign the agreement in Doha in early September, however, came as a relief to the Afghan government, which could proceed without distraction to hold the presidential election. Sectors of the Afghan public also felt relieved, as they feared that the agreement's unknown provisions would lead to the return of the Taliban, including the re-imposition of their most retrograde policies on women, among others. The government congratulated Trump on his decision, which it hoped would lead to the scrapping of the entire process from which it had been excluded. The government had advocated a bilateral negotiation between Washington and Kabul over the US troop withdrawal and a political negotiation between it and the Taliban, which the latter refused.

Hopes that the election would greatly strengthen the government's hand seemed misplaced, however. An apparent turnout of less than 20 percent meant that whoever was elected would have at best a weak endorsement from a traumatized and skeptical electorate. Instead of accelerating the vote count and making it more transparent, the introduction of biometric verification added a new hurdle to certifying the vote count— reconciling the biometrically verified votes with the paper ballots and eliminating hundreds of thousands of ballots that could not be so reconciled. The concentration of votes for two strong candidates, Ashraf Ghani and Abdullah Abdullah, and particularly the lack of strong Pashtun competitors for President Ghani, made a first-round victory more likely, but not inevitable.

The fact that Bolton rather than Khalilzad resigned after Trump's announcement, plus the White House readout of a November 21 call by President Trump to Pakistan prime minister Imran Khan, in which the president was reported to have expressed the hope that the prisoner-hostage exchange would "contribute to furthering the peace process in Afghanistan"[10] indicated that the delay was likely to be temporary. Trump confirmed the resumption of the process during his Thanksgiving visit to Bagram Air Base on November 28, 2019, but as this book went to press, the content of that resumption was still ambiguous.

Anyone who has reached this point in the book needs no further guidance to construct an argument that the continuation of armed conflict in Afghanistan may be inevitable. Nonetheless, that is now less certain than at any other time over the past forty years. Most of Afghanistan's neighbors have reached a consensus on the need for a settlement. Despite skeptics and hardliners everywhere, the Afghan government, the Taliban, and constitutional opposition all agree on the principle of a negotiated settlement, as does the US. The domestic political situation in the US remains a wild card, and to that known unknown, we must add a multitude of unknown unknowns. But as foreseen in a Quranic passage with which the Tunisian scholar Ibn Khaldun (1332–1406) concluded many of his works, "There are signs for those who can discern them."[11]

10. https://www.voanews.com/south-central-asia/officials-trump-thanks-pakistani-afghan-leaders-release-western-hostages.
11. Quran, 3:190.

CO-AUTHOR BIOGRAPHIES

Nematullah Bizhan is a Lecturer in Public Policy at the Development Policy Centre, Crawford School of Public Policy, Australian National University, and a Visiting Lecturer at the University of Papua New Guinea. He is also a Senior Research Associate with the Global Economic Governance Program at the Blavatnik School of Government and University College, Oxford University. Previously, Nematullah was a Research Fellow at the Blavatnik School of Government, undertaking research on the role of identities and networks in establishing state legitimacy and effectiveness, and, in association with the Oxford-LSE Commission on State Fragility, Growth and Development, he worked on state fragility and international policy. His research interests include public policy, international development, and state building as well as post-conflict reconstruction. Nematullah was an Oxford-Princeton Global Leaders Fellow, an Australian Leadership Awardee, and a Fulbright Scholar. Nematullah contributed to development programs and reforms that helped Afghanistan's immediate post-2001 recovery. He served as Afghanistan's Youth Deputy Minister; Founding Director General for Policy and Monitoring of Afghanistan National Development Strategy; Head of the Secretariat for the Joint Coordination and Monitoring Board; and Director General of Budget at the Ministry of Finance. As a civil society activist, he has also contributed to promoting accountability and civic participation in decision-making processes.

Antonio Giustozzi is an independent researcher born in Ravenna, Italy, who earned his PhD from the London School of Economics and Political Science (LSE). He is the author of several books on Afghanistan: *War, Politics and Society in Afghanistan, 1978-1992, Koran, Kalashnikov and Laptop: The Neo-Taliban Insurgency, 2002-7, Empires of Mud: War and Warlords in Afghanistan, Policing Afghanistan* (with M. Isaqzadeh), *The Army of Afghanistan, The Islamic State in Khorasan,* and *The Taliban at War* (Oxford). He also authored a volume on the role of coercion and violence in state-building, *The Art of Coercion,* one on advisory missions, *Missionaries of Modernity.* He edited a volume on the Taliban, *Decoding the New Taliban,* featuring contributions by specialists from different backgrounds, and another on DDR processes, *Post-Conflict Demobilisation, Disarmament and Reintegration: Bringing State-Building Back In.*

David Mansfield is recognized as one of the preeminent experts on the drugs economy of Afghanistan. He is one of the few people who has conducted fieldwork in rural Afghanistan for more than two decades, and who continues to do so amid the current challenging security conditions. His recent work has moved up the value chain and offers unique insights into ephedra/methamphetamine production, the workings of heroin laboratories, and cross-border smuggling networks. David has worked as a technical advisor to the government of the United Kingdom in its role as lead nation (and subsequently partner nation) on counter-narcotics, as well as worked for a variety of different national, bilateral, multilateral, and non-governmental organizations. He has supported the World Bank, Asia Development Bank, and the European Commission in integrating the drugs issue into their rural development programs in Afghanistan, and he designed, researched, and drafted the Special Inspector General of Afghanistan Reconstruction's Lessons Learned report on counter-narcotics. David has a doctorate degree from the School of Oriental and African Studies, London, and is the author of the book *A State Built on Sand: How Opium Undermined Afghanistan* (Oxford).

BIBLIOGRAPHY

The list below is based on the comprehensive bibliography assembled by Christian Bleuer for the Afghanistan Analysts Network (https://www.afghanistan-analysts.org/publication/other-publications/afghanistan-analysts-bibliography-on-afghanistan/). This list includes mainly single-authored books, but much valuable material is found in articles, book chapters, and organizational reports, all of which are cited in Bleuer's bibliography.

1. Abirafeh, Lina. *Gender and International Aid in Afghanistan: The Politics and Effects of Intervention.* Jefferson, NC: McFarland, 2009.
2. Abou Zahab, Mariam, and Olivier Roy. *Islamist Networks: The Afghan-Pakistan Connection.* New York: Columbia University Press, 2006.
3. Adamec, Ludwig W. *Historical Dictionary of Afghanistan.* Lanham, MD: Scarecrow Press, 2012.
4. Aggarwal, Neil Krishan. *The Taliban's Virtual Emirate: The Culture and Psychology of an Online Militant Community.* New York: Columbia University Press, 2016.
5. Aharon, Sara. *From Kabul to Queens: The Jews of Afghanistan and Their Move to the United States.* Mt. Vernon, NY: Decalogue Books, 2011.
6. Ahmad, Aisha. *Jihad & Co.: Black Markets and Islamist Power.* New York and Oxford: Oxford University Press, 2017.
7. Ahmed, Akbar. *Millennium and Charisma Among Pathans.* Abingdon, UK: Routledge, 1976.
8. Ahmed, Akbar. *Pakhtun Economy and Society.* London: Routledge and Kegan Paul, 1980.

9. Akbar Agha, Sayyed Mohammad. *I Am Akbar Agha: Memories of the Afghan Jihad and the Taliban.* Berlin: First Draft Publishing, 2014.

10. Amin, Agha H., David J. Osinski, and Paul Andre DeGeorges. *The Development of Taliban Factions in Afghanistan and Pakistan: A Geographical Account.* Lewiston, NY: Edwin Mellen Press, 2010.

11. Amir Abdul Rahman Khan. *Autobiography of Amir Abdul Rahman Khan.* Manchester, UK: 2016.

12. Ansary, Mir Tamim. *Games without Rules: The Often Interrupted History of Afghanistan.* New York: Public Affairs, 2012.

13. Armstrong, Sally. *Bitter Roots, Tender Shoots: The Uncertain Fate of Afghanistan's Women.* Toronto: Viking Canada, 2008.

14. Auerswald, David P., and Stephen M. Saideman. *NATO in Afghanistan: Fighting Together, Fighting Alone.* Princeton, NJ: Princeton University Press, 2014.

15. Azoy, Whitney. *Buzkashi: Game and Power in Afghanistan.* Philadelphia: University of Pennsylvania Press, 1982.

16. Barakat, Sultan, ed. *Reconstructing War-Torn Societies: Afghanistan.* London: Palgrave Macmillan, 2004.

17. Barfield, Thomas. *The Central Asian Arabs of Afghanistan.* Austin: University of Texas Press, 1981.

18. Barfield, Thomas. *Afghanistan: A Cultural and Political History.* Princeton: Princeton University Press, 2010.

19. Barry, Michael. *A History of Modern Afghanistan.* Cambridge: Cambridge University Press, 2006.

20. Barth, Frederick. *Political Leadership Among Swat Pathans.* LSE Monograph Series. Atlantic Highlands, NJ: Humanities Press, 1959.

21. Bergen, Peter, and Katherine Tiedemann, eds. *Talibanistan: Negotiating the Borders Between Terror, Politics, and Religion.* New York: Oxford University Press, 2012.

22. Bhatia, Michael Vinay, and Mark Sedra. *Afghanistan, Arms and Conflict: Armed Groups, Disarmament and Security in a Post-War Society.* New York: Routledge, 2008.

23. Bird, Tim, and Alex Marshall. *Afghanistan: How the West Lost Its Way.* New Haven: Yale University Press, 2011.

24. Bizhan, Nematullah. *Aid Paradoxes in Afghanistan: Building and Undermining the State.* New York: Routledge, 2017.

25. Bradford, James T. *Poppies, Politics, and Power: Afghanistan and the Global History of Drugs and Diplomacy.* Ithaca, NY: Cornell University Press, 2019.

26. Brodsky, Anne. *With All Our Strength: The Revolutionary Association of the Women of Afghanistan.* New York: Routledge, 2003.

27. Brown, Vahid, and Don Rassler. *Fountainhead of Jihad: The Haqqani Nexus, 1973–2012.* London: Hurst, 2013.

28. Burde, Dana. *Schools for Conflict or for Peace in Afghanistan.* New York: Columbia University Press, 2014.

29. Canfield, Robert L. *Faction and Conversion in a Plural Society: Religious Alignments in the Hindu Kush.* Ann Arbor: University of Michigan, 1973.

30. Caroe, Olaf. *The Pathans: 500 B.C.–A.D. 1957.* 1958. Reprint, London: Kegan Paul International, 2000.

31. Cavanna, Thomas P. *Hubris, Self-Interest, and America's Failed War in Afghanistan: The Self-Sustaining Overreach.* Lanham, MD: Lexington, 2015.

32. Centlivres, Pierre. *Un bazaar d'asie centrale: Forme et organization du bazaar de Tashqurghan.* Wiesbaden: Ludwig Reichart, 1972.

33. Centlivres, Pierre, and Micheline Centlivres-Demont. *Afghanistan on the Threshold of the 21st Century: Three Essays on Culture and Society.* Princeton, NJ: Markus Wiener Publishers, 2010.

34. Chandrasekaran, Rajiv. *Little America: The War Within the War for Afghanistan.* New York: Alfred A. Knopf, 2012.

35. Chouvy, Pierre-Arnaud. 2010. *Opium: Uncovering the Politics of the Poppy.* Cambridge, MA: Harvard University Press, 2010.

36. Coburn, Noah. *Bazaar Politics: Power and Pottery in an Afghan Market Town.* Stanford, CA: Stanford University Press, 2011.

37. Coburn, Noah. *Losing Afghanistan: An Obituary for the Intervention.* Redwood City, CA: Stanford University Press, 2016.

38. Coll, Steve. *Directorate S: The CIA and America's Secret Wars in Afghanistan and Pakistan, 2001–2016.* New York: Penguin, 2018.

39. Coll, Steve. *Ghost Wars: The Secret History of the CIA, Afghanistan, and Bin Laden, from the Soviet Invasion to September 10, 2001.* New York: Penguin, 2004.

40. Collins, Joseph J. *Understanding the War in Afghanistan: A Guide to the Land, the People, and the Conflict.* New York: Skyhorse Publishing, 2013.

41. Cordesman, Anthony H. *Afghanistan at Transition: The Lessons of the Longest War.* Lanham, MD: Rowman & Littlefield, 2015.

42. Cortright, David. *Ending Obama's War: Responsible Military Withdrawal from Afghanistan.* Boulder, CO: Paradigm Publishers, 2011.

43. Cowper-Coles, Sherard. *Cables from Kabul: The Inside Story of the West's Afghanistan Campaign.* New York: Harper Press, 2011.
44. Crews, Robert D. *Afghan Modern: The History of a Global Nation.* Cambridge, MA: Harvard University Press, 2015.
45. Dam, Bette. *A Man and a Motorcycle: How Hamid Karzai Came to Power.* Utrecht: Ipso Facto, 2014.
46. Dobbins, J. F. *After the Taliban: Nation-Building in Afghanistan.* Lincoln, NE: Potomac Books, 2008.
47. Dorronsoro, Gilles. *Revolution Unending: Afghanistan, 1979 to the Present.* New York: Columbia University Press, 2005.
48. Doubleday, Veronica. *Three Women of Herat.* Austin: University of Texas Press, 1990.
49. Dyvik, Synne L. *Gendering Counterinsurgency: Performativity, Embodiment and Experience in the Afghan "Theatre of War."* New York: Routledge, 2016.
50. Eager, Paige Whaley. *Waging Gendered Wars: US Military Women in Afghanistan and Iraq.* New York: Routledge, 2016.
51. Edwards, David B. *Before Taliban: Genealogies of the Afghan Jihad.* Berkeley: University of California Press, 2002.
52. Edwards, David B. *Caravan of Martyrs: Sacrifice and Suicide Bombing in Afghanistan.* Berkeley: University of California Press, 2017.
53. Edwards, David B. *Heroes of the Age: Moral Fault Lines on the Afghan Frontier.* Berkeley: University of California Press, 1996.
54. Edwards, Lucy Morgan. *The Afghan Solution: The Inside Story of Abdul Haq, the CIA and How Western Hubris Lost Afghanistan.* London: Pluto Press, 2011.
55. Eide, Kai. *Power Struggle over Afghanistan: An Inside Look at What Went Wrong, and What We Can Do to Repair the Damage.* New York: Skyhorse, 2012.
56. Emadi, Hafizullah. *Dynamics of Political Development in Afghanistan: The British, Russian, and American Invasions.* London: Palgrave Macmillan, 2010.
57. Emadi, Hafizullah. *Repression, Resistance and Women in Afghanistan.* Westport, CT: Praeger, 2002.
58. Ewans, Martin. *Conflict in Afghanistan: Studies in Asymmetric Warfare.* New York: Routledge, 2005.
59. Fayez, Sharif. *An Undesirable Element: An Afghan Memoir.* Berlin: First Draft Publishing, 2014.

60. Felbab-Brown, Vanda. *Aspiration and Ambivalence: Strategies and Realities of Counterinsurgency and State Building in Afghanistan.* Washington, DC: Brookings Institution Press, 2013.
61. Felbab-Brown, Vanda. *Shooting Up: Counterinsurgency and the War on Drugs.* Washington, DC: Brookings Institution Press, 2009.
62. Ferdinand, Klaus. *Afghan Nomads: Caravans, Conflicts and Trade in Afghanistan and British India, 1800–1980.* Copenhagen: Rhodos International, 2006.
63. Fry, Maxwell J. *The Afghan Economy: Money, Finance, and the Critical Constraints to Economic Development.* Leiden: Brill, 1974.
64. Gall, Carlotta. *The Wrong Enemy: America in Afghanistan, 2001–2014.* New York: Houghton Mifflin Harcourt, 2014.
65. Gates, Scott, and Kaushik Roy. *War and State-Building in Afghanistan: Historical and Modern Perspectives.* London: Bloomsbury, 2016.
66. Girardet, Edward. *Killing the Cranes: A Reporter's Journey Through Three Decades of War in Afghanistan.* White River Junction, VT: Chelsea Green Publishing, 2011.
67. Girardet, Edward, and Jonathan Walter et al., eds. *Afghanistan: Essential Field Guide to Humanitarian and Conflict Zones.* Geneva: Media Action International, 2004.
68. Giustozzi, Antonio. *Afghanistan's Endless War: State Failure, Regional Politics, and the Rise of the Taliban.* Seattle: University of Washington Press, 2001.
69. Giustozzi, Antonio. *The Army of Afghanistan: A Political History of a Fragile Institution.* London: Hurst, 2015.
70. Giustozzi, Antonio, ed. *Decoding the New Taliban: Insights from the Afghan Field.* New York: Columbia University Press, 2012.
71. Giustozzi, Antonio. *Empires of Mud: Wars and Warlords of Afghanistan.* New York: Columbia University Press, 2009.
72. Giustozzi, Antonio. *Koran, Kalashnikov and Laptop: The Neo-Taliban Insurgency in Afghanistan.* New York: Columbia University Press, 2008.
73. Giustozzi, Antonio. *War, Politics, and Society in Afghanistan: 1978–1992.* Washington, DC: Georgetown University Press, 2000.
74. Goodson, Larry P. *Afghanistan's Endless War: State Failure, Regional Politics, and the Rise of the Taliban.* Seattle: University of Washington Press, 2001.
75. Gopal, Anand. *No Good Men among the Living: America, the Taliban, and the War through Afghan Eyes.* New York: Metropolitan Books, 2014.

76. Grau, Lester W., ed. *The Bear Went over the Mountain: Soviet Combat Tactics in Afghanistan*. New York: Routledge, 2003.
77. Green, Nile, ed. *Afghanistan's Islam: From Conversion to the Taliban*. Oakland: University of California Press. 2016.
78. Grima, Benedicte. *The Performance of Emotion Among Paxtun Women: "The Misfortunes Which Have Befallen Me."* Austin: University of Texas Press, 1992.
79. Gurcan, Metin. *What Went Wrong in Afghanistan?: Understanding Counter-insurgency Efforts in Tribalized Rural and Muslim Environments*. Solihull, UK: Helion and Company, 2016.
80. Hagen, E., and J. F. Teufert. *Flooding in Afghanistan: A Crisis in Threats to Global Water Security*. Springer, 2009.
81. Hamid, Mustafa, and Leah Farrell. *The Arabs at War in Afghanistan*. London: Hurst, 2015.
82. Hanifi, Shah Mahmoud. *Connecting Histories in Afghanistan: Market Relations and State Formation on a Colonial Frontier*. Palo Alto, CA: Stanford University Press, 2011.
83. Haroon, Sana. *Frontier of Faith: Islam in the Indo-Afghan Borderland*. London: Hurst, 2011.
84. Harpviken, Kristian Berg. *Social Networks and Migration in Wartime Afghanistan*. London: Palgrave Macmillan, 2009.
85. Harpviken, Kristian Berg, and Shahrbanou Tadjbakhsh. *A Rock Between Hard Places: Afghanistan as an Arena of Regional Insecurity*. London: Hurst, 2016.
86. Hastings, Michael. *The Operators: The Wild and Terrifying Inside Story of America's War in Afghanistan*. Boston: Little, Brown, 2011.
87. Hodes, Cyrus, and Mark Sedra. 2013. *The Search for Security in Post-Taliban Afghanistan*. New York: Routledge.
88. Ibrahimi, Niamatullah. *The Hazaras and the Afghan State: Rebellion, Exclusion, and the Struggle for Recognition*. New York: Oxford University Press, 2017.
89. Isby, David. *Afghanistan: Graveyard of Empires: A New History of the Borderland*. New York: Pegasus, 2010.
90. Jalali, Ali Ahmad. 2017. *A Military History of Afghanistan: From the Great Game to the Global War on Terror*. Lawrence: University Press of Kansas, 2002.
91. Jalali, Ahmed Ali, and Lester W. Grau. *Afghan Guerilla Warfare*. Oxford, UK: Osprey, 2002.
92. James, Eric. *The Military-Humanitarian Complex in Afghanistan*. Manchester, UK: Manchester University Press, 2016.

93. Jankowski, Jacob E. *Corruption, Contractors, and Warlords in Afghanistan*. Hauppauge, NY: Nova Science Publishers, 2011.
94. Jettmar, Karl. *The Religions of the Hindukush*. Vol. 1: *The Religion of the Kafirs*. Rev. ed. London: Oxford / IBH Publishing, 1986.
95. Johnson, Chris, and Jolyon Leslie. *Afghanistan: The Mirage of Peace*. London: Zed Books, 2005.
96. Johnson, Robert. *The Afghan Way of War: How and Why They Fight*. New York: Oxford University Press, 2011.
97. Johnson, Thomas H. *Culture, Conflict, and Counterinsurgency*. Palo Alto, CA: Stanford University Press, 2014.
98. Johnson, Thomas, and Wali Shaaker. *Taliban Narratives: The Use and Power of Stories in the Afghanistan Conflict*. New York: Oxford University Press, 2018.
99. Jones, Seth. *In the Graveyard of Empires: America's War in Afghanistan*. New York: Norton, 2009.
100. Joya, Malalai. *A Woman Among Warlords: The Extraordinary Story of an Afghan Who Dared to Raise Her Voice*. New York: Scribner, 2009.
101. Kakar, Hassan. *Afghanistan: The Soviet Invasion and the Afghan Response, 1979–1982*. Berkeley, CA: University of California Press, 1997.
102. Kakar, Hassan. *Government and Society in Afghanistan: The Reign of Amir 'Abd al-Rahman Khan*. 1979. Reprint, Austin, TX: University of Texas Press, 2014.
103. Kalinovsky, Artemy M. *A Long Goodbye: The Soviet Withdrawal from Afghanistan*. Cambridge, MA: Harvard University Press, 2011.
104. Khan, Riaz M. *Afghanistan and Pakistan: Conflict, Extremism, and Resistance to Modernity*. Baltimore, MD: Johns Hopkins University Press, 2011.
105. Koofi, Fawzia, and Nadene Ghouri. *The Favored Daughter: One Woman's Fight to Lead Afghanistan into the Future*. London: Palgrave Macmillan, 2012.
106. Koplik, Sara. *A Political and Economic History of the Jews of Afghanistan*. Leiden: Brill, 2015.
107. Lamb, Christina. *Farewell Kabul: From Afghanistan to a More Dangerous World*. New York: William Collins, 2015.
108. Lamb, Christina. *Not a Shot Fired: The War on Terror in Afghanistan*. Harper, 2008.
109. Lovewine, George. *Outsourcing the Global War on Terrorism: Private Military Companies and American Intervention in Iraq and Afghanistan*. New York: Springer, 2014.

110. Maley, William, ed. *Fundamentalism Reborn? Afghanistan and the Taliban*. New York: New York University Press, 1998.
111. Maley, William, and Susanne Schmeidl, eds. *Reconstructing Afghanistan: Civil-Military Experiences in Comparative Perspective*. London: Routledge, 2014.
112. Maley, William. *The Afghan Wars*. London: Palgrave Macmillan, 2002.
113. Maley, William. *Rescuing Afghanistan*. London: Hurst, 2007.
114. Maley, William. *Transition in Afghanistan: Hope, Despair and the Limits of Statebuilding*. London: Routledge, 2018.
115. Malik, I. Hafeez. *Pashtun Identity and Geopolitics in Southwest Asia: Pakistan and Afghanistan Since 9/11*. London: Anthem Press, 2016.
116. Malik, I. Hafeez. *US Relations with Afghanistan and Pakistan: The Imperial Dimension*. New York: Oxford University Press, 2008.
117. Malkasian, Carter. *War Comes to Garmser: Thirty Years of Conflict on the Afghan Frontier*. New York: Oxford University Press, 2013.
118. Manoori, Ukmina, and Stephanie Lebrun. Translated by Peter E. Chianchiano Jr. *I Am a Bacha Posh: My Life as a Woman Living as a Man in Afghanistan*. New York: Skyhorse, 2014.
119. Mansfield, David. *A State Built on Sand: How Opium Undermined Afghanistan*. New York: Oxford University Press, 2016.
120. Marsden, Magnus. *Trading Worlds: Afghan Merchants across Modern Frontiers*. London: Hurst, 2016.
121. Marsden, Peter. *Afghanistan: Aid, Armies, and Empires*. London: I. B. Tauris, 2009.
122. Martin, Mike. *An Intimate War: An Oral History of the Helmand Conflict*. London: Hurst, 2014.
123. Maurer, Kevin. *Gentlemen Bastards: On the Ground in Afghanistan with America's Elite Special Forces*. New York: Berkley Books, 2012.
124. McFate, Montgomery, and Janice H. Laurence, eds. *Social Science Goes to War: The Human Terrain System in Iraq and Afghanistan*. New York: Oxford University Press, 2015.
125. Mercille, Julien. *Cruel Harvest: US Intervention in the Afghan Drug Trade*. London: Pluto Press, 2013.
126. Misdaq, Nabi. *Afghanistan: Political Frailty and Foreign Interference*. London: Routledge, 2006.
127. Monsutti, Alessandro. *War and Migration: Social Networks and Economic Strategies of the Hazaras of Afghanistan*. London: Routledge, 2005.

128. Mousavi, Sayed Askar. *The Hazaras of Afghanistan: An Historical, Cultural, Economic, and Political Study.* New York: St. Martin's Press,1997.

129. Mukhopadhyay, Dipali. *Warlords, Strongman Governors, and the State in Afghanistan.* New York: Cambridge University Press, 2013.

130. Murtazashvili, Jennifer Brick. *Informal Order and the State in Afghanistan.* New York: Cambridge University Press, 2016.

131. Nagamine, Yoshinobu. *The Legitimization Strategy of the Taliban's Code of Conduct: Through the One-Way Mirror.* New York: Springer, 2016.

132. Najimi, Bashirullah. *Gender and Public Participation in Afghanistan: Aid, Transparency, and Accountability.* New York: Springer, 2018.

133. Nawa, Fariba. *Opium Nation: Child Brides, Drug Lords, and One Woman's Journey through Afghanistan.* New York: Harper Perennial, 2011.

134. Neumann, Ronald E. *The Other War: Winning and Losing in Afghanistan.* McLean, VA: Potomac Books, 2009.

135. Nichols, Robert. *A History of Pashtun Migration, 1775–2006.* New York: Oxford University Press, 2008.

136. Nojumi, Neamatollah. *American State-Building in Afghanistan and Its Regional Consequences: Achieving Democratic Stability and Balancing China's Influence.* Lanham, MD: Rowman & Littlefield, 2016.

137. Nojumi, Neamatollah. *The Rise of the Taliban in Afghanistan.* London: Palgrave, 2002.

138. Nojumi, Neamatollah, Dyan Mazurana, and Elizabeth Stites. *After the Taliban: Life and Security in Rural Afghanistan.* London: Rowman & Littlefield, 2008.

139. Nordberg, Jenny. *The Underground Girls of Kabul: In Search of a Hidden Resistance in Afghanistan.* New York: Crown Publishers, 2014.

140. Nunan, Timothy. *Humanitarian Invasion: Global Development in Cold War Afghanistan.* New York: Cambridge University Press, 2016.

141. Olesen, Asta. *Islam and Politics in Afghanistan.* London: Curzon, 1995.

142. Orywal, Erwin. *Ethnischen Gruppen Afghanistans: Fallstudien zu Gruppenidentität und Intergruppenbeziehungen.* Wiesbaden: L. Reichert, 1986.

143. Partlow, Joshua. *A Kingdom of Their Own: The Family Karzai and the Afghan Disaster.* New York: Knopf Publishing, 2016.

144. Ponzio, Richard. *Democratic Peacebuilding: Aiding Afghanistan and Other Fragile States*. New York: Oxford University Press, 2011.
145. Pstrusinska, Jadwiga. *Secret Languages of Afghanistan and Their Speakers*. UK: Cambridge Scholars Publishing, 2013.
146. Rais, Rasul Baksh. *War Without Winners: Afghanistan's Uncertain Transition*. New York: Oxford University Press, 1995.
147. Rashid, Ahmed. *Descent into Chaos: The U.S. and the Disaster in Pakistan, Afghanistan, and Central Asia*. New York: Penguin, 2009.
148. Rashid, Ahmed. *Pakistan on the Brink: The Future of America, Pakistan, and Afghanistan*. New York: Penguin, 2012.
149. Rashid, Ahmed. *Taliban: Militant Islam, Oil, and Fundamentalism in Central Asia*. New Haven: Yale University Press, 2000.
150. Robertson, George Scott. *The Kafirs of the Hindu-Kush*. London: Laurence and Bullen, 1896.
151. Roy, Arpita Basu. *Human Security in Afghanistan: Reconstructing an Alternative Notion of Security for Afghanistan in the South Asian Security Paradigm*. Kolkata, West Bengal: Maulana Abul Kalam Azad Institute of Asian Studies, 2014.
152. Roy, Olivier. *Afghanistan: From Holy War to Civil War*. Pennington, NJ: Darwin Press, 1995.
153. Roy, Olivier. *Islam and Resistance in Afghanistan*. Cambridge, UK: Cambridge University Press, 1990.
154. Rubin, Barnett R. *Afghanistan from the Cold War through the War on Terror*. New York: Oxford University Press, 2013.
155. Rubin, Barnett. *The Fragmentation of Afghanistan: State Formation and Collapse in the International System*. New Haven, CT: Yale University Press, 1995.
156. Rubin, Barnett. *The Search for Peace in Afghanistan: From Buffer State to Failed State*. New Haven, CT: Yale University Press, 1995.
157. Rubin, Barnett R., and Jean-Frédéric Légaré-Tremblay. *L'Afghanistan sur le point de bascule*. Montréal: Nota Bene, 2009.
158. Russian General Staff. Translated and edited by Lester W. Grau and Michael A. Gress. *The Soviet-Afghan War: How a Superpower Fought and Lost*. Lawrence: University Press of Kansas, 2002.
159. Rynning, Sten. *NATO in Afghanistan: The Liberal Disconnect*. Palo Alto, CA: Stanford University Press, 2012.
160. Saikal, Amin. *Modern Afghanistan: A History of Struggle and Survival*. 2nd ed. London: I. B. Tauris, 2012.
161. Schetter, Conrad. *Ethnizität und Ethnische Konflikte in Afghanistan*. Berlin: Dietrich Reimer, 2003.

162. Schurman, H. F. *The Mongols of Afghanistan: An Ethnography of the Mongols and Related Peoples of Afghanistan.* The Hague: Mouton, 1962.
163. Shahrani, M. Nazif, and Robert L. Canfield, eds. *Revolutions and Rebellions in Afghanistan: Anthropological Perspectives.* Institute of International Studies, University of California, Berkeley, 1984.
164. Shinn, James, and James F. Dobbins. *Afghan Peace Talks : A Primer.* Arlington, VA: RAND Corporation, 2011.
165. Shroder, John F. *Natural Resources in Afghanistan: Geographic and Geologic Perspectives on Centuries of Conflict.* Boston, MA: Elsevier, 2014.
166. Shroder, John F., and Sher Jan Ahmadzai. *Transboundary Water Resources in Afghanistan.* Boston, MA: Elsevier, 2016.
167. Siddique, Abubakar. *The Pashtun Question: The Unresolved Key to the Future of Pakistan and Afghanistan.* London: Hurst, 2014.
168. Singh, Deepali Gaur. *Drugs Production and Trafficking in Afghanistan.* Washington, DC: Pentagon Press. 2007.
169. Sinno, Abdulkader. *Organizations at War in Afghanistan and Beyond.* Ithaca, NY: Cornell University Press, 2008.
170. Smith, Graeme. *The Dogs Are Eating Them Now: Our War in Afghanistan.* Berkeley, CA: Counterpoint Press, 2015.
171. Stenersen, Anne. *Al-Qaida in Afghanistan.* New York: Cambridge University Press, 2017.
172. Strick van Linschoten, Alex, and Felix Kuehn. *An Enemy We Created: The Myth of the Taliban / Al-Qaeda Merger in Afghanistan, 1970–2010.* New York: Columbia University Press, 2011.
173. Suchanek, Christiane. *Digging into Chaos: Security Sector Reconstruction and State-Building in Afghanistan.* Baden-Baden: Tectum, Wissenschaftsverlag, 2018.
174. Suhrke, Astri. *When More Is Less: The International Project in Afghanistan.* New York: Columbia University Press, 2011.
175. Tanner, Stephen. *Afghanistan: A Military History from Alexander the Great to the Fall of the Taliban.* New York: Da Capo Press, 2002.
176. Tapper, Nancy. *Bartered Brides: Politics, Gender and Marriage in an Afghan Tribal Society.* New York: Cambridge University Press, 1991.
177. Thompson, Edwina A. *Trust Is the Coin of the Realm: Lessons from the Money Men in Afghanistan.* New York: Oxford University Press, 2011.
178. Tomsen, Peter. *The Wars of Afghanistan: Messianic Terrorism, Tribal Conflicts, and the Failures of Great Powers.* New York: PublicAffairs, 2013.

179. Tondini, Matteo. *Statebuilding and Justice Reform: Post-Conflict Reconstruction in Afghanistan*. New York: Routledge, 2010.
180. Walter, Ben. *Gendering Human Security in Afghanistan: In a Time of Western Intervention*. New York: Routledge, 2017.
181. West, Bing. *The Wrong War: Grit, Strategy, and the Way Out of Afghanistan*. New York: Random House, 2011.
182. Williams, Brian Glyn. *The Last Warlord: The Life and Legend of Dostum, the Afghan Warrior Who Led US Special Forces to Topple the Taliban Regime*. Chicago, IL: Chicago Review Press, 2013.
183. Zaeef, Abdul Salam. *My Life with the Taliban*. Edited by Alex Strick van Linschoten and Felix Kuehn. New York: Columbia University Press, 2010.

INDEX

For the benefit of digital users, indexed terms that span two pages (e.g., 52–53) may, on occasion, appear on only one of those pages.

CPSIA information can be obtained
at www.ICGtesting.com
Printed in the USA
BVHW071230021022
648344BV00001B/2